Hitler's Children

Gerald Posner is the author of
Mengele: The Complete Story,
Warlords of Crime: Chinese Secret
Societies – The New Mafia and *Bio-*
Assassins. He lives in New York City
with his wife, Trisha.

Hitler's Children

GERALD POSNER

Mandarin

A Mandarin Paperback
HITLER'S CHILDREN

First published in Great Britain 1991
by William Heinemann Ltd
This edition published 1992
Reprinted 1992
by Mandarin Paperbacks
Michelin House, 81 Fulham Road, London SW3 6RB

Mandarin is an imprint of the Octopus Publishing Group,
a division of Reed International Books Limited

A CIP catalogue record for this title
is available from the British Library
ISBN 0 7493 1085 5

Printed and bound in Great Britain
by Cox & Wyman Ltd, Reading, Berks

To all victims of Nazi aggression

Acknowledgements

While this book is based on eleven in-depth interviews, significant research was also required on the backgrounds of the Nazi parents, and it was necessary to verify the information given by the children. I have, at various times, relied upon original World War II documents maintained in German and US archives; on copies of trial transcripts and the appended evidence; on books and articles, unpublished theses and legal briefs; on interviews with historians; and, extensively, on documentation available through the United States Freedom of Information Act. Prior to every interview, I constructed my own biography of the Nazi parent. In cases where the child presented new information, I checked his or her recall independently against documentary evidence. At no time did I accept the children's recollections as the final historical word, although their memories proved remarkably accurate.

Dozens of people have assisted my work during the past two years, and it would take a separate chapter to thank all of them. Instead, I wish to acknowledge those who made a distinctive and often invaluable contribution.

Special gratitude is due to Anne Webber, producer of Yorkshire Television in London, who unselfishly assisted me from the inception in sharing her accurate and extensive research. Dr Robert Wolfe, of the National Archives and Records Service in Washington, DC, helped me, as he has done in the past. Dr David Marwell, director of the Berlin Document Centre, is one of the most knowledgeable authorities on the Third Reich, and his insights were important. Elliot Welles, of the Anti-Defamation League in new York, generously placed the resources of his office at my disposal.

Irene Münster in Buenos Aires and Dr Wolfgang Neugebauer in Vienna were willing to pursue leads, even if these often proved fruitless. Several people intervened in cases where they might have influence with children of the Reich, and I thank particularly Christian Brandt and Dr Paul Schmidt-Carell, both in Hamburg; Peter Black, in Washington, DC; and Dr Günther Deschner, in Nuremberg. Also, several journalists tried to locate additional children of prominent Nazi parents; I am most indebted to Terry Gould of the Canadian Broadcasting Company and to Harvey Rowe of Berg, Germany.

Jan Levie, Günther Bergmuehl, Claudia Steinberg, Eberhard Glöckner, Susan Bronfen and Ute Spleth had linguistic skills which surmounted any barriers I found in my path. I am most grateful for their work on faded wartime documents and letters written in Germany's arcane old script.

Pam Bernstein, my agent and friend, helped me find a publisher and editor who recognized the project's uniqueness and its potential contribution to literature about the Third Reich.

Mere words are empty expressions in thanking Robert Loomis, my editor. He not only encouraged the development of this idea but also proved a steady source of inspiration. His guidance helped me through the project's difficult stages, and his advice stimulated my writing. I am fortunate to have worked with him.

Finally, last but certainly not least, I pay tribute to my wife, Trisha. As she has in the past, she was my constant and cherished source of motivation. From helping me with the research to reading and criticizing innumerable rough drafts, she lived with this book from its inception. She is my ingenious partner, without whom this book would not be possible.

Contents

Hitler's Children

CHAPTER 1

Breaking the Wall of Silence

On a blistering June afternoon in 1985, dozens of journalists gathered around a small, dusty graveyard in Embu, Brazil. They were attracted by persistent mid-morning rumours that the federal police had discovered the gravesite of the elusive Nazi fugitive, Auschwitz's Dr Josef Mengele. Lumbering around the tombstones was a stocky man in his mid-fifties, police chief Romeu Tuma. Dressed in a well-worn black suit, he barked orders in Portuguese and ran his hands nervously through his oily hair as he tried to direct the disorganized police and coroner's officials. Suddenly one of the three gravediggers hit the top of a wooden coffin with his pick, and Tuma rushed to the edge of the grave. The crowd rustled to attention. The police chief ordered the casket smashed open, and as journalists and onlookers crowded around in a ghoulish ring, they saw mud-coloured bones and remnants of clothing inside the simple wooden box. A forensic pathologist leaned into the grave and pulled a decaying skull from the casket. As he held it high so that reporters could take pictures for the evening news feeds, Tuma seemed confident. 'That's the "Angel of Death",' he muttered as he watched the cameras follow the swivelling skull.

Only days later, five thousand miles away in Munich, a tall, good-looking man, recently turned forty, approached the modern office complex of *Bunte* magazine. The young man was dressed in a dark grey double-breasted suit, and he carried a thick black attaché case. Inside were some five thousand pages of diaries and personal letters written by the world's most wanted Nazi, Josef Mengele. The man carrying the fugitive's papers had no doubt about their authenticity and no apprehension about providing them to a national magazine for publication. He was

Mengele's only son, Rolf, ready to close the file on his missing parent. The time had come to let his father go public.

Bunte knew it had a great scoop in the Mengele papers, if they were authentic. However, after the Hitler diaries scandal, when *Bunte*'s competitor *Stern* paid millions of dollars for forgeries purporting to be the Führer's missing wartime papers, *Bunte* was not taking any chances. Its editors selected a five-member panel to judge the historical accuracy of the Mengele writings, while the US Federal Bureau of Investigation and its West German counterpart subjected the paper, ink and handwriting to a barrage of scientific tests. *Bunte* sent a representative to Brazil, where I was serving as consultant to ABC News on the Mengele case, and asked me to join the panel. I abandoned my South American investigation and flew to Munich. Four internationally recognized historians of the Third Reich were already there. Although I was the panel's only non-PhD, I compensated by bringing the largest known private archive of Mengele documentation, some twenty-five thousand pages. For two weeks we scrutinized each page of the fugitive's writings; more important, we had access to a member of the Mengele family: his son, Rolf. He sat across a table from the panel and patiently answered hundreds of questions about his father. It was my first contact with a child of a Nazi murderer.

At first, convinced his 'feelings are no different from any child to any parent', Rolf thought he had nothing to say about his father. He soon realized he had underestimated the depth of his emotion for the man who abandoned him at the age of four, then taunted him for years from South American hide-outs. After several frank discussions, Rolf Mengele's complex feelings ranged from criticism and condemnation to a family loyalty which compelled him to protect his father from many hunters.

I was surprised to discover a young professional who was tormented by his father's past. Rolf's attempts to cope with a heritage over which he had no choice, and his efforts to understand what drove his father to such acts of savagery and cruelty, consumed large parts of his life. Once, during a series of questions about his family relationship, he paused and said wearily, 'You know, I would have preferred another father.' As I witnessed Rolf Mengele's conflict, I realized it was not easy to be sentenced to life as the child of a Nazi war criminal. In postwar

West Germany, with its economic miracle of the 1950s and 1960s, Nazis were a dark, past shadow better forgotten. Children like Rolf Mengele had to cope with their fathers' deeds on their own, without the help of German society.

The conversations that June sparked my curiosity about whether other children of prominent Nazis felt the same as Mengele's son. Or was Rolf's outlook coloured by the fact that his father deserted him and was a fugitive? Would some of the children reject criticism and instead ape their parents' hateful beliefs? I knew that several books had studied the children of concentration camp survivors, but at that time I was not aware of any attempt to study the children of the perpetrators. How had these children dealt with the crimes against humanity and their fathers' roles in those crimes? I knew the answers could be found only by locating a group of surviving children of prominent Nazis and persuading them to talk openly.

My first task was locating the children. Information requests to German government archives and prosecutors' offices were rejected under their privacy laws. The US government and Interpol provided no help. Nazi-hunters like Simon Wiesenthal had information on the criminals, especially the remaining fugitives, but virtually none on the children. I went to the Berlin Document Centre, the world's largest repository of Nazi archives; it maintains more than fifty million pages, including all the original Nazi party and SS personnel files. These files revealed only whether someone had a child at the time he or she joined the party, not whether the children were still alive, much less where they might live or under what name. Almost all requests to reporters at magazines, newspapers and television stations either went unanswered or were politely answered with an 'I'm sorry we can't help you' form letter.

Most frustrating was that people who might have useful information were not willing to help. Wolfgang Löhde, an adventurer who discovered the Third Reich's millions of counterfeit British pounds in Austria's Lake Toplitz, had travelled around the world meeting old Nazis. He never answered my letters. Jochen von Lang, a famous *Stern* reporter who had written books on prominent Nazis and led the 1965 Berlin hunt for Martin Bormann's remains, ignored my letters until they became so persistent that he finally replied, claiming total ignorance and offering no assistance. I even tried enlisting the help of Gerd Heidemann, the ex-*Stern* reporter who was jailed for complicity in the Hitler diaries fraud. Although he was discredited as a reputable journalist, there was no doubt his fascination with Nazis had led him to a select group of ex-officers and their offspring. He had even purchased Luftwaffe chief Hermann Göring's yacht, the *Carin II*; and prior to his unmasking in the diaries fiasco, the yacht was the scene of splendid parties for former Nazi officials. He finally answered, through his son, that he had had 'enough of Nazi shit', and also refused to help.

In the end I resorted to slow research at the US National Archives. Many wives of war criminals were detained in Allied camps for several months after the war. When released they had to register their new residences with the occupying forces. The files were not well organized but they eventually provided leads to some of the children I wanted to locate. The only problem was that the information was almost forty-five years old. But when I returned to West Germany, the information from the archives proved invaluable. In some cases the children were still in the same city, and I found them by dialling every listing of the family name in the phonebook. Sometimes a neighbour remembered the family and knew where they had next moved. By going to that town, I was one step closer to the child. More often than not the information stopped short of final success, but methodical research eventually yielded an address list of almost thirty children of prominent Nazis, scattered mostly in Germany, with a few in Austria and one in Brazil. As can be imagined, I guarded that list as though it were gold.

Now I had to convince some of those thirty to discuss their parents. I feared that many of them might have developed a standard negative to interview requests, and that I had somehow to persuade them my project was different from and more deserving than those they had rejected in the past.

One hurdle I quickly encountered was a cultural one. In the United States, tell-all programmes and books are common. It is not unusual to turn on the television one afternoon and see the children of serial killers or alcoholics talking about their childhood and their parents. But this candour is frowned on in many European countries. Over forty years had passed since the war. All the children had new lives, some had different names, and many preferred to forget the past. Now an American, a co-citizen of those responsible for judging and in some cases executing their parents, was tracking them down and asking them to discuss intimate personal details about their fathers, for publication. This scenario guaranteed I would get some doors slammed in my face.

A second obstacle which reduced the number of children who might be interviewed was my decision that none of the participants could remain anonymous. Those who spoke to me had to do so under their real names, with their fathers clearly identified and discussed. By this time I had discovered that two other books on the children of Nazis were under way, and in both cases the authors guaranteed anonymity to induce the children to speak.[1] In my view, that was a fundamental problem. Without knowing the parent's identity, or what he did during the war, it was difficult to understand fully what the child had endured. To be the daughter of SS chief Heinrich Himmler was quite different from being the son of Colonel Claus von Stauffenberg, the officer who planted the bomb which almost killed Hitler. I also thought it important to understand how the child knew his or her parent. Mengele's son, for instance, was born in 1944; his father left Germany when the boy was barely five. Rolf did not even know his father was alive until he was sixteen, and met him only once as an adult. Grand Admiral Karl Dönitz's daughter, on the other hand, was in her thirties during the war and was extremely close to him, visiting him regularly. Would a son who never really knew his father find it easier to condemn him than a daughter who knew her father into her middle age?

Unfortunately, because of my insistence on real names, many of those I contacted refused any cooperation. Heinrich Himmler's daughter was typical of a small group who completely ignored all my letters and telephone calls. Reportedly involved in neo-Nazi activities, she even rebuffed the efforts of a German professor who was on friendly terms with her husband. 'She will probably take her memories with her to her grave,' the professor told me when his last appeal failed. Some dismissed me curtly in blunt and unequivocal language. Others declined to be interviewed but provided tantalizing, brief glimpses of their feelings towards their fathers.

The daughter of Artur Seyss-Inquart, Reich commissioner for the Netherlands, who was executed at Nuremberg, wrote a series of revealing letters about 'Our beloved father . . . an idealist often misunderstood. He was a German patriot who only wanted his country's best. . . . We loved our father with his idealistic ideals. . . . To us his past life is sacrosanct. Our father's life is ours and nobody else's concern.'

Klaus Barbie, the 'Butcher of Lyon', currently in a French prison, has one daughter, Ute.[2] Brought up with her father in his Bolivian hide-out, she did not know about his SS past until the early 1970s, when he was unmasked as a fugitive. She did not like the idea that I was seeking children of prominent Nazis like Göring, Hess and Dönitz. 'My father was a low-ranking officer, with no decision-making authority,' she told me. 'If I allow you to put him in a book with such important officials, people will think my father had similar authority. I can't do that.' After she told me her relationship to her father was a 'normal' one, she added: 'My father, through unlucky circumstances, was chosen from thousands of SS-Obersturmführen [first lieutenants] to be used as a symbol of the "Third Reich" and of National Socialism. He drew, as *Der Spiegel* once correctly wrote, the black lot. I have, though, been equipped with enough reason to see through the hypocrisy of this absurd theatre which was camouflaged as legal proceedings.'

Similarly, Irmgard, one of Martin Bormann's children, refused to be interviewed but described her relationship with her father as 'very normal, nothing different from any other family'. In an earlier public statement she insisted he was 'good and very caring' and that she had unsuccessfully searched for a husband like her father. She is convinced that her father 'simply tried to put into practice what he believed Hitler wanted. I don't judge him, because judgement is always relative.'

Understandably, those who were interested in the project wanted to meet me before making a final decision. I decided to approach each child with candour – what was it like for them to grow up in a Nazi family? Even at that late stage some decided not to participate. One was Dr Karl Adolph Brandt, the only son of Hitler's personal physician, executed at the 'doctors' trial' after the war.[3] Dr Brandt actually allowed me to stay at his house for two days, with his wife and two of his three adult children. He shared with me unpublished diaries and letters from his father, written in prison, as well as private wartime photographs of his father with Hitler. Although Dr Brandt is articulate and proud of his father, he finally refused to be interviewed for a reason that had not occurred to me. 'I don't want to be part of your book where my only connection to the other people who are interviewed is that our fathers had some close relationship to Hitler,' he told me when we parted.

One of those who cooperated did so reluctantly. As a result, the information from Edda, the only daughter of Hermann Göring, is limited. In her first letter she said she had only a 'loving memory' of her father, and would therefore grant an interview. But she also wanted more details from me, including the amount of her fee. When I informed her that I never paid for information, she answered saying that an accident prevented her from seeing me during my next trip to Munich. I implored her for a meeting. She grudgingly set a time. Although hesitant at first, she finally talked to me for several hours about her feelings for her father. Then she told me that to obtain more information I would have to agree to a fee and give her the right to reject what I wrote. I declined and as a result she refused to meet me again or to have acquaintances provide further information.

Wolf Hess, the only son of Deputy Führer Rudolf Hess, who flew to Scotland in 1941 only to spend the next forty-six years of his life in prison, met me three times before deciding to participate. One of his early objections was the opposite of that raised by Klaus Barbie's daughter. Whereas she was concerned that her father would seem too important in a book with officials like Hess, Göring, and Frank, Wolf Hess was concerned that his father would be tarnished in a book which associated him with people like Mengele and Eichmann. 'You should keep your book only to the highest-ranking officers,' he urged me. I was surprised to discover that, a generation after the war, the sons and daughters still tried to maintain some distinctions based upon rank and conduct. Despite his objections, he eventually met me in Munich for a complete and far-ranging interview.

The daughter of Hjalmar Schacht (the former president of the Reichsbank, who was one of three defendants acquitted at the main Nuremberg trial) was reluctant to speak about her father and undecided until the last moment. She had turned down all earlier interview requests, and even after meeting me she wavered. She decided to discuss her parent openly only during the last days of my final German research trip.

Besides Hess, Mengele, Schacht and Göring, the others who finally agreed to speak included two sons of the governor-general of Poland, Hans Frank; the daughter of Grand Admiral Karl Dönitz; the son of Karl Saur, the first assistant to Albert Speer and the technical director of the armaments ministry; and the son of Colonel Claus von Stauffenberg, the young officer who planted the briefcase bomb which almost killed Hitler on 20 July 1944. In addition to these children of prominent wartime figures, there are two cases where the parents are virtually unknown but the stories told by their daughters are particularly compelling.

Obviously, this is not a selected group, but merely those children who decided to speak on the record. Yet they constitute an interesting cross-section of the Third Reich. Among their parents are five principal architects of Nazism, all of whom were defendants at the main Nuremberg trial. Two of those (Göring and Frank) were convicted and sentenced to be hanged; one (Hess) was given a life sentence and died in 1987 in Spandau Prison; another (Dönitz) was sentenced to ten years and was released in 1956; and one (Schacht) was acquitted. As for the parents of the other children, one (Stauffenberg) was executed by Hitler during the war; one (Mengele) was a fugitive until his 1979 death in Brazil; one (Drexel) was convicted in 1975 of murder; and two (Saur and Mochar), although fervent Nazis, were never charged with crimes.

The often haunting wartime recollections of the sons and daughters of prominent Nazis are powerful reminders that Hitler's crimes have claimed many victims. Together their stories provide a rare view of how children of Nazi SS troops and non-criminal German soldiers react to the Final Solution and their fathers' roles in the 'Thousand-Year Reich'.

CHAPTER 2

'A Thousand Years of Guilt'

Hans Frank was no longer nervous. The former governor-general of Poland, who fidgeted constantly during the Nuremberg trial, was tranquil the night of his execution. He was kneeling in prayer when the guards arrived at his cell for the walk to the gallows. At a few minutes after 1 a.m. on 16 October 1946, two GIs and a priest accompanied him through the prison wing and a darkened hallway to the open gymnasium. His hands were manacled behind his back. As he entered the gym, the brilliant, stark lighting made his eyes blink, but he managed a smile, the only one of the condemned defendants to do so.

His gaze immediately settled on three black gallows standing in a row. Alfred Rosenberg and Ernst Kaltenbrunner were already hanging, not yet dead. Frank glanced towards several tables packed with witnesses, reporters and Allied officials. He took a deep breath of the damp air, saturated with cigarette smoke and the aroma of coffee, before hurrying up the thirteen steps. A lieutenant-colonel asked Frank his name as he guided him to the middle gallows. There the United States Army's official hangman and two volunteers waited. They replaced the handcuffs with black shoelaces and asked Frank for his final words. He followed advice given him by the priest: 'I pray to God to take my soul. May the Lord receive me mercifully. I am grateful for the treatment I have received in prison.'

Sergeant John Woods, a red-faced, overweight Texan who had hanged 347 men in his fifteen-year career, stepped forward and placed the noose over Frank's head. At the same time, an assistant strapped his ankles together with a GI belt. A large black hood was dropped over his head. An American colonel made a short cutting motion with his hand and Woods pulled the lever. Through his hood Frank shouted 'Jesus have mercy!' as he plunged from view as if sucked into hell.

Hans Frank was forty-six years old when executed. He was a well-educated attorney, highly cultured and cultivated, but his background did not prevent his being guilty of crimes against humanity. His statements about the extermination of the Jews and the eradication of Polish society are among the most brutal recorded during the war. How someone with his background ended up on the gallows for his crimes has fascinated historians and anguished his family.

Frank had five children. Sigrid, the eldest, lives under a married name in South Africa. Brigitte, the third child, died in 1981, at the age of forty-six. She had cancer but the family suspects suicide. She always vowed not to live longer than her father. Michael, the middle brother, is the most supportive of his father, believing many of the Nazi crimes are exaggerated.

I interviewed the two remaining brothers in separate, far-ranging conversations. Niklas Frank, the youngest of the brothers, was born on 9 March 1939. Though he is gregarious and warm, he has a harsh opinion of his father. 'I hate him,' Niklas says. 'You cannot imagine how much I hate him.' In 1987, Niklas published a book about his father, *My Father, A Reckoning*. It met a torrent of criticism in Germany because of the unbridled disgust Niklas directed at his father. Among other appellations he called him a 'weak, vain, characterless little creature', a 'cowardly puppet', a 'slimy hypocrite and fool', a 'murderer'. Besides speculating as to whether his father was a 'latent homosexual', Niklas described him as 'a pathetic arse-kisser' who was 'harebrained' and a 'numbskull'. While the book was highly emotional, Niklas's harsh style added to the critical uproar. He fantasized about his father in sex scenes with Hitler, described masturbatory dreams about Hans Frank's execution, and depicted vividly horrific images of his parents in hell. He detests his mother as much as his father, 'except she wasn't as effeminate as he'. Of all the children I interviewed, he is the only one who truly despises his parents. He is the only child who, without hesitation, answered yes to the question of whether he would turn his father in if he were a fugitive.

Frank's eldest son, Norman, was born on 3 June 1928, and was his father's favourite child. He is quiet and introspective, physically and emotionally very different from the convivial Niklas. He is shorter than his six-foot younger brother. Slightly hunched, often in pain from an ulcer and assorted physical problems, this very thin sixty-two-year-old man spends most of his time inside the darkened study of his Bavarian home, his eyes sensitive to light. Norman loved his father deeply. He still does today, but felt betrayed when, after the war, he learned the nature of his father's role. 'It all changed when I saw the first pictures from Auschwitz; when I knew what had really happened,' Norman recalls. Today, he is perplexed by the contradictions raised by his father's life. When we first met, he showed me two pictures of his father: an idyllic one of the entire family and another of Hans Frank at Nuremberg escorted by a white-helmeted American GI. These two photos represent Norman's basic conflict – the contrast between a loving and respected parent and a war criminal. Norman is tormented by his father's legacy.

'He cries for his father often,' his wife, Elizabeth, says. 'His father has ruined his life. He doesn't think he has a right to be happy after what his father did.'

'I think of him every day,' Norman says. 'But I could never write a book like Niklas did. I am happy he did it for himself. But I think of my father differently.'

These contrasting brothers have had to cope with the same heritage. Their father, Hans Frank, the second of three children, was born into a middle-class Catholic family on 23 May 1900, in Karlsruhe. His father was a disbarred lawyer, 'a weakling and a womanizer', Norman says; 'deceitful', according to Niklas. His mother abandoned the family to live with a German professor in Prague, and as a teenager Hans Frank was shuttled between his parents. Because of his youth, he served only a year in World War I, but never at the front line. By 1919, as a Munich university student, Frank joined the right-wing Deutsche Arbeiterpartei (German Workers' Party), and, when it merged into the Nazi party in 1923, he automatically became a storm trooper. His diary from the period shows him obsessed with German culture, viewing German science, literature and music as superior to all others. He was a rabid nationalist, pompously commenting on the decline of Western civilization and the necessity for a strong Germany.

During this time Frank met his wife, Brigitte. She was a typist at the Bavarian State Parliament and was five years older than he. After an eight-month courtship they married. Niklas views his mother as 'a sly she-devil who knew what she wanted, and got it'. Even on their honeymoon, she took along her lover (their relationship was unknown to Frank), the son of a Hamburg shipping magnate. There are photographs of Brigitte and her lover on the honeymoon, with Frank, a 'spineless jerk' according to Niklas, behind the lens. Norman differs from his brother's harsh view of a manipulative mother. 'As time passes, I love my mother more and more,' he says. 'She did know what she wanted but she worked for it. She was very strong, by far the stronger personality in the marriage. My father was scared of her, but she was not frightened of him.' Frank, who fought a bitter divorce battle during the war, wrote a letter about her while imprisoned at Nuremberg. In the letter, addressed to his mother, he said he only married Brigitte because of 'an erotic intoxication' and that ever since he had been in 'mental slavery'. Mistakenly, the letter was sent to Brigitte. Niklas remembers she was enraged and 'wanted to tear down the Nuremberg walls to get at him'. Father Sixtus O'Connor, the Catholic priest at the prison, later told Niklas, 'Even in prison, he was still afraid of your mother.'

But in the late 1920s, the strain on the marriage was not evident. Frank was consumed with his career. In 1927, one year after he qualified at the German bar, he saw an advertisement in a Nazi newspaper seeking a lawyer to defend party members. He accepted the case and the defendants received light sentences. It guaranteed his work as a Nazi attorney, 'a revolting loud-mouth', according to Niklas. Frank defended hundreds of Nazis, mostly in cases involving beatings of communist rivals. In one case, he called Hitler as a witness. The future Führer was impressed with Frank, an effective and persuasive orator, whose image was only slightly marred by a high-pitched voice. Hitler retained him as his personal attorney, and he represented the Nazi leader in over 150 lawsuits. Frank was even entrusted with research to disprove the rumour that Hitler had Jewish blood. Niklas says, 'My father was stupidly proud of these legal accomplishments to the very end.'

Frank was rewarded for his loyal legal work with rapid promotions. By 1930 he was Reichsleiter (leader) of the Nazi party. In three years, when Hitler became chancellor, Frank was given a host of important positions, including president of the Academy of German Justice (which he founded) as well as of the International Chamber of Law, and he was appointed Bavarian minister of justice. During this time of zooming professional fortunes, the Franks started a family. In 1927, their first child, Sigrid, was born. Norman arrived the next year. His first memories are from 1932, when he was four and the Nazis became the largest party in the German parliament. 'My earliest memory of my family is that I only had a mother,' he recalls. 'My father was always busy, and I later learned it was the time of much political fighting. Our house was definitely upper middle class, very big, with large rooms all nicely decorated. Both my sister and I had nannies, but I don't remember them at all. I only remember my mother.'

Norman entered school in Munich in 1934, at the age of six. That year turned out to be a crucial one for his father. During June, Hitler decided to purge the leadership of the SA, an organization of two and a half million storm troopers. He had Ernst Röhm, his longtime friend and supporter, arrested, together with hundreds of other SA officials. On 30 June, Hitler flew from Bonn to Munich to oversee Röhm's arrest. All the SA leaders were delivered to Munich's Stadelheim prison, under Frank's legal jurisdiction. Six-year-old Norman remembers the day: 'I was in the chauffeured Mercedes with my father on the Night of the Long Knives [the name given to the SA purge], on a road near Munich. Hitler came to the car and put his head into our window and spoke to my father.'

Matters came to a head two days later when Hitler sent SS troops to the Stadelheim prison to execute summarily some of the SA leaders, even though no charges had been brought against them. Upset, Frank telephoned Hitler and then Hess. As minister of justice, and in his jurisdiction, Frank protested at such sentences without a trial. Hitler would hear none of it. He screamed at Frank that the prisoners were only at Stadelheim because 'I had no other secure place to put them. They are merely your guests. I and the Reich have full power over them, not Bavaria.' Frank backed down. He turned over nineteen men to the SS executioners. Röhm was slaughtered in his cell the following day. What Norman saw in the car only two days earlier had been the beginning of his father's complicity in murder.

'This was the moment that my father sold himself,' said Norman. 'It was absolutely his moment of corruption, when he went on his knees before Hitler. From that moment on it was a question of money and power and he wasn't a lawyer any more. I know that he regretted this decision. I know it as only a son can know it. My father suffered because he was such a weakling. He couldn't be strong against Hitler.' About this incident, Niklas totally agrees with his brother, but is characteristically harsher: 'He knew the law and he walked all over it, all the more disgraceful. From that moment on he was coopted, he had blood in his throat, on his hands, in his soul, and on his conscience.'

While Frank acquiesced in the SA purge, his initial hesitation disappointed Hitler. The following January, the Führer appointed Frank a full Reich minister, but without any portfolio. It was a position of great prestige but virtually no power. However, it necessitated a move to Berlin. Norman, then seven, has distinct memories of the next four years in the Third Reich's capital. 'My father was moving up in rank. I knew he was important. I had to know. We had three big limousines with chauffeurs and adjutants and all that. Even from the licence-plate numbers I knew my father was special. We had a very large villa with a great garden. But no one was around. I had to play with the chauffeurs. In their spare time between work they taught me to box and smoke cigarettes. I also played tennis by myself against the wall. My father was always away and my mother seemed either pregnant or in the hospital. And even when my mother was at the house, because she was a minister's wife she always attended many official functions. She was never around either. I didn't have any friends from school because our villa was so isolated that nobody ever came over. I was close to my older sister, but she was more outgoing than me, and since she had a lot of friends she stayed away from the house. It was very nice in Berlin, very peaceful, but also very lonely.'

Norman found refuge in reading. His father was also an avid reader of a wide range of books, including history, philosophy, and literature. 'During that time the most important book I read was *Tom Sawyer* and *Huckleberry Finn* – they were both in the same volume,' recalls Norman. 'It ruined me for the rest of the

Third Reich. My mind was always with Jim and the Mississippi River. It was so special to me, had such an impact on me. It was such a different world than the one I knew, the Indians, everything. It seemed strange but wonderful. I read it at nine and I still remember it clearly. I had a good imagination, and could see the scenes very well. I would rather have been there than in Berlin.'

Although Norman thought Mark Twain's world was remarkable, he was not aware that his own childhood was quite unusual. Because of their high position, his parents frequently entertained important Nazis. Norman met Goebbels at the propaganda ministry, Göring at the Munich Carnival, and Himmler in Munich. Mussolini, a close friend of his father, visited their Berlin home. 'Mussolini was the only one I didn't like. The others were all very nice to me. Göring struck me as very clever, very smart. But I didn't like any of those gatherings. I hated them. It was usually very embarrassing because I would spill my hot chocolate or something like that. I was taught to be quiet, correct, very well mannered, but I was always afraid of doing something wrong. On those big evenings with sixty or more guests, I would have to stand in line and greet everybody. It was terrible. I would try to get to the kitchen and hide with the personnel. I was a very private person in a very public house.'

Norman is still embarrassed by an occasion when he was selected to present a bouquet of flowers to Mussolini on his arrival at the train station. Hundreds of party dignitaries were awaiting Il Duce's appearance, and Norman was terrified of making a mistake that would disgrace both him and his father. 'I told my mother that I would rather eat rotten peaches than give the flowers to Mussolini,' he recalls. She relieved him of the dubious honour.

In the little time he did see his parents, Norman formed firm opinions about them. He remembers that both had tempers, but were controlled and seldom fought in front of him. There was little affection or religion in the household. 'My father was very intelligent, very witty, more educated than my mother, but she was smarter than him in daily life, in assessing people,' he says. 'They were different. He was a lawyer, a pianist, a writer, a connoisseur of the fine arts. He played classical music on the piano or organ for hours each day. He could hear it once and play it.

My father was not a day-dreamer. He was very practical, and I remember even in the beginning he spoke about politics at the dinner table. He was reckless and said things he should have kept to himself. I always felt he was never convinced the Germans would win the war. Even in the beginning I believe he had his doubts. He did everything he had to, anything that was his duty, but I don't think he believed in eventual victory.'

But Norman is the only family member who senses any initial doubt by his father. Frank's Berlin colleagues say he approached his work with zeal and was dedicated to National Socialism. He was slavishly addicted to Hitler.

During the 1936 Olympic Games, Hans Frank and Norman attended the opening ceremonies. But Frank's work was so hectic that an adjutant took the eight-year-old to the rest of the games. 'My favourite part was Jesse Owens, because he won three gold medals. At the time I did not know of the resentment in the Nazi hierarchy towards Owens as a black. But this was not the case among the German people. They all liked him. He is the only thing I remember of those games. I have forgotten the opening ceremonies, which are supposed to have been quite spectacular.'

In school, Norman says, his father's rank did not produce preferential treatment. 'The boy next to me in class was Jewish. I knew he was Jewish – we couldn't go to the same religious classes together because I was Catholic and he was Jewish. So we used to take long walks together. We liked each other. In 1938 he disappeared. I never knew, at that time, why he was gone. No one asked a question or said a word. But I did not think it was unusual because the school had many children of diplomats, and people always came and left.'

Nineteen thirty-eight was also the year of Kristallnacht (the 'night of broken glass'), the November terror when bands of Nazis destroyed thousands of Jewish businesses and synagogues. Again, Norman remembers the event and his father's reaction. 'My father had flown in from Munich and I went with my mother to pick him up in the car. When he came to us, the very first thing my mother said was "Hans, did you have anything to do with this?" And he quickly said, "No, I promise you I have nothing to do with it." People like my mother, like any decent German, were shocked by it. People did not like that type of destruction. But it was very clever of Hitler because at the time none of us knew he was behind it; we thought it was Goebbels. It was no longer the real Third Reich from that point on. It was a war against so many groups and people.'

Norman and Niklas differ sharply over whether their parents liked the high-profile Berlin life-style in the Nazi inner circle. Norman bases his feelings upon his own observations while living with them. Niklas has read his parents' writings, interviewed many witnesses and studied hundreds of documents from the period. Norman believes his parents had a 'duty to be public. But they would have preferred their privacy. My father would rather read than entertain those guests. My mother would have preferred that my father had remained a lawyer, with a small practice, in a little town. That is what she wanted and what would have made her happy. Naturally, any woman is proud if her husband achieves such a career, but it wasn't her desire. I watched and I heard things in our house. I know this was the case.' Only after 1940 did Norman notice a change in his father. 'In Poland, it became important for him to accumulate power and wealth, but not before.'

Niklas considers both his parents greedy for power and wealth from the earliest days. 'My mother loved the power, positions, money and status,' Niklas says. 'She loved her power over my father, over the personnel, over the Jews in the ghetto.' He condemns them both for a 'monumental career of raking in the loot' in their roles as governor-general and first lady of conquered Poland. 'There she assembled a small warehouse of furs,' says Niklas. 'She demanded to be called "Frau Minister". Yet, even from 1933 to 1939 I can imagine her greedily bustling about, out buying dresses, having tea at the Carlton, and riding with her friends in the big Mercedes.' As for his father, Niklas has no doubt that his love of prestige and power utterly corrupted him: 'He sold his soul to become important again. He was politically a dead man before his appointment as governor-general. He was striving for a position like that while he was in Berlin.'

The culmination of their father's career came on 26 September 1939, only seven months after Niklas's birth. Hitler appointed Frank governor-general of occupied Poland. In Berlin, Frank fell on one knee in front of his wife and said, 'Brigitte, you are going to be the queen of Poland.' While his wife and family returned to their home in southern Bavaria, near the stunning lake and mountain village of Schliersee, Frank headed east to Cracow. There, the thirty-nine-year-old governor-general established his headquarters in a castle on the Vistula river. The castle, stuffed with antiques and rare art, was considered a holy site, the place where Polish kings were crowned in earlier centuries and where their tombs were carefully preserved. As he settled into his new home, overlooking Cracow and the Polish countryside, Frank modelled his new kingdom on the Nazi state. Shortly after his arrival, he established the tone of his administration: 'Poland will be treated like a colony. The Poles will become the slaves of the Greater German Empire.' During his nearly six-year rule Hans Frank destroyed Poland as a national entity and exploited its human and material resources. He declared German the official language, walled in the Jewish ghettos, confiscated Jewish and Polish property, expropriated national art treasures, and allowed huge quantities of food and delicacies to be sent home to Schliersee at a time when most of Europe was hungry. Polish workers were forcibly shipped to Germany to assist the war effort. The Nazis sent the bulk of the Polish harvest to Germany, while the average Pole subsisted on six hundred calories a day. Frank tried to transform the Catholic Church into a Nazi tool, saying that 'priests will preach what we wish, and any priest who acts differently, we shall make short work of him. The task of the priest is to keep the Poles quiet, stupid, and dull-witted.' Thousands of Polish priests were arrested, and 850 died in Dachau.

Frank's ruthless tone appealed to the most thuggish elements in the SS and police. He declared: 'After the war is over you can make mincemeat out of the Poles and the Ukrainians and anything else hanging around here as far as I am concerned.' He bragged to a Berlin journalist, 'If I were to have one poster printed for every seven Poles I'm going to have shot, all the trees in Poland couldn't provide enough paper.'

His implementation of Hitler's policies towards Jews was particularly brutal. In the spring of 1940, Frank told a meeting of division chiefs that 'it can no longer be endured for our generals to have to live in houses where the only other lodgers, beside the generals, are human vermin – Jews'. He promised to rid Cracow of Jews, disinfect the ghetto, and build German housing surrounded by 'good German air'. Over the next few years, Frank championed the harshest Nazi measures against Jews.

On the first anniversary of assuming power in Poland, he told his officers that their families in Germany should not worry about them. Conditions had drastically improved since so many 'lice and Jews' had been eliminated. His seminal address came in a government session at the castle. In a rousing talk he said, 'Now as to the Jews, and I am telling you this quite candidly, there must be a stop put to them, one way or another. As far as the Jews are concerned, I shall henceforth use as my one guiding principle the assumption that they are to disappear. . . . We must obliterate the Jews wherever we find them and whenever the opportunity is afforded us. . . . We cannot shoot these three and a half million Jews, we cannot kill them with poison, but we can proceed with the necessary steps which somehow or other will lead to their successful extermination.' By December 1942, 85 per cent of Poland's Jews had been transported to concentration camps, most of which were under Frank's jurisdiction.

For Niklas, his father's statements are the most difficult to live with. 'I don't even think he was an anti-Semite,' Niklas says. 'It was expected of him and he instantly became one. He was such an opportunist and so weak during that time. He wanted to appear so tough to Hitler and the rest. It is almost impossible to read these statements because of the anger and bitter shame I feel, yet I read them over and over again. It is incredible that a person who could love Chopin, Beethoven, was a friend of Richard Strauss, had tears in his eyes when he read Christmas stories, could say those words. To me, those sentences are as evil as the murders committed by the SS.'

For Norman, his father's statements are as if they came from somebody else. 'He never spoke like that in front of the family. In my youth I had not been educated in anti-Semitism, neither by my parents nor by anyone else. There was no talk about Jews in our family, but very much so in the official media. However, as a young man, one did not have any interest in such things. Those anti-Semitic feelings, and the idolization of the extermination of the Jews which my father articulated more than once, but always in front of a large audience, did not come from his soul. Rather, they were his commitment to official policies. to identify yourself as a National Socialist, this hatred of the Jews became the surrogate for a political programme.

'When I read my father's words after the war, I was just ashamed. It was not the father I loved. It's such a contradiction in him, I can't understand it. How could he be so cultured and good to me and then say things so stupid and hateful?' Norman shakes his head, near tears.

Some of Hans Frank's colleagues later tried to defend him by blaming the crimes on Himmler and the SS. They claimed Frank only gave 'tough' talks when the SS was present, so he would not appear soft on the extermination policies. They argue that he had no direct control over the concentration camps, which were under SS jurisdiction. They are quick to point out that the largest camp, Auschwitz, was outside of the governor-general's boundaries.[4] There is little doubt that Frank disliked Himmler and his hand-picked man in Poland, Friedrich Krüger. He often tried resisting the SS orders and criticized their arbitrary and 'nonjudicial' incarcerations. However, most of Frank's conflict with the SS was not because of moral objections, but rather a fight for ultimate control in the general administration, as well as an attempt to discredit an SS inquiry into corruption by Frank and his wife.

The SS investigated Frank and his wife for shopping in the ghetto and forcing Jews to sell at very low prices or give free gifts. 'My mother used to say that the Jews in the ghetto made the most beautiful camisoles,' Niklas remembers. The Franks took food, art, icons, Russian jewellery, furs, gold, marble, antiques and rare carpets. Some of it ended back at their Bavarian home in Schliersee. Frank employed the same art agent ('art-theft agent', says Niklas) as the insatiable Göring. Once he learned of the SS inquiry, Frank faked invoices to cover his trail, but the SS eventually concluded that the entire Cracow administration was riddled with corruption.

However, the corruption investigation did not come to a head until 1942. Until then, Frank was busy with the tumultuous task of administering Nazi Germany's largest occupied zone. During the beginning he was alone, his family still in Germany. Norman had returned to Bavaria when his father went to Poland in 1939. Although his father visited during holidays, they saw each other only sporadically during 1939–40. 'During my stay in Bavaria I met my wife-to-be, only I didn't marry her for another twenty years,' Norman says.

In March 1940 Norman was transferred to a boarding school. The introverted child still had difficulty making friends at his new school. 'And now my sister was separated from me. But being separated from her did not make me more alone, I was just as lonely when I was with her.'

While his father established the decrees to render Poland a German slave state, Norman heard about the war in school. 'They told us about the war, especially about the German victories. I remember the fall of France was a big event. But I was never excited by the military. Many of my schoolmates dreamed of fighting in the army, but not me. I didn't play those games. For me, a good goal in hockey or one of my books was far more exciting. Instead of going into the war I would have preferred going down the Mississippi with Huckleberry Finn.'

In March 1941 the Nazis completed a school in Cracow and Hans Frank summoned his thirteen-year-old son. 'I would have liked to have stayed in Bavaria, but at least I was going to be reunited with my father. To me, his position, governor-general, was just another military position.' But Cracow was different from Norman's expectations. 'It was much warmer than I imagined. I thought people never got out of furs in Poland. It was much nicer than I expected. Cracow was very pretty, but castle life was dull and uninspiring because of the war. Berlin was much more exciting because it was during peace. Except for the castle, my life in Berlin was grander.'

Although Poland surprised Norman, the youngster's biggest surprise was his father. 'It had been six months since I last saw him, the longest separation I had ever had. When I saw him, I could tell that he was under a lot of pressure. His health was good, but he was much more serious, much less joking. For my father, it had all changed. He was dead – he just didn't understand it yet.'

While Brigitte visited occasionally with Niklas and the other children, Norman was mostly alone with his father. 'Since my mother didn't like to travel much with small children, she didn't come that often. So it was just me and my father and the staff, and we never saw them. My father wanted me there with him so he would have a sense of family. My older sister was also around sometimes, but she was always out with some boyfriend and we hardly ever saw her.'

Norman attended a high school for Germans and Volks-deutsche (Poles of German blood). His grades suffered: he quickly deteriorated from a good student to 'a terrible one. Only sports mattered to me.' Every day he bicycled to the school. 'I knew the whole town very well, and the ghetto had been shown to me. To me it was just part of the town. I don't remember any walls or fences around it like in Warsaw. I didn't think it was unusual because I had been told it had been there before my father arrived and the Poles wanted it that way. There was no sign that said GHETTO or anything like that.'[5]

Norman also saw the Warsaw ghetto on one occasion. He remembers 'incredible pushing and shoving. Jews, as super-visors, were in their own uniforms. There were two clearly distinct classes. One still had something, while the other was at the beginning of misery.'

Niklas, eleven years younger than Norman, also has two distinct and harrowing memories from his trips to the ghetto. 'I was in the back of the Mercedes, accompanying my mother on one of her buying trips. There was her adjutant, and a driver, and my nurse. I had my nose to the window looking at everything and I remember all the grown-ups seemed scared and the children were staring at our car. I asked my mother why they all looked so cross, and why they had stars [Stars of David] on their clothes and who were the men with whips. "Oh, never mind, you wouldn't understand. Enjoy the ride." That's what she told me. And when the car stopped, I looked out of the window and an older boy was standing outside staring at me. He must have been ten or older because he had the star on his right arm, and later I learned that all children over ten had to wear it. And I made faces at him and he looked very sad and then ran away. I remember feeling very victorious against this older and bigger boy. Only later did I realize how poor his situation was, and that he probably did not survive. Then I felt shame.

'Another time, I was with my nanny. And there is a memory of a house, a dimly-lit corridor, and one of the aides picked me up so I could see through a peephole. There was a young woman near a wall and she was staring at the floor. "See the wicked witch in there," the aide said. I started crying. "She won't hurt you," he assured me. "She'll be dead anyway soon." Many years later I discovered she was a famous member of the resistance who had escaped from a concentration camp. She was killed.

'These are the pictures I bear with me.'

Norman is also troubled by chilling memories. He still vividly recalls an event early during his Cracow stay. He was playing football when suddenly he heard men loudly singing the banned Polish national anthem, and then the nearby sound of gunshots. He asked a supervisor what was happening. ' "They are shooting the Poles," he told me.' Later Norman asked his father about it, but Hans Frank became furious and dismissed the conversation. 'He said it was war and I shouldn't ask about it,' Norman recalls sadly.

Not all memories are as depressing for the brothers. In Cracow, as in Berlin, Hans Frank entertained some of the Third Reich's most prominent officials. Both sons remember parties at the castle. Visitors included propaganda minister Josef Goebbels and party ideologue Alfred Rosenberg. 'There were also movie stars, musicians, opera singers and artists from Germany, Norway, Sweden, all types and places,' Norman recalls. 'Cracow was far away from the war and it was safer to perform there. For my father, who loved culture, this was important. I also found it interesting.'

Norman also travelled with his father around Poland. Often, their private saloon car passed one of the concentration camps which dotted the countryside. 'We always passed Auschwitz if we came from Vienna,' Norman recalls. 'I didn't know at the time it was Auschwitz, but I knew it later because we had travelled an hour from Cracow and it was very large. I never thought anything about the camps, it never even registered. I thought it was normal for a war. I knew they were KZs [shorthand for *Konzentrationslager*, concentration camp], with barbed wire and all, and I thought they were prisoner camps. Only after the war did I discover what happened there.'

The only suggestion Norman had that something more sinister was taking place came at school. A classmate had drawn a picture of a Jew entering the top of a mill and coming out as bars of soap. The teacher thought the drawing was so good it was passed around the class. Already rebuffed by his father when he tried to ask about the shooting of Poles, Norman did not mention the drawing to his father. 'But I felt then that something terrible was happening,' he recalls.

Niklas remembers a single trip to a barbed-wire enclosure, which he now knows was the perimeter of a concentration camp. 'These skinny men were being made to get on the back of a donkey and it kept throwing them. I thought it was hilarious. The uniformed man was nice to me, giving me hot chocolate. That's all I remember.'

But Hans Frank did not take his children, even Norman, on all his trips from Cracow. Official records show that in a twelve-month span (mid-1942 to mid-1943), Frank was away for 170 days. 'During many of those times I was left in the castle by myself, with the domestic staff. It was like Berlin, in that I was alone again, but this time I was grown up [he was fifteen years old]. I kept to myself. I was embarrassed about everything, never made any statements, was always very quiet.'

Unknown to Norman, his father, a womanizer, had rekindled a romance with a childhood sweetheart in Germany. He used every excuse to visit his 'beloved Lilly'. Although Norman was aware the relationship between his parents had 'cooled', he was not aware that his father wanted to end the marriage. In 1942, Frank wrote Brigitte a letter in which he vaguely spoke about 'blood and mountains of corpses'. It was his way of confessing his knowledge of the extermination of the Jews. In order to spare her the consequences, he offered to make 'the greatest sacrifice a husband can make, a divorce'. She saw through the charade and refused. While the children were kept in the dark, their parents conducted a vicious divorce battle. Brigitte accused her husband of being a 'schizophrenic' suffering from a 'psychosis, the result of his sexual adventures'. She wrote letters to Hitler's aides complaining about Hans and implying that he was disparaging Himmler. In turn, Frank generated rumours that his wife was involved in fur-smuggling with her own lover, a close Frank friend, the governor of Radom, Dr Karl Lasch.[6] He also implied that Niklas was really Lasch's son. Niklas says that his mother did accumulate a warehouse of furs, that Lasch was her lover, and that he often wondered whether he was Lasch's son. Although the divorce battle amused Frank's enemies, Brigitte eventually appealed to Hitler, who ordered a halt to the squabbling. The marriage continued despite the couple's almost total estrangement. In retrospect, Norman views his father as the victim. 'The few women he had were not very nice to him,' he says. 'Only his mother was nice to him. Even the girlfriend he saw during the war, she was not good for him either.'

The child who more acutely sensed the marital strain at this time was Niklas, even at five years of age. He remembers going to Poland by train, 'in my father's saloon wagon. A car would take us to the castle, I can see myself sitting in it. I remember one time at Kressendorf [the Franks' weekend castle outside Cracow] that my father was standing at the top of the steps and he waited for me and my mother to go up to him. He was waiting there like a king, and I could sense that my mother was furious that he didn't come down the stairs to greet her. And at the same time I felt afraid of my father.'

At the main castle in Cracow, Niklas and his brother Michael played hide-and-seek 'around the graves of the kings of Poland. This is a very good memory for me. And now I find it unbelievable we were allowed to do that, and I am ashamed.' Another game he played at the castle was pedalling his small toy wagon into the Polish servants. 'I would wait around a corner and when I heard them walking nearby, I would push out as hard and fast as I could and slam into their legs. And they would be furious, but have to look down at me and smile because I was the governor-general's son. I was very aggressive. Today, I would say it was reaction to the poor atmosphere created by the extremely bad marriage of my parents. I don't remember my parents arguing, but I know they did not seem normal to me. I can't describe it exactly, but I never had the feeling of being happy or anything like that. I have tried to call back my memories of the time, all my feelings. I don't have any particular situation in mind, but I know it wasn't good.'

While Niklas took out the frustrations of an unhappy household in hostile games, Norman became more introverted. 'We never played with Norman,' Niklas recalls. 'He was already a grown-up to us. I remember Norman around this time playing the role of an old man with a stick, all hunched over and walking like a very old man. He would be alone in a field and do this for hours. I think he did it both during the war and after. That was his game.'

Niklas does not remember his father showing any affection to him or the rest of his family. 'I remember nothing during this period,' Niklas says. 'No hugs, no "I love you." ' Instead, he remembers his father once teasing him: 'He would say, "Who are you, little stranger? What are you doing here?" ' One of the few times Niklas remembers an outburst of emotion was a mild slap in the face when he accidentally broke his father's eyeglasses. In contrast, while Norman does not remember his father being demonstrative, he recalls him as very warm. He does not remember any corporal punishment. 'He felt guilty that he was away from me so much, so when he was at the castle, he tried to make up for it. He never hit me. I never saw that type of anger in him. If anything, by 1942, he wasn't concerned with all the family intrigue any longer, he was more concerned with his work. He had pulled back totally and was withdrawn.'

Nineteen forty-two was a significant year for the Frank family. Norman was nearly fourteen and membership in the Hitler Youth was mandatory. 'Fortunately, I was in Cracow, in Berlin, in Schliersee, all over, so they never knew where I was and I never did any duties,' Norman says. 'I only had to wear the uniform and that was enough. I had nothing else to compare it to and at the time I thought it was just another part of normal existence in a war.' But Norman's difficulty with the Hitler Youth was minor compared to problems faced by his father. On 5 March 1942, Frank was summoned to Himmler's private rail coach, which had travelled to Poland for the occasion. With Himmler was a hated Frank opponent, Obergruppenführer [Lieutenant-General] Hans Lammers, and Hitler's secretary, Martin Bormann. Himmler kept notes on the meeting. The three Nazi officials confronted Frank with evidence of his corruption-riddled administration. In return for dropping the investigation, Frank gave the SS control over all police, providing them free rein in the general administration. Frank thus abdicated much of his power in Poland to Himmler.

Norman saw his father react to his political problems by taking refuge in music and reading. 'He began composing again, and playing the piano almost every night, sometimes for hours. I would sit and watch. It was just the two of us.'

But Frank harboured a deep resentment of the SS for their strong-arm tactics. In June and July 1942, in Germany, he gave four remarkable speeches in which he called for a return to constitutional rule, a firm role for an independent judiciary, and a halt to many of the SS's arbitrary arrests and detentions.[7] Norman attended one of the university talks. While the speeches were enthusiastically received by German students, the Nazi hierarchy was furious. Hitler stripped Frank of his party posts and restricted any future speeches to Poland. For Frank, his attempt to undermine Himmler's popular support within the party had backfired. Although he boldly offered to resign as governor-general if Hitler had lost confidence in him, the Führer let him stay. 'That made my father very happy,' says Niklas, 'as he told my mother.'

Norman believes his father gave the 'brave' talks because 'he was against the SS terror and as a lawyer knew a state could not exist without laws'. He does not see the speeches as the culmination of a rivalry with Himmler for power. Even Niklas admits the speeches took *chutzpah* but he condemns his father for having the 'nerve to leave a raped country, talk about justice in Germany, and then return to Poland and get the murder machine going again. He should have just resigned, not stayed if Hitler wanted him to.' Niklas says that his father's four speeches on behalf of justice were nothing compared to one he gave a few days later, on 1 August 1942, in Poland. There he spoke to assembled troops and to Ukrainian and Polish delegations. He thanked Hitler for giving him control of 'this ancient nest of Jews', so that armed with shovels and insect powder he had made it possible for 'a German to live here in comfort. Jews, yes, we still have a few of them around, but we'll take care of that.' He joked about how the town he was in had once had thousands of 'unbelievably disgusting . . . Jews of such hideous repulsiveness', but now he could not find any. 'Don't tell me that you've been treating them badly?' The stenographer's notes show the audience reaction was 'great hilarity'. Niklas considers this speech incredible, especially since it came within days of Frank's seeming appeals in Germany for a return to a system of law and order.

The August speech was not an isolated exception. Frank continued to propel the murder machine. By the end of 1942 he told the police, 'In several years Poles will no longer be in existence.' The following spring he still called Jews the 'greatest peril' while threatening to kill a hundred Poles for every German killed. At the same time he complained about the insufficient manpower supplied to complete his deadly task: 'When the Bolsheviks plan to annihilate people, they send at least two thousand Red Army troops into every village where the people are to be exterminated. But to send us only ten thousand police troops for the whole administration of Poland, and then order us to finish off fifteen million people . . . that just can't be done.' At Belvedere Castle in Warsaw he told fellow Nazi officials, 'There is no reason to be squeamish when we hear about seventeen thousand people being shot. May I remind us, everyone gathered here, that each and every one of us already has his place on Roosevelt's roster of war criminals. I have the honour of being number one. We are all, as it were, accomplices, speaking from the perspective of world history.'

'It is sentences like that which brought about his death,' says Niklas. 'And I must go on living with them.'

During the time Hans Frank was encouraging the Nazi crimes in Poland, Norman was unaware of his father's dark side. 'To me he was merely in an important military position, worked most of the day and always seemed to be involved in some type of official function. He was still the same father to me, still good to me. Except for his personal withdrawal, I saw nothing unusual about his behaviour.' According to Niklas, there was a reason for his father's withdrawal. 'The war was being lost,' he says. 'Many of the Nazis who were so brave when they were marching across Europe were now quite frightened as it turned against them.'

On 6 June 1944, the Allies landed in Normandy. The Russians were moving westwards at a quickening pace. Norman was at the second Frank castle, at Kressendorf, when the Allies assaulted the French coast. Hans Frank was in Cracow. 'We all really expected this news. We knew they would be coming at some time, but we just didn't know when and where.' During the autumn of 1944, Norman was sent to a German school in Czechoslovakia, farther away from the advancing front. 'But my father called me back to Cracow for the Christmas holidays that year. When I saw him again he was resigned to defeat. Anyone who didn't know several months after the Allied landings that this was the end had to be an idiot. For my father, the war had been lost for years. Events were just now confirming the inevitability of defeat.'

However, while Frank might have shown his defeatism to Norman, he exhibited a far more confident and aggressive public face. When Italy fell in August, he said, 'The ultimate lines of combat have been clearly drawn: on the one hand, the swastika, and on the other, the Jews.' Some of his most vicious statements came during the final months of 1944. He promised that the Nazi party would outlive Jews. 'When we began here, there were three and a half million of them; now, all that is left is little more than a few groups of Jewish labourers. All the others have, shall we say, emigrated.' In another address he claimed that his consolation in case of military defeat would be 'that I will be able to say triumphantly that I have killed two million Polacks'. Frank spent part of his final year as governor-general unsuccessfully trying to organize an anti-Jewish congress in Cracow, dubbed 'Antisemitropolis'.

Yet Frank never revealed this side of himself to Norman. He felt most comfortable with his eldest son and drew closer to him as his government crumbled. 'I left Cracow on the sixth of January,' Norman recalls. 'My father left eleven days later, when the city fell to the Russians.'

On 17 January 1945, after several weeks of destroying files, HANS Frank left for Schliersee. His private car was attached to a train which also carried some of Poland's greatest art treasures, including a Raphael of a young boy and Leonardo da Vinci's oil 'Lady with an Ermine'. Niklas remembers the da Vinci hung in his father's office suite at the castle. 'I thought it was ugly,' he recalls. 'I thought she was holding a rat. Only later did I learn it was a da Vinci.' Frank later told his American interrogators he had taken the pictures so that they would not be looted while he was away. 'The Raphael was saved but the da Vinci has never been found. It's probably hanging in some farmer's house in Bavaria,' says Niklas sarcastically. 'Maybe my mother traded it for some butter and eggs after war. She knew as much about art as my father knew about the truth.'[8]

During his escape to the west, Frank gave a gluttonous three-day party in a Silesian castle, an event which infuriated the Nazi hierarchy in Berlin when the news reached them. It was not the type of behaviour that instilled confidence in hungry soldiers fighting with limited ammunition.

Norman saw his father on 25 January at the family home in Schliersee. 'He was the same to me,' he recalls. 'My mother was simply waiting for the Americans. She was convinced peace would come and they had not done anything wrong. She really expected a normal life would soon return.'

According to Norman, Hans Frank spent nights with the family but established auxiliary headquarters of the administration in a former café in neighbouring Neuhaus. Niklas has only one distinct memory from the period before his father's arrest. He recalls the family, including his father, standing beside their house watching hundreds of Allied planes on the way to bomb nearby Munich. 'We just watched the skyful of silver machines in silence. It seemed endless.'

Norman, then seventeen years old, recalls the day of his father's arrest. 'I saw my father every night. On May fourth, I visited him, together with my sister, only one hour before his arrest. We went by bicycle and had a coffee with him. The Americans were very close. He was quite calm. Three of his co-workers were with him. My father had his diaries with him and was convinced they would prove his innocence. While we had coffee he said, "I think I am the last minister who is still free, still sitting in freedom drinking coffee." '

'He knew he was about to be arrested,' Niklas says. 'Earlier that day he gave my mother a thick bundle of money [fifty thousand Reichsmarks]. There was no kiss, no affection. It was just like a pay-off to a whore.'

An hour after Norman's visit, an American, Lieutenant Stein, arrived and arrested the governor-general. The arrest did not seem unusual to Norman. 'I wasn't surprised by it. All of Germany was being detained and my father had been a high official, so I expected it. We never knew where he was until September, almost five months later. That's when they moved him to Nuremberg and we heard on the radio that there would be a trial.'

When Frank was arrested, he voluntarily surrendered all forty-two volumes of the official diaries he kept while governor-general.[9] They included all transcripts of his speeches, trips, receptions, government meetings, and conferences. He had unwittingly provided the Nuremberg prosecution with the bulk of the evidence against him. Frank naïvely thought the books would establish his opposition to Himmler and vindicate him. Even he was surprised at the trial when many of his nastiest speeches were introduced into evidence. 'Some of the words are terrible,' he told the tribunal. 'I myself must admit that I was shocked at many of the words which I had used. It was a wild and stormy period filled with terrible passions, and when a whole country is on fire and a life-and-death struggle is going on, such words may easily be used.' Niklas is 'eternally grateful' that his father surrendered his diaries. 'They jog my memory whenever my wrath begins to flag. All I need do is flip through them for a while.'

Upon Frank's arrest he was taken to Miesbach prison. The American soldiers had just seen pictures of the concentration camps and they wanted vengeance. Frank was a symbol of the twisted skeletons on the newsreels. They formed a double line nearly seventy feet long and beat him as he walked into the prison. That night he tried to commit suicide by slitting his throat with a rough implement left inside his cell. He was brought to Berchtesgaden several days later, looking, according to a witness, like a 'bloody pulp'. Later he again tried to kill himself, slashing open his left arm.

By this time the Frank family had seen newspaper pictures of the concentration camps. 'It all changed then,' says Norman. 'From that moment on the war was lost, my father was lost. Until that time no one thought we had done anything wrong. I knew the pictures in the papers were real. I never thought it was Russian propaganda like a lot of other people. It was the truth and I knew it. American soldiers guarded our house after some displaced persons looted the home. After the pictures from Auschwitz, I felt it was all justified. It had not been a war. It was worse. These crimes changed everything.'

On Niklas the photos of mountains of bodies also made an indelible mark. 'One of my most distinct impressions and memories were the first newspaper pictures when I saw thousands of naked bodies in the concentration camp. I was not even seven years old. This has stayed with me all my life. Those pictures of death, of bodies, of small boys' bodies, and girls' bodies, and naked and all. I knew my father had been very important in Poland and that these camps were in the East. From the beginning I could imagine he had something to do with those pictures. It wasn't long before I knew the words "the Butcher of Poland".'

Soon after seeing the camp photos, Norman received the news of his father's first suicide attempt. 'It was about three days later on the news. Someone came running to me and said, "Your father is dead!" That's the first I heard of it. I felt nothing. Millions had died. My father had talked about it with me. I almost expected it. Then I found out he was alive and tried it again. I could imagine how badly he wanted to die.'

On 19 October 1945, the Allies presented the Nuremberg defendants with the war crimes indictments. Frank, charged under all four counts, burst into tears. The Frank family heard the news on the radio. When the trial started on 20 November, the family gathered to listen to the news summaries. 'I knew it was really serious because all the grown-ups around me were very sad and crying often,' Niklas recalls. 'I remember listening very often to the radio broadcasts of the trial. It was a very sad atmosphere. My mother would gather us around the radio – it was very important for us to be home at the right time so we didn't miss the broadcast. My father wasn't on until the spring of 1946, but my mother was still interested because she knew many of the other defendants.'

Frank presented an aggressive defence, blaming Himmler and the SS while minimizing his own authority. At the same time he played to the tribunal by criticizing National Socialism and Hitler. He claimed the trial testimony had 'shaken him' and he was baptized again into the Catholic faith. Proclaiming a new religious fervour, he accepted the 'dreadful responsibility' for the extermination camps even though he 'never installed one'. He told the judges that Hitler 'represented the spirit of evil on earth' and praised the tribunal as 'a God-willed world court, destined to examine and put an end to the terrible era of suffering under Adolf Hitler'. In the climactic ending of a monologue to the tribunal, Frank announced: 'A thousand years shall pass and still this guilt of Germany will not have been erased.' Francis Biddle, Roosevelt's attorney-general and the chief American judge at Nuremberg, called Frank's statements 'a cheap dramatic confession'. The other judges concurred and were unanimous in convicting him on two of the indictment's four counts.

'I thought it was fantastic when he said he was guilty in April of 1946,' Norman says. 'I think he said this for the German people, that he would take the responsibility for the crimes.

'Under the circumstances, which were almost impossible, it was a trial of the victors over the vanquished, but it was also necessary and fair. These were different crimes from anything else we had ever seen and they had to be judged. It is only a shame that the Nuremberg trials were not able to stop further crimes from being committed in this world.'

Before the verdict, in September 1946, Frank's family visited him in Nuremberg. It was a day set aside for the families of all the defendants. The smaller children went in with their mother. It was the first time Norman had seen his father since his May 1945 arrest. 'I remember Edda Göring and all the other children. It felt unusual at the prison. My father looked different, he was very thin. But he tried to be very calm, especially for my brothers and sisters. He told me to be strong and to always remember never to speak my mind unless I first thought carefully about what I would say. Put a stick in my throat if I was going to speak too freely. It had damaged him and he warned me about this. It was his parting advice to me.'

In contrast to Norman, who was satisfied with his final meeting with his father, Niklas was angry about the prison visit. 'I remember it very clearly,' he says. 'I was sitting on my mother's knees and he was sitting behind a window, next to a white-helmeted soldier, and he was friendly and laughing. It was my strongest impression of him because it was the last time I saw him. And I knew that it was the last time. And he said to me, "Ah, Niki, in three months' time we will have a wonderful Christmas Eve in our house." And I sat there thinking, "He is lying." He knew he was going to be executed. Why was he lying to me? Today, I know it was to comfort me and to appear happy so I could remember him in a later time as a better man or something like this. But I wish he had given me some advice, that he had said, "I am going to die, and I am guilty, and you will never meet me again, but here is something for your later life." That is the one thing that is really haunting me, following me.'

For many years Niklas was also angry over a prison prayer book his father left him, with an inscription wishing him God's protection. 'He misspelled my name as Nicki, with a c. He couldn't even spell my name right at the hour of his death. People shouldn't do things like that. I am no longer angry – just disappointed.'

On 30 September 1946, the court passed sentence on Frank. He seemed disoriented, facing the courtroom's rear wall until the GIs spun him around to face the tribunal. His hands trembled slightly and he fumbled with the earphones. When he heard the death sentence, he murmured, 'Thank you', the only defendant to utter a sound. Norman clearly remembers that day. 'We heard the death sentence live on the radio. We were all sitting around together. My mother didn't cry, she held back for the rest of us. We were all strong. My father was ready to die.'

Norman would not have preferred a life sentence for his father. 'For me it is better he is executed. It would have been terrible if my father was in prison like Hess. I would have had real trouble living with that. If I had to know all my life that every time I took a cup of coffee, or a walk, that my father was in prison, I couldn't have taken this. In that sense I am grateful he was condemned to die. A life sentence for my father would have been a life sentence for the whole family.'

For seven-year-old Niklas, the memory of his father's sentencing is not as clear. 'I don't remember hearing it on the radio,' he says, 'but I knew it, I knew he was sentenced to death. But I can't say from where. I understood what it meant. I understood that he would be hanged. You have to imagine, I was in the lowest grades of my school, and the whole village spoke about this, and in school it was always talked about. It was a very small town, and everyone knew who I was. Everyone knew my father had been sentenced to die.'

The news of how he would be executed was difficult for the family. 'The worst news for us was that he would be hanged,' Norman recalls. 'This was a surprise to us. We thought he would be shot like a soldier. He thought so too. It was unworthy for a people as decent as the Americans to give these men this unworthy death. It was the hardest for him.'

Niklas disagrees with his brother. He believes that hanging was justified. 'I know it is not so easy to die at the age of forty-six. I have passed that age and I know how young you can feel. To go to the gallows, it's hard. But I wished my father this death and fear of death, because he, and all the other Germans, gave this fear of death to millions of people, under their so-called great times.'

Niklas remembers his mother brought him the news of his father's death. 'My brother Michael, my sister Brigitte, and me, we three were taken to a kindergarten. A couple of days after my father was executed, my mother came to get us and said, "Let us make a little walk." And we went along with her, and she had very colourful clothes on, not black ones. And she said, "Now I must tell you that your father is dead. And it is a bad thing that he is dead, but as you can see by my clothes, I am not behaving like a widow, because it is the best for your father that he is dead now."

'And then my sister and my brother started crying very heavily, and I was only quiet. And my mother said, "Look, both of you, to Niki, he is not crying. Be like him." But I had the definite feeling that she was furious at me for not crying. It was like the time I felt her great anger directed at my father at the steps to the castle when he made her walk up to greet him. But now the anger was directed at me.'

Niklas never saw his mother cry over his father. 'She cried often after the war, but it had to do with our bad situation, not with him,' Niklas says. 'There were several years after the war when we did not know what was going on with our future.'

Niklas also did not shed a tear over his father's death. 'But even though I never cried, I felt very close to him on the anniversary of his death. This started for me around 1947 or 1948. I felt very close to his death. I would see my father going down a long corridor to the gallows and I created in myself a real fear of death. I was my father. I put myself in the same situation as him. It was as though I was looking at him in these images, but it was also me about to be hanged.'

While Niklas had difficulty adjusting to his father's execution, it was worse for Norman. Niklas clearly remembers his brother during this period. 'He was very sad. He had a lot of arguments with my mother. For me and Michael it was always very hard to go home from our games outside, because I feared the atmosphere at home very much. Often I could hear my mother screaming and crying at least thirty feet away. And since it was a small village, when the window was open you could hear her all around. It was very distressing and very hard on all of us, but I

think especially difficult for Norman. He was good to Michael
and me, and tried to be very funny to keep us happy. But he was
sad.'

Norman is very sombre when talking of his father's execution.
'I didn't cry at the time and that's half the reason I am so sick
with an ulcer,' he says. His wife, Elizabeth, interrupts him, 'Oh,
Norman, you did cry! You still cry for your father.' He dismisses
her and does not add anything.

During the summer of 1947, Brigitte Frank was incarcerated
for more than three months. She was put into an American
detention camp at Augsburg, together with many of the wives of
other prominent Nazis. Niklas and Michael accompanied her to
the railway station. 'I cried a lot when she was taken,' Niklas
recalls. 'But when I visited her at the camp it was quite exciting.
Ilse Koch[10] was there and was always singing the old Nazi songs.
My mother found that very funny. She was in good spirits and
looked better than when she went in. I remember this well. She
would say to us, "Look at me, look how tanned I am." Later she
would joke this was her last real holiday.

'It was not a bad time for us when my mother was in the camp.
Not at all. We were very happy because our Aunt Else took care
of us and she was very funny. Michael and I laughed at all her
efforts to educate us.'

While Niklas may have found the situation 'happy' and his
mother in good spirits, Norman has a quite different memory. 'I
saw my mother every week during the time she was in the camp,
and she got very sick. I was eighteen and had to take care of the
family. Food was very hard to get.'

One time an American GI, drunk on too many bottles of wine
from the Frank cellar, lined the family up against a wall and
waved his rifle, threatening to shoot them. Brigitte Frank coolly
told him not to shoot children. Michael was sobbing. But
Niklas's reaction was quite different. 'At that moment, I will
never forget it, I was on the side of the American soldier. I really
felt that he wasn't the criminal, but that we, our family, we were
the criminals. And from that moment, I have always felt like
that.'

Not every difficulty facing the Frank family was as clear-cut as
a soldier waving a gun. They were forcibly moved from their
large home to a very small, cold flat, and food was difficult to

find. Almost all their personal property was confiscated. Niklas remembers being sent out by his mother to beg for food, with a note pleading the family had nothing to eat. He came back with half a loaf of bread, and is still ashamed at the memory. Brigitte Frank sold some jewels she had hidden from the American army and the looters. They provided the family with enough money to live. Norman felt useless because he was unable to return to school or find a job. 'The worst part was they refused to allow me to go to school. When I tried, the German director said that no children of war criminals could attend. My elder sister could not go back, but she didn't care because she was married by then. All my younger brothers and sisters were allowed into schools. But I was left out. I couldn't get any work for the same reason. As the eldest son, these negative feelings were directed at me.'

In an effort to support her five children, Brigitte Frank turned to an unlikely source of income. Hans Frank wrote a book while in prison, a reminiscence of life in the Third Reich ('I have never been able to read more than a few pages at a time because of its insufferable vanity,' says Niklas). But Brigitte marketed the book under the title *Face to Face with the Gallows* and sold it by mail order to thousands of customers, including many former Frank colleagues and ex-Nazis. According to Niklas, the sales brought in more than two hundred thousand Deutschmarks, all untaxed. He says it also brought hundreds of letters, containing 'unctuous enthusiasm about the nostalgic garbage produced by my father'. After the book sales slowed, Brigitte marketed copies of Frank's prison letters to his family, together with a letter describing the family's economic plight. When that failed to bring in enough funds, Brigitte sold *The Cabin Boy of Columbus*, a short novel Frank wrote while governor-general.

During this time, Niklas wanted to learn about his father. He read newspapers and at the cinema saw weekly newsreels about the war. Whenever he found a book, he looked up his father's name in the index and immediately read the pages about him. 'So I got a lot of information about him,' Niklas recalls. 'From the very beginning there were no good lines about my father. It was always negative, but I always believed what I read about him. And I never had any wish to defend my father. It was always the complete opposite. I would always say my father is a criminal, and the others would say, "Oh no, poor man, victim of circumstances", and the like.

'One of my biggest mistakes, though, was that I never asked my mother any questions. I never asked anyone in the family. I kept it all to myself. I never wanted to talk to anyone about it.'

But Niklas is convinced his family would not have talked to him if he had asked. The only form of communication they tried were occasional séance sessions to contact his dead father. As a youngster, encouraged by his aunt's belief in reincarnation, Niklas once thought he found his father reincarnated as a neighbour's dachshund. After two frustrating weeks of talking to him and getting no answer, Niklas tied fifty firecrackers around the dog and blew him up. 'I guess it was how I was feeling about my father,' he says.

While Niklas was finding out about the war and his father's role, Norman was not. He had enough of his own memories. 'I did almost nothing during this time, just some private studies. But I never got the equivalent of a degree in anything. Nothing was important to me any more. I had not read my father's diaries at that time, although I did later. I have never read the trial transcripts.'

By 1951, twenty-three-year-old Norman was so frustrated with postwar Germany that he moved to Argentina. 'My sister had a friend there, so I decided to try it. I was in Buenos Aires and in the Andes for five years. It was a good time. I worked at all types of odd jobs. I really did everything, a miner, manufacturing, you name it. But in 1955 I had to come back to Germany because my mother was so sick. I had not seen my family in five years and when I arrived I wanted to go back to Argentina immediately. I didn't like Germany at all. The way Germany had developed – there had been so many changes. It was a new and prosperous Germany that had buried the past. I couldn't do that. But I stayed here and never went back to Argentina. In the beginning, I moved from job to job, always something different. Then I settled into television until my retirement. I married Elizabeth, whom I knew since a youngster. That helped me stay.'

When Norman returned to Germany in 1955, Niklas was on an island in the North Sea finishing high school. They worked at the same company during the holidays and spent a lot of time together. 'I always really liked Norman,' says Niklas, 'and when he returned I was happy. We had very little money, but we had an excellent time together. But I also knew he was sad during this period, a little afraid of being back in Germany.'

While Norman married in 1959, Niklas started nine years of disjointed university study, 'studying different subjects and finishing none'. During this time he began writing. While he studied law, history and sociology, and almost received a doctorate in German literature, he finally became a journalist. He has held diverse positions, including that of cultural editor at the German *Playboy*, but is now a senior correspondent at *Stern* magazine.

The brothers have their differences. Norman decided never to have children 'because after all I know, I don't think the Franks should go on'. Niklas has one child, a daughter, from his twenty-four-year marriage. 'Norman was unsettled after the war,' Niklas says. 'He never found his niche again. It was difficult for him.'

They also differ over whether it was an advantage or disadvantage to be the son of the governor-general of Poland. 'Growing up in Germany, it was an advantage to be the son of this criminal,' says Niklas. 'It is a degree of honour to have a father who was sentenced in the first big trial, not in the trials that came afterwards. To have such a famous criminal as a father, that was a distinction in Germany. I used to feel I was a famous little person by being his son. Not so famous perhaps as a Goebbels boy or a Göring child, and the most famous would have been Hitler's son, but with the position my father had, it was good to be his son. People thought me more interesting once they found out.'

Norman absolutely disagrees. 'During my life it was a disadvantage to be the son of the governor-general. I am thankful for a good father and a good upbringing, but it hurt me very much to have a father so prominent. Because I was the eldest son, and knew my father the best in the family, it affected me more and worse than any of my brothers and sisters.'

While Norman and Niklas differ on whether such a legacy was an advantage in postwar Germany, they agree their heritage has constantly been with them. For Niklas, his father 'was always part of my life when I just wanted to have my own' and Norman says, 'I think of my father daily.'

They have both tried to understand what drove their father to his crimes. Niklas studied everything published about him and interviewed many surviving colleagues for six years in preparation for his book. 'I still do not understand him,' he says. 'I have tried. He wasn't an ideologue. It was a career to him, and his ambition and weakness drove him. But still if he was alive there are a lot of questions I would ask him. A lot. I want the truth from him. I want him to tell me he is guilty. I know he wanted the big homes, the fine uniforms, all the luxury, but besides that I can't understand why he would do it. I hate him for it. I am furious at his weakness. When I used to meet his former colleagues and tell them I thought he was a criminal, they thought I was mentally deranged. They don't see it. To me it is so clear, only his motivation is hidden.'

Norman is as perplexed as his younger brother. 'I do not understand my father at all. I have tried so much to understand him. I can't understand that he allowed himself to become so corrupted for junk. It is such a contradiction in a man I love. On the one hand I have the image of a good father and the other is the man at the trial charged with crimes. And for me these two images belong together in my mind. When I visited him at Nuremberg, I had to accept this conflict, this contradiction. I saw that great intelligence can always come close to excess if it is mixed with ambition. Being highly educated does not shield you from horrible crimes.'

Norman would not have preferred another father, just a 'stronger' one. And though he is critical of his father's wartime role, he admits he would never have turned him in to the authorities if he was a fugitive after the war. 'No, I could never betray him. But that would have been terrible, maybe worse than if he had been in jail all his life.'

When I told Niklas of Norman's answers, he was not surprised. 'Norman is critical of my father, but he also has the deepest love for him. To me, my father has ruined Norman's life. I have never said this to him, but it is how I feel. I have said it many times to my wife. When my book was serialized in *Stern*, I later heard Norman was ashamed at work because he knew all his colleagues were reading the articles and nobody talked to him. No one knows how deeply he feels all this. I know him very well because after boarding school I lived with him and he acted as my father. I owe him a lot because when we started to talk about our father he told me the truth. He never told me a lie or claimed anything was exaggerated. Norman always encouraged me to seek the truth, but I could always tell he still loved our father.

'But I must thank him for letting me get to the facts. He allowed me to see the crimes of Germany and what our father had done. We share these thoughts, those of all the people killed. They are pictures in our brains, and we must both live with them to the end.'

CHAPTER 3

'Victors' Justice'

Wolf Hess is the only child of Rudolf Hess, who until his solo flight to England on 10 May 1941, was the deputy Führer of the Nazi party, and one of Hitler's closest confidants. Hess spent the last forty-six years of his life in prison, the longest imprisonment for any Nazi official, and that incarceration fundamentally affected Wolf Hess's views about his father, the Nazi party, World War II, and Allied justice. Of all the children interviewed, Wolf Hess is by far the most bitter and angry. He considers his father a 'man of peace' who was 'absolutely innocent' but was subjected to the 'improper and unfair justice of the victors'. His view of the Nazi period and his father's role has been challenged as revisionist. But the stocky, fifty-three-year-old makes no apologies for his opinions.

During our conversations, I learned that if revisionism was 'unmasking the falsehoods of what we Germans have been taught about our history', then Wolf Hess would not contest the categorization. He not only attempts to re-argue the basis of his father's conviction, but also the underlying truths of both world wars; and he concentrates on the most inhumane aspects of his father's multi-decade imprisonment. Rudolf Hess's 1987 death, deemed a suicide by prison officials, breathed new life into Wolf's lifelong struggle to assist his father – he is now leading a crusade to prove that his father was murdered by his Allied guards. He applies the same zeal to this cause as he did to his twenty years of effort to have his father released from prison on humanitarian grounds. For Wolf, being the son of a prominent Nazi has meant that his life was consumed by the knowledge of his father's past, and by a singular frustration caused by his 'illegal' imprisonment. 'My father had a unique lot,' according to Wolf, 'meaning that my life differed from other people. His courage as a prisoner in Spandau put an extra obligation on me, his son. Throughout all his years of imprisonment, the spiritual bond between my father and myself remained unsevered.'

Wolf's father, Rudolf Walter Richard Hess, was born on 26 April 1894, in Alexandria, Egypt, where his family had a successful import-export business, Hess & Co. The family was prosperous, maintaining a luxurious Egyptian villa and a German summer home. Rudolf Hess received a firm Teutonic upbringing. At the age of fifteen he enrolled in a German boarding school, and three years later in a Swiss commerce school. When World War I broke out, Hess, like millions of other young Germans, jumped at the opportunity of enlisting. He fought on the Western and Eastern fronts and was severely wounded in both 1916 and 1917.

Released from the army, twenty-four-year-old Hess enrolled in the University of Munich, but he was disheartened. Germany was in ruins and shackled by the terms of the Versailles Treaty. Wolf Hess understands his father's frustration and says he longed for 'justice'. Not only had the British expropriated the Hesses' import-export company, but, Wolf says, his father was concerned about 'the Fatherland more than the family's misery. Versailles was a turning point for my father. It was a peace of annihilation. Its terms were suppressive and destructive. From the beginning, my father, like most Germans, was shocked by it and knew he had to fight it. And from the outset, one man and one party proved they would not be subject to the victors' blackmail. That man was Adolf Hitler and the party, the National Socialist German Workers' Party [NSDAP].'

Hess first heard Hitler speak one night in April 1920. He rushed home shouting repeatedly, 'The man! The man!' That single meeting transformed Hess into a devoted follower. On 1 July 1920, he became the sixteenth member of the new Nazi party. Wolf Hess has thought about his father's motivation to become an early Nazi member and justifies it. 'My father was worried about the visible subjugation of Germany. He found in Hitler the one person he was convinced could restore Germany's rightful position. See, the Western powers' real aim was to destroy Germany in World War I, and afterwards they wanted to do the same. Now Hitler was building what his neighbours feared most – a unified Germany as strong as they were. In this way, my father was like millions of Germans, only he followed him [Hitler] with more dedication than the rest. His dedication was more to Hitler than to National Socialism.'

While it is true that eventually more than ten million Germans became NSDAP members, at the time Hess joined it was considered a radical, fringe group of a few hundred. And Hess's dedication went beyond that of a normal party member. Within a few months the two men had formed a close bond. In 1924, when both were convicted for the failed 1923 Beer Hall Putsch against the government and sent to Landsberg prison, Hess became Hitler's closest companion. He edited *Mein Kampf*, and upon their release he became Hitler's private secretary; he increasingly acted as the Führer's alter ego in dealing with party questions and as a result built a personal following. From 1925 to 1932, Hess was constantly at Hitler's side, from fund-raising meetings with German industrialists to mass rallies. In hundreds of official portraits from the period, next to Hitler is Hess; the deputy has such bushy eyebrows and so angular a face that he looks harsh, almost fierce.

When Hitler assumed power in 1933, Hess was appointed a minister of the Reich. According to Wolf, 'My father was still one of Hitler's closest confidants, one he trusted without reservation.' Wolf also emphasizes that while his father held a powerful position, he never used his rank to enrich himself or his family, and remained a private man of modest expectations, in contrast to some other Nazi leaders. This is an accurate portrayal; Hess was the opposite of Göring, who could not acquire wealth quickly enough to satisfy his greed.

Hess's first commitment was to the party, and he showed this during the early years of National Socialist rule. The Nazis revolutionized most aspects of German government, and of judicial and social life. The Nazi philosophy was encoded in laws based upon an underlying racial theory of 'Aryan' superiority mixed with a heavy dose of anti-Semitism. In 1935, Hess was a principal signatory of the Nuremberg Laws, which divided the population into 'Reichs Citizens', with full legal rights, and 'State Subjects', primarily Jews, who lost many statutory protections. Marriage between Aryans and Jews, and their sexual relations outside marriage, were prohibited. Jews were forbidden to fly the German flag. The Nuremberg Laws made it clear that Jews were no longer considered equal under German law. The London *Times* called the law the 'most complete disinheritance and segregation of Jewish citizens . . . since medieval times'.

Yet, even in this case, Wolf Hess rationalizes rather than criticizes his father's role in such notorious laws. He says it is 'of interest to consider what the well-known Jewish philosopher and writer Hannah Arendt says in her book on the Eichmann trial . . . :[11] 'Israeli citizens, religious and non-religious, seem agreed upon the desirability of having a law which prohibits intermarriage. . . . There was something breathtaking in the naïveté with which the prosecution denounced the infamous Nuremberg Laws of 1935, which had prohibited intermarriage and sexual intercourse between Jew and German. The better informed of the correspondents were well aware of the irony. . . .' Wolf views them as merely providing the segregation constantly sought by Orthodox Jews. He is earnest in this rationalization, convinced they were not bad in themselves, only in the way some Nazis used them.

Wolf Hess admits that 'the Nuremberg Laws were intensified under the influence of many an NS [National Socialist] leader' but he adamantly argues that his father 'advocated in many instances properly balanced treatment of Jews'. He believes his father supported the Madagascar solution, a plan for the expulsion of all European Jews and their relocation to a new homeland, the island country of Madagascar, in the Indian Ocean off Africa. He cannot imagine his father supporting or assisting mass extermination. To buttress his claim that his father provided 'balanced treatment of Jews', he cites the example of Albrecht Haushofer. Haushofer was the son of one of his father's closest friends, Professor Karl Haushofer, who was one-quarter Jewish by virtue of a grandparent on his mother's side. Under the Nuremberg Laws, Haushofer was subject to all the brutal consequences of being a Jew in Nazi Germany. Hess 'Aryanized' his friend and gave the family a 'letter of safe conduct'.[12] The same applied to the family of Thomas Mann, whose father-in-law, a professor of mathematics in Munich, was Jewish. 'My father kept his hand above him,' says Wolf, 'and finally enabled the family to leave Germany, taking most of their property with them.' Wolf can cite no other cases in which his father aided Jews trapped by the laws he helped to promulgate.

While Hess was verbally as anti-Semitic as any other major Nazi, he did not have the stomach for physical brutality, much to the disdain of some of his more thuggish colleagues. Hess became known as the conscience of the party. He did not want the coming war, but he deluded himself into thinking that Hitler was a man of peace, and that the Allies were responsible for eschewing peace. Today Wolf echoes his father's beliefs of an earlier generation: 'Hitler rightly considered the unification of Austria, the Saarland, the Sudetenland and Danzig into the Third Reich to be German domestic matters. These had been unjustly taken away in 1919.' Wolf contends that Churchill and Roosevelt deliberately developed a course of conduct which led to war with Germany. He argues that it was the Western commitment to Poland that forced Hitler to prepare for battle, since 'Hitler was now faced with encirclement, a deadly danger to the German Reich. Peace was no longer solely in his hands.'

As Wolf sees it, the Allies could have negotiated a peace with Hitler, but they deliberately set the stage for conflict 'hoping that a revolution led by the resistance would replace Hitler'. He contends it is 'nonsense' to claim the Allies were serious about protecting Poland from attack, since Britain and France never declared war on Russia, which had attacked Poland as part of the Molotov-Ribbentrop Pact. He views the attack on Poland only as an excuse for an Allied declaration of war. He also champions a German justification for moving against Poland: 'To help the German citizens who the Poles were murdering by the thousands in the months prior to September 1939. There are hundreds of examples where Germans had been slaughtered by the Poles just because they were Germans.'

In 1937, while Hitler was making preparations for his coming attacks, Rudolf Hess was diverted for a short time. His wife was pregnant, and on 18 November, while he was at the Berghof, Hitler's imposing mountain retreat, Hess received the news that he had a son. He named his son Wolf Rüdiger. ('Wolf' was the nickname of Hitler in the early days of political struggle.) Hess was intensely proud of his new son. Hitler was his godfather ('I remember nothing of Hitler,' says Wolf) and attended the pagan

NSDAP 'naming ceremony', only six days after Göring had aggravated the party chiefs by having his daughter christened at a religious service.

From Wolf's birth until his father's flight to Scotland, there are two commonly published reports about Rudolf Hess that his son adamantly disputes. One is that part of the motivation for his flight was that the build-up to the war had brought Hess's personal eclipse in the Nazi party and that Hitler had distanced himself from his former friend. Some historians have judged the flight as an attempt to restore Hess's high standing. 'That is completely wrong,' says Wolf. 'While it is true that Hitler was more engaged in foreign affairs, the personal relationship between the Führer and my father remained unchanged. They simply did not see each other as often as before, which does not mean that their friendship deteriorated.'

A second report that he strongly contests links Hess to a fervent belief in astrology, the occult, homoeopathic medicine, and fringe philosophies. The basis of the stories is clear. In his diaries, Felix Kersten, Himmler's masseur-psychoanalyst, said Hess was 'a vegetarian who surrounded himself with clairvoyants and astrologers and despised official medical views'. Albert Speer, the Nazi minister of armaments, published a widely repeated story that Hess was so particular about his food that he refused to eat with Hitler at the Reich Chancellery unless he brought his own 'biologically dynamic' food. Reports by his English captors paint the picture of a paranoid hypochondriac, and Dr Douglas Kelley, one of the Nuremberg prison psychiatrists, wrote that Hess told him that in late 1940 one of his astrologers had predicted he was ordained to bring about peace. Gustav Gilbert, a Nuremberg psychologist, added to the published reports of Hess's purported reliance on psychics.

'These are ridiculous lies and inventions,' insists Wolf. 'These are nonsense, simply dumb stories that have already been disproved. The story told by Speer has been repeated many times, but this doesn't make it correct. There are numerous witnesses who have said this is not true. The people who have told these stories have never taken the trouble to read my father's approximately four thousand letters from the period of 1908 to 1987. These letters are indisputable [proof] that all the stories invented by my father's enemies are only stupid lies. I know from my mother and from my own discussions with him that there is no truth to them. There are two important things to keep in mind. When my father's peace mission to England was not successful, and Hitler had to discredit the flight to the German people, some officials tried to do so by spreading these stories of reliance on astrologers and so forth. They were exaggerated and invented by liars. For instance, Kersten also wrote that my father kept magnets under his bed. Kersten was never even in our house in Munich and it is unknown where he obtained his "knowledge". My mother just laughs at the idea of magnets under my father's bed.

'As for the British and the Nuremberg trial, there is absolutely no doubt. It was part of a coordinated effort to discredit my father after the war. They tried to show he was either stupid or crazy. It was part of how they tried to distort history, to cover their own mistakes and maliciousness. They have a reason to make him look as though he is crazy. If they present him to the world as deranged then it is easier for them to say, "See, we could not accept the terms of a lunatic." I really resent this British propaganda, which had one aim in those days: to show how brilliant the British were and how stupid the Germans. The course of history proves the contrary. Britain is now a third-rate country which still does not understand that it was among the losers of World War II. It is impossible to emphasize enough that these stories about magnets, extraterrestrial powers, hypochondria and exaggerated vegetarianism are completely and utterly false.'

What is undisputed about Hess in the period before his flight is his geopolitical view of the world. 'He said, like many other people in Britain, that the way Churchill was going would mean the loss of the British empire and spreading bolshevism into the heart of Europe,' says Wolf. 'Events proved him right!' Hess could not understand why Britain would not ally itself with Germany. Wolf believes that his father's political view of a British-German alliance was at the heart of his motivation for the flight. 'The main motive was to restore peace and stop the Second World War. I was once able to put to him a historical question, through unofficial channels in Spandau. The question was: "Can we assume that there would not have been the attack on Russia if your peace mission to Britain had succeeded?" The answer was, "Yes, of course!" I have this in writing!' This answer from Hess to his son directly contradicts the British and Soviet interpretation of the flight, which was that Hess intended to strike a separate peace with England so Germany would have a free hand in fighting Russia.

Advised by Albrecht Haushofer, who was in contact with a high-ranking Royal Air Force officer, the Duke of Hamilton, Hess decided to fly to Hamilton and present his peace initiative. 'It is still unknown why he flew to see Hamilton,' says Wolf, 'rather than, for example, to Lloyd George whom he knew and who had visited my father in his home in 1936. Albrecht Haushofer, who was an important man in the resistance against Hitler, might have had a hand in misleading my father.'

On 10 May 1941, Hess climbed into a twin-engine Messerschmitt fighter he had had fitted with extra fuel tanks, and once airborne headed straight for the Duke of Hamilton's Scottish estate over nine hundred miles away. He left behind his wife, Ilse, and Wolf, then three and a half. 'I can still see his worried face as he pulled me out of the garden pond, and I can still hear his comforting voice as he disentangled me, screaming in panic, from a bat that had caught itself in my hair. He carried it to the window and released it into the night. These are the only personal memories I have of my father from that time.'

Hess's navigation, even at night and without modern equipment, was so efficient that he came within twelve miles of Hamilton's estate. 'How could a lunatic have managed to reach that target?' asks Wolf with an ironic grin. Hess parachuted to the ground and, finding a farmer in a nearby field, politely asked to be taken to the duke. Churchill initially refused to believe the news that Hitler's deputy had arrived in the country to strike a separate peace, but when British officials met Hess, they heard an unrealistic proposal they had rejected many times in the past. Hess predicted eventual German victory; he offered the British peace and support in maintaining their empire in return for Nazi hegemony over the European continent.

Churchill refused even to meet Hess, and immediately arrested him as a prisoner-of-war instead of treating him like a cabinet minister, as he demanded. As a result, Wolf Hess harbours some of his deepest resentment for Churchill. He agrees with his father's concept that Churchill did not understand that the 'issue of the twentieth century was not the balance of power in Europe, but rather the balance of power in the world. . . . [B]y his lack of statesmanship he destroyed not only the British empire but also the fundamentals of Europe, which he left to the harmful influence of American banking interests and communist destruction.'

While he reserves harsh judgement for Churchill, Wolf does not turn as critical an eye towards Hitler. Using an assortment of circumstantial evidence, he concludes that while Hitler did not know of the exact date of his father's flight, he knew of the mission, and with some reservations approved it. It is true that Hess had an adjutant deliver a letter to Hitler the morning after his flight, informing him of the mission and stating that if anything went wrong, 'you can drop me at any time – say I am mad'.

While this is what Hitler did, his reaction indicates that the Hess trip caught him unawares. Dr Paul Schmidt, Hitler's translator, remembers that when Hitler heard the news it was 'as though a bomb had struck the Berghof'. General Keitel found Hitler pacing in his library, pointing to his head and mumbling that Hess must have gone crazy. Hitler told Göring and other officials that he could not recognize Hess in the note he had received. 'Something must have happened to him,' Hitler told Keitel, 'some type of mental disturbance.' Hitler detained Messerschmitt, from whose company airfield Hess had taken off, as well as incarcerating dozens of men on Hess's staff. For several days the British did not release any word of Hess's arrival and Hitler hoped that he had not made it, that his plane had crashed into the North Sea. When the British finally announced that he was a prisoner, Hitler was deflated. Within two weeks, he gave a speech in which he ordered that Hess be struck from the memory of the Nazi party, that all pictures of him be removed from every NSDAP office, and that all who assisted him be severely punished. Within a year Hess was officially eliminated from the party. Although nothing happened personally to the Hess family, his wife, Ilse, watched helplessly as adjutants, orderlies, secretaries and drivers were arrested. Some stayed in concentration camps until 1944. She later recalled that 'it was a bitter pill we had to swallow, day after day, year after year'. None of this sounds like the actions of a man who had approved of the flight 'in principle', but Wolf Hess believes that Hitler's harsh measures were planned in advance in case the flight and peace proposal did not succeed.

When it was apparent that the British would not negotiate with Hess, he made his first suicide attempt, on 15 June, a month after his arrival. He threw himself from a second-storey landing but only succeeded in breaking his thigh. Afraid of another suicide attempt, as well as of a Nazi rescue effort, the British isolated Hess on a remote country estate with a large contingent of troops, a doctor, and several psychiatrists. Hess became convinced he was being poisoned. In the dining room, where he sometimes ate with British officers, he demanded an exchange of plates or a random shuffling of the plates. He kept pieces of food for later chemical analysis, and when he arrived for the 1945 Nuremberg trial, he brought dozens of envelopes containing suspect food. Hess filled more than fifteen notebooks with observations of his health. During his British confinement he suffered a series of illnesses. The British deemed the illnesses 'psychosomatic', but Wolf says that is 'nonsense'. He views as the smoking gun a 15 September 1949 letter in which a Spandau captain acknowledges destroying 'for security reasons' the drugs that had been given to Hess during his English imprisonment. 'And the diaries of the warders, between 1941 and 1945, have been published,' says Wolf, 'and prove that he was given drugs and was poisoned!'

Wolf Hess believes the British treatment of his father was calculated to lead to his physical and mental deterioration. 'The food they gave him was often inedible,' he says. 'They kept the light on in his cell all night, and the guard would noisily make rounds to keep him awake. He thought the continuous air-raid sirens on the roof were set off to drive him mad. This subtle terror, plus nutritional defects, led to physical ailments. The British wanted to substantiate the widespread notion that my father was mad.'

Wolf Hess even speculates that his father was duped into the flight as the result of an elaborate operation organized between British intelligence and the German resistance, part of Churchill's 'black propaganda' intended to embarrass his father and Hitler and to scare Stalin into thinking that Germany and Britain might strike a separate peace. Recently declassified KGB documents show that the Russians agree with Wolf's hypothesis. The British intelligence agencies adamantly deny any involvement. But the possibility that the British secret service may have played a role in luring Hess to England does not diminish Wolf's certainty that his father was on a 'mission of peace'.

But the Allies, according to Wolf, 'did not want to make the peace mission public since they would look rather like warmongers instead of peace angels'. As a result, on 30 August 1945, Hess was one of the first twenty-two defendants charged as war criminals. But because of his 1941 flight to England, the case against him was not an easy one. The worst Nazi atrocities were committed in Russia and in the concentration camps, when Hess was in a British prison. He was not present at any of Hitler's conferences when the grand plans for aggression were discussed. He had been out of the inner power circle during the crucial first two years of the war. But still Hess was charged under all four counts of the Nuremberg indictment: conspiracy to wage aggressive war, crimes against peace, war crimes and crimes against humanity. The crux of the case against him was that he was an early and slavish follower of Hitler and had loyally supported the repressive measures taken against Jews. As far as Wolf Hess is concerned, the charges against his father were totally unjustified.

'Nuremberg violated all principles of international law and equality. The Allies had no right to pass judgement on German nationals on German soil. It was only a case of the victors judging the vanquished. They already knew who would be found guilty; the trial was just a sham. I believe that they even included some defendants [Hjalmar Schacht, Franz von Papen, and Hans Fritsche] to be in the trial so they could be acquitted. By doing that, it gives the trial the appearance of fairness, so people must conclude that if some were found not guilty, the other defendants must have really been guilty. It was totally arbitrary. Don't you think the Allied bombing of Dresden and the American nuclear bombings of Hiroshima and Nagasaki, when Japan was already defeated, qualified under the Nuremberg definition of war crimes – "the wanton destruction of towns and villages"? There were a lot of examples like this. And the Americans went too far in this trial. They accused not only the SS, Gestapo and SA as being "criminal organizations", but they also included the general staff, the Reich government and the Wehrmacht command. In this way they made the Third Reich look like a criminal consortium of Chicago gangsters. Nuremberg was like a super-Versailles.'

Wolf Hess believes that Nazis responsible for Holocaust crimes should have been tried by German courts. 'Germany did not need Allied courts and newly invented laws.'

Although many of the defendants in 1945 may have agreed with the sentiment that the Nuremberg trials represented victors' law, they had no choice but to submit to the court's jurisdiction. Hess was the last defendant to be transferred to Nuremberg, arriving on 8 October 1945. By then the fifty-one-year-old Hess, gaunt and slightly hunched, had been in a British prison for four and a half years. The British knew he was going to be a difficult defendant when in January 1944 he wrote a letter to his wife, Ilse, claiming, 'I have completely lost my memory; everything in the past has become blurred as if it lies behind a grey fog. I can no longer remember even the most commonplace things. Why this has happened I don't know.' At Nuremberg, Hess continued to hide behind a wall of 'amnesia'. Although prosecutors were very sceptical of his memory loss, Hess put on a convincing show during the interrogations and at the trial – he failed to remember his flight to England and did not recognize Göring (much to the latter's anger) or a photo of his good friend Professor Karl Haushofer or any of his secretaries. When shown a photograph of himself to-gether with Ilse and Wolf, he recognized them but could not re-call any details. Courtroom spectators were split between those who felt sympathy for the pathetic-looking man who sat in the courtroom for hours on end reading books and showing no ap-parent interest in the proceedings, and those who thought he was cunning and knowing, an actor playing out a great hoax. Wolf Hess claims he knows the truth: 'He was pretending to have lost his memory, and he succeeded in fooling all of them. He actually remembered everything very well, and I found out in later years through his letters that his memory was really quite sharp. But he refused to participate in this so-called trial and this was the best way of avoiding it. If he didn't like what he saw in court he would sever his memory from recognizing the person or the document. It was very clever. If all the defendants had taken the attitude of my father, then the whole farce would have collapsed.'

Although Wolf believes his father's guilt was already pre-determined, there is little doubt that Hess's 'amnesia' backfired and influenced the tribunal's final decision. As a result of his failure to recall almost anything of significance, Hess's contribution to his defence was perfunctory, although Dr Alfred Seidl, his attorney, made all the necessary legal arguments protesting his client's innocence. Even here Wolf objects: 'Dr Seidl was not able to introduce many of his exhibits and he was limited in his arguments. He was forced by the "court" to cut out about one-quarter of his defence speech. The "court" censored his speech and allowed only the passages they felt not to be harmful to them. It was a farce.'

However, Dr Seidl had also decided to omit some parts of the defence. When Hess encouraged him to ask questions about 'mesmeric forces', Seidl refused. No witnesses were called. Hess refused to testify in his own behalf. Yet the Hess defence still produced one of the trial's biggest bombshells, when Seidl introduced the secret protocol of the 1939 Soviet-German Non-Aggression Pact. The protocol revealed that Stalin and Hitler had agreed to divide Eastern Europe between them, with Poland being the first victim. Its introduction appeared to be a brilliant move, because it threatened to destroy count one of the indictment, conspiracy to wage aggressive war. If the count was justified, then the Soviet Union was one of the conspirators and should not be judging the Nazis for the same crimes. If the Soviet Union was not guilty, then the Nazis could not be held to a higher standard. In the deliberations, the tribunal ignored this dilemma, but the revelation of the protocol still dealt a major propaganda blow to the Russians. They blamed Hess for the disclosure and never forgave him.

Hess also did not help his own case when he was given an opportunity to make a final statement. It was his first statement at the trial, and it surprised courtroom personnel because his mental state had supposedly been worsening, with an inability to remember from one day to the next. Hess presented a rambling discourse, criticizing some of his co-defendants for their 'shameless utterances about the Führer' and comparing the proceedings to Moscow's purge trials of the 1930s. Since the Russian trials, he proposed, a mysterious mesmeric force was present in the world and had infiltrated the minds of some of the German leaders as well as the 'personnel in the German concentration camps'. Citing testimony from Field Marshal Erhard Milch, he even claimed that during the last years the 'Führer's eyes and facial expressions had something cruel in them, and even had a tendency towards madness'. Göring kept tugging at Hess's sleeve and whispering 'Stop! Stop!' Hess ignored him. Finally, after twenty minutes, the tribunal interrupted him and encouraged a rapid conclusion. Hess complained that when testifying he was not asked all the questions he wanted to answer. Then he concluded in a firm voice: 'I was permitted to work for many years of my life under the greatest son whom my people have brought forth in their thousand-year history. I am happy to know that I have done my duty to my people, my duty as a German, as a National Socialist, as a loyal follower of the Führer. I regret nothing. If I were to begin all over again, I would act again as I acted, even if I knew that in the end I should burn at the stake. No matter what people may do, I shall some day stand before the judgement seat of the Eternal. I shall answer to Him, and I know that he will judge me innocent.'

Hess's lack of repentance did not help him during the judges' deliberations. He generated no sympathy. None of the judges was willing to consider leniency for a man who publicly reaffirmed his faith in Hitler and was proud he had no regrets. While the two Russian delegates voted for execution, the two Americans, and one each of the British and French judges, voted for life imprisonment. One French delegate wanted to give him twenty years, and the final British judge abstained, not wanting to sentence a defendant he deemed mad. The final sentence was life in prison.

Wolf Hess is angry about the verdict. 'The judgement was ridiculous. It was a sham. He was exonerated from the criminal charges of "war crimes" and "crimes against humanity". He was the only defendant who – apart from conspiracy – was found guilty only of so-called "crimes against peace". Of all people! Since he was the one person who tried to achieve peace at great personal risk to himself, I find it preposterous that he was found guilty of "crimes against peace". That decision is the best demonstration of the absurdity of the trial. My father accepted the verdict with great calm, because he had been expecting it for some time.'

Shortly after the sentencing, the Allies allowed family members to visit the defendants. Hess was the only one who refused to see his family. He wrote to his wife, 'I have firmly refused to "meet" you or anyone else under circumstances I consider quite undignified.' Wolf understands his father's position. 'He would not show the victors he accepted their dictates and wishes. It would have been humiliating to him to have seen us in that way. It is very clear to me. He saw visiting as a moral concession to those who took it upon themselves to sit in judgement upon him.'

After the sentencing, Wolf contends, his father was 'treated as a convict. The American guards removed all reading and writing material from his cell. And during the winter cold, the heating was turned off for nearly three days, all of which led to my father becoming sick.' On 17 October 1946, Hess suffered a violent attack of intestinal cramps. Wolf Hess relies on prison records to show that his father had to make seven requests for a doctor before one arrived five hours after the start of his attacks. Although he was given bicarbonate of soda, the next day the American guards refused to give him his medicine, and, Wolf claims, 'The pains were so severe during the night that he groaned loudly, and the American soldiers who crowded to his cell door revelled in his cramps and mimicked his groans.' Over the next few days Hess was moved to several new cells; each one, according to Wolf, 'was unheated and had a broken window'. He believes that this conduct by the American guards was 'special treatment which was not only inhuman, but at times grotesque'. His father obviously agreed, because on 20 October 1946, he submitted a fourteen-point petition complaining of deficiencies and harassments. But before any of those issues were addressed, Wolf says, 'on 18 July 1947, my father and his companions in misfortune were moved to Berlin-Spandau'.

Spandau, a fortresslike building built by the German Kaiser in 1876, was intended to house six hundred prisoners. Under Hitler it served as an interrogation centre for political prisoners. In 1947 the seven convicted and surviving Nazis were Spandau's only inhabitants. Each was referred to only by a number, and Hess became, for the next forty years of his life, Prisoner Number 7.

Wolf criticizes the conditions at Spandau as 'very difficult', including coarse clothing, a primitive six-foot-by-nine-foot cell, little sleep, and military rules that required constant deference to the 'victors'. The four Allied powers took control of the prison alternately. Besides the changing military guards, a permanent staff of seventy-eight – including cooks, doctors and orderlies – watched over the seven prisoners. Wolf says the first year was one of the worst, 'dreadfully bleak', until new directives were issued in December 1948. After that date, among other changes, the prisoners could speak to one another without incurring punishment. After 1956, they could receive one fifteen-minute personal visit each second month, and if sick could remain in bed without violating the rules.

While his father adjusted to life in Spandau, Wolf was adapting to life in postwar Germany. His mother, Ilse, was imprisoned by American authorities in June 1947, at an internment camp at Göggingen, near Augsburg. 'The only reason for her arrest was that she was the wife of Rudolf Hess,' says Wolf bitterly. 'I found it cruel and unjust. I lived with my grandmother, and frequently visited the concentration camp where my mother was held.' She was released after fifteen months, but his separation from her caused him to harbour more resentment of the Allies and their intrusion into his family. 'Even at that young age, I knew my father was in prison because we had lost the war, and that's how the victors decided it was going to be.'

By 1950, Wolf complains, conditions at Spandau had deteriorated again. Censorship of all correspondence was 'onerous', visits from solicitors were still banned, and the prisoners' sleep was constantly interrupted by noisy guards and bright lights. Although Wolf admits that some of the rules were relaxed over the next decade (for instance, Dr Seidl eventually visited his client on six occasions), the general atmosphere at Spandau was 'oppressive'. Yet one item did not change in those early years of Rudolf Hess's life sentence. He still steadfastly refused to allow his family to visit. Just as he had turned them away after the Nuremberg sentencing, he again refused any personal contact, although he did correspond. It was in one of Hess's letters, in 1951, that Wolf saw signs of sadness in his father. Rudolf Hess's mother had died in October; when he was finally informed of the death, he wrote to his family, 'It is a sad world, full of suffering lurking in the background, always ready to drop on us suddenly, culminating in the "immense solemnity of the hour of death".'

'Only by reading between the lines,' Wolf says, 'can you see some of what he had to endure in his innermost self. But even with all the mental torments that were inflicted upon him, he never uttered a single word of complaint, of despair, of hopelessness. Being separated from his family was very difficult for us, and especially for him, since he was in prison. But he would not capitulate nor bow to the victors. Certainly we were disappointed that he would not see us, but we knew his time in Spandau was hard, so we honoured his wish.'

During the mid-1950s, Hess watched as the number of prisoners dwindled to three. Konstantin von Neurath, the protector of Bohemia and Moravia, was the first to be released in 1954. He was eighty-one; his fifteen-year sentence had been reduced to eight years because of his poor health. He lived another two years. In 1955, Erich Raeder, former grand admiral of Hitler's navy, was released after serving nine years of a life sentence. The reason for the early release was also bad health, but he lived another three years in freedom. In 1956, Grand Admiral Karl Dönitz was released after serving his full ten-year sentence. Finally, in 1957, Walther Funk, Schacht's successor as Reichsbank president and minister of economics, was set free from a life sentence after serving eleven years. His health also prompted his release, and he lived another three years. The fact that three of these four were released early gave the family hope that similar treatment might one day be given to Rudolf Hess.

It was also during this period in the mid-1950s that Wolf began learning about his father and the war. German newspapers and magazines carried numerous stories about the Third Reich. Initially, Wolf drew his information from these sources. He did not learn about the period at school. 'The Allies wanted the German teachers to teach a new version of National Socialist history,' he recalls. 'But good German teachers would always find some way around this requirement, like saving it until the bell to end the class, and then starting the next class with a different subject.'

Wolf graduated from high school in 1956 and visited South Africa the following year. That visit unexpectedly helped to change his outlook towards his father. 'I discovered that the conditions in South Africa were quite different from what had been presented to us in the German newspapers. I was quite surprised by this and decided that I had better take a more critical scrutiny of what I had learned about the Third Reich and about my father's life from the media.' He now sought advice from his mother, studied books more closely, and had conversations with men who had been Nazi party members. Wolf's opinions started crystallizing during his early twenties. Slowly, he came not only to feel he understood what drove his father, but to be proud of who his father was, and how he 'nobly' served his 'unjust' sentence. When in 1959 Wolf was called for compulsory service in the German army, he refused. He claimed that one of the main reasons for his father's imprisonment was his signature of the 16 March 1935 law creating the military draft. As long as his father was in Spandau, he refused to be part of the German army, 'which according to the victors at Nuremberg represented a "crime against peace" '. Although two examining boards rejected his claim, his position received substantial press attention. As a result, the German government did not use police action against the twenty-two-year-old son of the former deputy Führer. He never served in the army.

In 1962, Wolf completed his civil engineering studies at the Munich Technical University, and in the summer of 1964 he passed his civil-service examination and became a government engineer. At this time, the twenty-seven-year-old professional was pleased not only that his own career was finally settled, but that his father's release might be forthcoming within a couple of years. On 1 October 1966, both Albert Speer and Baldur von Schirach would finish serving their twenty-year sentences. At that point, the Allies would either have to maintain Spandau as a one-prisoner fortress or possibly grant Hess an early release, as they had done for Neurath, Raeder, and Funk, the latter two of whom had, like Hess, received life sentences. Ilse Hess hoped that the release of the other two prisoners 'would inevitably be followed, logically and humanely, let alone as a just outcome – after twenty-five years of imprisonment – by the break-up of the Spandau prison and the release of my husband'. But Ilse and Wolf were to be disappointed. On 1 October 1966, Speer and von Schirach left the prison gates at nearly midnight, in a crowd of onlookers and press. Amid the flash of press lights, someone shouted, 'Freedom for Rudolf Hess!' and then the gates slammed shut. Prisoner Number 7 was the last convict. Wolf is certain 'these surely must have been the most dreadful days and weeks my father ever experienced at Spandau'.

Ilse Hess suggested that since he was in isolation, her husband should agree at least to allow Wolf to visit. His written response was as inflexible as ever: 'Now, as ever, I want no reunion behind prison walls and in the presence of others, neither with you nor with Wolf. Apart from the emotion, this is a matter of dignity.'

However, at this point, the family decided it was time to abandon restraint. Even though Rudolf Hess was adamant that he should never appear to ask the Allied governments for mercy, his family issued a 'Declaration to All Thinking People of the World' on 1 October 1966. The declaration asked that the Nuremberg sentence be considered discharged after twenty-five years and stated, in part, that Hess's long imprisonment was a 'cruel situation, hitherto unknown in the annals of modern law, [and] was neither foreseen nor desired by the Nuremberg Court'. The fate that had befallen him was for his family 'a subsequent aggravation of the sentence originally imposed, and is perhaps a more dreadful process of extinction than even the executions at Nuremberg'.[13]

Ilse and Wolf Hess sent their plea to the Pope, to the heads of the four Allied powers, to the UN Human Rights Commission, and to the World Council of Churches. 'It was time to form an organization,' Wolf recalls. 'It was time to abandon our discretion and the pursuit of the strictly legal path.' The Pope, the World Council of Churches, and the Soviet government ignored the plea. The UN Human Rights Commission claimed it had no jurisdiction. The United States, France and Britain said they would consider the request.

In addition to issuing the declaration, by January 1967 Wolf had also formed the Hilfsgemeinschaft 'Freiheit für Rudolf Hess' ('Freedom for Rudolf Hess' Support Association), an international citizens' group in favour of releasing Hess. Wolf fondly remembers his first public activism on behalf of his father. 'It was overdue. We had to arouse public opinion by beating the drum.' Eventually, the association gathered more than four hundred thousand signatures in forty countries. The signatories included Hartley William Shawcross, the British prosecutor at

Nuremberg, as well as Lord Geoffrey Lawrence, the president of the International Military Tribunal. Some of those who supported release made it clear they did not excuse or like the man they were championing. Typical of this group was Simon Wiesenthal, the Vienna-based Nazi-hunter, and Bernard Levin, a well-known British journalist who was also Jewish. In a September 1989 attack in the London *Times* on Wolf Hess's 'shameless and disgusting' public comments, Levin said: 'I believe I was the first British journalist to publicly urge clemency for [Hess]. . . . Clemency is independent of justice; the campaign for Hess's release should not, and for me did not, have passed over in silence what Hess the Nazi in power actually did.' While Wolf Hess is grateful that people like Levin, whatever their motivations, supported his efforts to free his father from Spandau, he dismisses Levin's personal attacks as 'hateful . . . untrue and injurious'.

While Wolf tried to influence public opinion in his father's favour, Dr Seidl, his Nuremberg defence attorney, attempted to improve the conditions in Spandau. Included in Seidl's nine-point proposal of 'special privileges' was that Hess should be allowed to wear a watch, spend sixty minutes in the garden instead of thirty, have a bell in his cell to ring a guard in case of illness, be able to make his own tea or coffee as well as take more than a single weekly bath, and be able to decide for himself when he turned off his cell light. The Allies acknowledged receipt of Seidl's letter but did not make the changes for another four years.

In 1969, seventy-five-year-old Hess's health took a turn for the worse. In mid-November, he complained of unbearable stomach pains and refused food, lying in bed and groaning all day. Only after four days was he taken to the British Military Hospital in Berlin, where a special 'Hess suite', serviced by its own elevator and equipped with extra security, was waiting for him. There doctors determined that he had a perforated duodenal ulcer. But the four custodial powers considered it unnecessary to inform the Hess family. Wolf recalls how he learned of his father's illness: 'I was away on business and heard the news on the radio. I immediately telegraphed Federal Chancellor Willy Brandt and demanded my father's transfer to a German hospital and treatment by a German doctor. The victors rejected both requests.'

While he was treated in the hospital, American, British, Russian and French soldiers guarded the empty Spandau prison. For Wolf Hess, that showed that 'Spandau was a ludicrous symbol of a victor's right that had lost its point'.

But, unknown to Wolf, a fundamental change was taking place in his father. Faced with death, Rudolf Hess viewed the decision not to see his family in a different light. On 8 December 1969, he wrote to the Spandau directorate requesting 'a visit from my wife and son, if possible on the morning of 24 December. It is the first visit for twenty-eight years, and I therefore request that no witnesses be present in the room at the beginning of the visit.' Hess offered to allow the Allies to tape-record the entire meeting, promised not to shake hands with his wife or son, and asked if during the half-hour of allotted time they could take a Christmas lunch, 'with witnesses present'. The Allies approved the request for a meeting, but none of the privileges.

'It was quite a moment when we learned that my father had asked to see us,' Wolf recalls. 'I learned of it in a telephone call from the American director, and we were all excited. We had so many feelings. There was of course excitement and joy, however suppressed by the knowledge of the inhuman circumstances in which the visit would take place and the fact that my father was kept as a prisoner. It had been twenty-eight years, and we did not know when we might ever see him again. When we [Wolf and his mother] arrived at the hospital, there were several dozen reporters, but we drove past them into an enclosed area. Then we were taken to the visitors' waiting room on the third floor, past numerous soldiers with machine guns, and there were the four directors. The Russian director was the only one who refused to shake our hands. Then they presented us with the nine-point prison regulation we had to sign before we could see my father. Although I found all of the regulations offensive, I particularly objected to two rules – the one that required that we be frisked like criminals before any meeting, and the one that said we would lose our visiting privileges if we spoke to the press. The Russian director, Colonel Toruta, said that if my mother and I did not sign the regulations, we would be turned away. All the directors tried to persuade me to change my mind. They even had my mother and me leave the room while they argued among themselves. Finally when they had us back in, they said it was an ultimatum. Either we signed it or left without seeing my father. So I had no choice. I signed it, they did not frisk us, and later I spoke to the press anyway. They never blocked me from seeing my father.'

That first meeting was emotional, yet the atmosphere was also stiff – a result of the long separation and the presence of the four prison directors. Hess was in a twelve-foot-square room, off a corridor with four guards with machine guns. Wolf distinctly remembers the event. 'When we entered the room, he was sitting at a table that was placed in the middle. My mother started to move towards him, but I reminded her that handshaking was not allowed. He looked surprisingly well. Although he was thin, he was not emaciated, and his face had a good colour, maybe from the blood transfusions. Although the four directors and a warden sat around us, we had a good talk with him. He was very alert. We all controlled ourselves very well given the situation. I could tell my mother was on the edge of tears, but my calmness helped control her. I had become used to exerting self-discipline over the years and this came in handy for this meeting.'

The warden started to give a countdown when only five minutes were left. As Wolf and Ilse Hess left, they glanced back to see Rudolf Hess leaning against the table and waving. The barrier had been broken. Hess had decided that contact with his family was more important than the appearance that he had capitulated to the 'victors'.

Hess's illnesses kept him in the hospital for several months. During this time, the media took interest in the story, and pressure built for possible freedom, especially in Great Britain. But the effort failed. 'All hope was brutally dashed on 13 March 1970,' Wolf angrily recalls. 'Barely recovered from a dangerous illness and aged seventy-seven, Rudolf Hess was returned to the Allied prison. All the protests and all the pressure from the public were in vain. In Spandau, the cynics were triumphant.'

By returning Hess to prison, the Allies further inflamed Wolf's feelings that his father was subjected to 'cruel and false imprisonment. If the Nuremberg "victors' law" was genuine law then Spandau would be filled with the politicians responsible for more than one hundred and forty wars and forty million dead since the end of the Second World War. This double standard did not affect their conscience.'

Over the next seventeen years, Wolf Hess was an untiring advocate for his father's release. Moreover, Dr Seidl filed legal initiatives with the Spandau administrators, with the four governments responsible for the prison, with European and international human rights commissions, and with the West German courts. None of the legal actions worked. Wolf is not surprised, since 'they had no intention of releasing him. He had become a symbol of the foreign powers' domination over Germany. Dr Seidl was not even allowed to speak about legal matters arising from the detention. Even the most simple questions of civil law could not be discussed. And when Dr Seidl became a state secretary in the Bavarian ministry of justice in 1974 and had to relinquish my father as a client, the Four Powers rejected our next suggestion as counsel, Dr Ewald Bucher, a retired federal minister – a fine example of Allied justice!'

Each year the British, Americans and French claimed that they were willing to release Hess, but that the Soviets rejected the proposal. No one can prove this is the case, because the meetings of the Four Powers were secret and the minutes never made public. Wolf Hess believes the public impression is false. In his view, none of the three Western powers wanted his father released, especially the British, 'who clearly have something to hide. They just used the Russians as an excuse.'

During the 1970s and 1980s, Wolf Hess travelled to numermes countries and repeatedly visited Washington and London to try to effect his father's release. At the time he received many promises of assistance from journalists, members of Congress and Parliament, the British foreign secretary, and other public figures. Today he feels 'they were all merely words. In retrospect I must doubt the sincerity of what I heard in every case. They were all hypocrites.' Not everyone he met promised to help. On one of his US visits he scheduled a meeting with the staff of Jacob Javits, trying to enlist the Jewish senator's support for his father's release. As the meeting started another staff member entered the room and began 'screaming at me that I had no right to even be there. "Six million are dead because of people like your father." I left. It was the only time I ever encountered such a reaction. At least this man was not a hypocrite.'

But while Wolf continued to try to turn positive words into effective action, he also visited his father when allowed by the

Spandau rules. But the long imprisonment wore the family down. Wolf views the Spandau conditions as having 'relentless consequences in not only physical but also psychological and emotional terms. Apart from the deprivation of freedom, the main instruments of psychological torture were censorship and the regulations on correspondence and visits.' Hess was not allowed to watch any TV programme or read any material about the Third Reich, Nazism, Nuremberg, or Spandau.

'My father was, and is, an important historical figure who could have made important statements from first-hand experience about the entire development of National Socialism, the outbreak, as well as the continuation of the war,' says Wolf. 'The behaviour of the Allies, who completely cut him off, did not only cheat his son of the answers to many questions, but also all people truly interested in history were deceived. It would, for example, have been of great interest for historians if my father had the possibility to report the content of his four-hour talk with Hitler, five days before his departure to England. All points of view for the political and military situation and actions of the Reich's government were surely discussed in this talk. A disclosure would surely hold more substance for the historical understanding of the later events than the repetition of dumb English propaganda aphorisms such as Hess being a psychopath and, on top of everything, very stupid.

'But they wanted to stop precisely this factual examination of the truth. Because on the victors' side they knew that through the testimony of a truly involved person, who, on top of everything, proved his honest commitment to peace, much of the postwar propaganda and the Nuremberg farce would begin to crumble. I am not angry about this. Rather, I recognize the intention behind the behaviour and know why the Allies, and particularly the British, had to prevent my father from speaking freely.'

Not only was Hess's access to information about the war and National Socialism restricted, but even mundane contact with his family was severely monitored. He was allowed to write only a single letter each week, to an immediate family member. The maximum of 1300 words was always censored. The same restrictions applied to letters from the family. Once a month – twice in the Christmas month of December – he could receive a single visit of one hour from an immediate family member. The visit had to be applied for two weeks in advance and the time and date were set by the Spandau authorities. Generally all four directors were present at any family meeting. While the conversations were in German, interpreters were also present. Any personal contact was forbidden. If any of these regulations were violated, the meeting was immediately halted. On one occasion, when Hess was again hospitalized, Wolf instinctively reached out and grabbed his father's hand for a quick but firm handshake. It was the first and last time he had touched his father since the age of three. As a result of that handshake the British officially reprimanded him and placed him on notice that any further prohibited activity could get him banned from visiting his father.

'Eventually, I learned how to play their game,' Wolf recalls. 'I would wait to bring up prohibited subjects until the last minute of our meeting. It would always take them by surprise and by the time they reacted, our meeting was finishing anyway. They cancelled two visits but never banned me totally from further visits.' Wolf visited his father 102 times prior to his 1987 death, for a total of four days of accumulated time, always in the presence of guards and prison wardens. In addition to hundreds of letters, it was the only way he came to know his father. 'During all the long years it is true I had a father, but in the end I did not have him, because the situations under which we corresponded, or rather conferred, were controlled through the rules of his imprisonment. There was not a single truly moving father-son discussion in which I could ask him about things on my mind. That was true for human problems a young man wants to discuss with his father, and particularly for historical issues.'

On 22 February 1977, Wolf says 'the cup of suffering was full for the old man' and his father tried to sever one of his arteries with a knife. He came close to death, but a long recuperation appeared successful; then, on 28 December 1978, he suffered a stroke which left him nearly blind in the right eye and with damaged vision in the left one. 'The doctor's diagnosis was the best argument for my father's release,' recalls Wolf. 'The patient had a diseased heart, a painful rupture of the abdominal wall and fluid in his legs. He suffered a cough, bladder problems and general exhaustion. No one knew how much longer he would live as he was already eighty-four years old.'

Because of his deteriorating health, Rudolf Hess then did something which shocked the Four Powers. On 4 January 1979, at the urging of Wolf and Dr Seidl, Prisoner Number 7 wrote to the Spandau directors and for the first time personally asked for freedom. His appeal was brief: 'Because of the poor state of my health, and because I would like to see my two grandchildren, I request that I be released from imprisonment. I am convinced that I have only a short time to live, and I wish to point out that in three other cases [von Neurath, Raeder, and Funk] there was premature release.' Hess's plea was followed by forty days of silence, until he was orally informed that the application was rejected. Wolf is still bitter about the decision. 'The Four Powers had missed this unique chance to come out of the affair with some of their self-proclaimed humanity intact.'

The following year, in November, Rudolf Hess again appealed for early release. 'By now he had an image of his freedom,' Wolf states. 'He imagined a small house in the country with an open view and good books. He wanted peace and quiet to read and reflect. He even thought he could easily do without a car.' After three weeks, the Allies again rejected the appeal. In August 1982, at the age of eighty-eight, Hess had a life-threatening attack of wet pleurisy. This was complicated with dramatic deterioration of his heart caused by two small heart attacks. He complained incessantly of breathing difficulties, intestinal cramps, and visible skin rashes. In this state, Hess decided to add conditions to his plea for release, in the belief that certain promises could allay the misgivings of the Four Powers. He informed the directors that he would agree, upon his release, to express no political or historical views, and to avoid any political involvement. This time the three Western powers answered in writing, all rejecting his latest plea. Once again, the Soviets completely ignored the request.

Despite the setbacks, Wolf Hess never abandoned hope that his father would be free. His efforts to obtain his father's release continued unabated. 'I never stopped believing that the victors might finally show some humanity,' he recalls. 'I always thought that when he was sick, or there was a big birthday, like eighty, eighty-five, or ninety, they might let him go.' Then on Monday, 17 August 1987, Wolf received a telephone call at his Munich office. It was from a German reporter based in Berlin who asked if he had heard the rumour that his father was dead. He said no and then quickly put the phone down. No one from Spandau had contacted him, but he knew the rumour might nevertheless be true. 'My father was ninety-three, we all knew it could happen any time,' he says. 'The Four Powers had failed to contact us before when he was in the hospital. They could be slow this time too. I decided not to call them. If he was dead, I knew they would soon call.'

At six o'clock, still unsure of whether his father was alive or dead, Wolf left the office and drove home. At six-thirty he received the telephone call he dreaded. Since the United States had custody of Spandau, it was from the American director, Darold W. Keane. The conversation, in English, lasted only a few seconds. 'I am authorized to tell you that your father expired at sixteen-ten today. I am not authorized to give you any more details.'

Wolf telephoned Dr Seidl. Together they flew to Berlin the next morning and drove straight to Spandau. They were not allowed into the prison, but instead met by Keane, who informed them they would receive information in half an hour. In thirty minutes, Keane returned to inform Wolf they were delayed and that he should go to an hotel and await further contact. Two hours later, after Wolf had telephoned several times, Keane called back with the news that his father's death was judged a suicide. 'That's a lie, I knew it immediately. For the first time the Russians, under Gorbachev, had indicated they might be changing their mind about releasing my father. In March 1987, they had agreed to see me for the first time about his release. My father knew about these Russian movements. Why would he kill himself when he was closer than ever to being free? It made no sense, and after I learned about how they said he killed himself, I knew it was murder.'

According to the first official account, Rudolf Hess had asked his accompanying American guard to let him go into a small garden house in the rear of the prison grounds. When he did not return in several minutes, the guard went inside and found the ninety-three-year-old man with a cable tied around his neck, having strangled himself. The cable was an electrical wire that the Allies claimed had been negligently left there. In a second version given a few days later, the Allies said that Hess hanged himself with an extension cord provided for a reading lamp in the garden house. 'It had occurred to them,' says Wolf, 'that the sudden finding of a leftover cable could not coincide with the writing of a "suicide note" they alleged to have found three days after his death in one of his pockets.'

Rudolf Hess was a frail man of ninety-three; he was nearly blind, had difficulty walking, and was acknowledged by his doctors as unable to do almost anything requiring strength, even tying his shoelaces. The form of death, and its taking place in a matter of a few minutes, seemed highly unlikely for a man in his condition. The British laid the groundwork for conspiracy buffs when they destroyed the 'death cable' and the garden house, with all its forensic evidence, within a few days of the death. Within two weeks, bulldozers broke down the walls of the 111-year-old prison, on its way to total demolition in less than a month. The Allies performed their own autopsy and confirmed that the death was a suicide. The body was flown to a US military airbase, Grafenwöhr, near Nuremberg, and turned over to the family. That was a relief to Wolf Hess. Up until 1982 the Allies had planned to burn Hess's body and scatter the ashes so a gravesite would not become a neo-Nazi rallying point. In 1982 they changed that policy and promised to return the body to the family for burial. Until they delivered the body, Wolf was uncertain they would keep their word. But instead of taking his father's corpse and burying it immediately, he decided to have an autopsy completed by an internationally renowned German pathologist, Professor Wolfgang Spann. His conclusion flatly contradicted the one reached by the British doctor, Professor James Malcolm Cameron. Numerous and substantial differences existed between the two autopsy reports. Whereas the Allies claimed suicide, the German doctor now concluded that Rudolf Hess was murdered.

Dr Hugh Thomas, a former British army doctor who examined Hess in Spandau in 1973, examined the photographs of the dead body. Based upon his review, he also concluded Hess was murdered. 'If a person hangs to death, you would expect that the line of the cord would run diagonally across the back of his neck. But the photographs of Hess [taken by Professor Spann] show a mark straight across. The line also continues around the front of the neck, suggesting he was killed by strangulation rather than hanging.'

But with the destruction of the death scene, a follow-up examination was impossible. The Allies closed the file as a suicide; their strongest argument was the question why anyone would want to kill a ninety-three-year-old prisoner. Wolf Hess believes he has the answer. 'The strong possibility of a Russian consent to his release left the British with the shock that he could talk freely. This could not happen, so he had to be silenced forever. Also, not always the best people were used as guards at the prison. For instance, in 1988, two former British guards were arrested for stealing my father's original flying suit he wore on his 1941 flight and then trying to sell it to me for three hundred thousand dollars. Murder is only another step up the criminal ladder. I think the British had the most to gain from his death. If the British don't have anything to hide, why have they closed the file on my father until the year 2017? What did he know that scared them so? I think the British arranged to have him killed while their good friends, the Americans, ran the prison.

'The truth cannot be permanently suppressed. I view the hectic attempts of the Allies with a certain irony, even though I know that this behaviour finally robbed me of my father and let him become the victim of a murder conspiracy. With this murder, the Allies only took a further step towards exposing themselves. The murder will be traced back to them and will, with an even greater certainty, shatter them more than the imprisonment of my father has already done.'

For Wolf Hess, the strain of his father's death was too much. His decades of efforts to free his father had ended in failure. His father died a prisoner, exactly what he had hoped to avoid. The fifty-year-old Wolf Hess had a stroke following his father's death, but his physical condition has improved faster than the emotional scars left by his father's plight.

With his father's death, he no longer has to watch his words, afraid that he might incense the Four Powers and lengthen his father's prison stay. His anger at the Four Powers is mixed with glee at German unification. 'How much my father would have enjoyed seeing the unjust victors' construction of a divided Germany fall to pieces!' exclaims Wolf.

In the living room of his large house near Munich, he has a 1932 drawing of his father. Sitting in a large sofa near the picture, he spoke of his current feelings. 'Maybe it's time we tried some Allied war crimes. What about the aggression on Egypt in 1956 by Britain, France, and Israel, or US aggression in Panama or Soviet in Afghanistan? Nuremberg was a big mistake, and history will show that. The Americans came here in World War I and Wilson didn't know what he was doing and they carved up Europe. Then after World War II, they still put their nose in everyone's business, in things they knew nothing about. The victors split Germany, gave away German land, and now it's all coming back at you. It's the same as Versailles – if you push something down hard enough, it will come back at you like an explosion. That's what is happening now in Germany, even though Mr Ridley,[14] advocating the thinking of Mrs Thatcher, believes he can turn back the clock with ridiculous statements. These people are the last ones of a bygone era. The future is with the first ones of tomorrow, and the Ridleys and Thatchers are not among them.

'I always predicted reunification in my lifetime. Germans are sick of having to feel ashamed to say they are proud to be German. Now it's all changing. The Soviet Union is crumbling, and the great American "melting pot" is melting over with crime and drugs and racial hatred. Germans know that Americans, British and French in the West, and Russians in the East, are still occupying our country. We want them all out. Then it will return to the Europe of old, with a powerful and large Germany in the middle. Even our lands the victors gave away after the war will come back. Now, the price for unification is to sign a treaty guaranteeing the present Polish border. But wait some years. Sooner or later that land will return where it belongs, to Germany. The Poles have run their former blossoming land into a dry, grass-covered land. With their economy in ruins, they must depend on financial aid. The German nation will not continually nourish these people who have stolen our property. The Americans should remember what Abraham Lincoln once said: "Nothing is settled unless it is settled in a just way." '

Wolf Hess is more adamant about the defence of his father than at any time in the past. He claims to have received thousands of letters and says 'ninety-nine per cent are positive'. He is encouraged by letters he receives about his father from German high schools. 'They show the right type of interest and understand what really happened. To me, this is a promising sign for German youth.'

While others felt sympathy for the Hess family, Wolf clearly demonstrates that the family, or at least he himself, felt anger and resentment at the long imprisonment. He provides the strident defence that his father failed to provide himself at Nuremberg. He is a shrill voice reminding us that some children of prominent National Socialists identify totally with their fathers' plight and philosophy and view them as the victims, not the criminals.

'It was an advantage for me to grow up as the son of Rudolf Hess,' he says. 'It was never a disadvantage. People liked my father, he was the "conscience of the party", and as a result they liked me. And the longer he was in prison, the more sympathy people felt for all of us.'

As Wolf Hess finished his last conversation with me, he summarized his hard feelings for the future. 'The American efforts have failed. They wanted history to know that every German was a Nazi and that every Nazi was bad so that the Germans collectively felt guilty. That was ridiculous and we now know it. The title "war criminal" for my father means nothing. In some years history will take a different perspective on these so-called crimes and my father will be seen in a proper and good way. It will be seen that the former Allies, the victors of World War II, are anything but the host of morality, justice, and humanity, as which they made themselves judges over Germany. It's changing already. You cannot hide the truth for ever.'

CHAPTER 4

'A Loud Dictator'

There are National Socialists who served in important posts in the Third Reich, but whose names are unrecognized by the general public today. Their importance to Nazi Germany is overlooked because they were not charged with crimes after the war, but instead returned to quiet lives. Many of these men held positions of immense power, far more critical to the Nazi war effort than some who achieved postwar notoriety, like Adolf Eichmann, Klaus Barbie, and Josef Mengele. That they lack notoriety does not mean their families have had an easy time coping with their Nazi legacy.

One such case is that of Karl Saur and his family. Not only was Saur a committed Nazi, chief of the crucial technical department in Albert Speer's armaments ministry, but he was a trusted friend of Hitler, so much so that he was one of the few men named in Hitler's will, which appointed him Speer's successor. Yet while Speer was convicted at Nuremberg as a major war criminal and spent twenty years in prison, Saur was a free man by 1948. The contradiction in treatment is emphasized when their careers are compared.

Karl Saur had six children. Klaus is his second-youngest child, born on 22 July 1941. He had almost two decades after the war to judge his father, including a brief time when they worked together. 'I never felt a close connection to him,' says Karl. 'I am quite negative on my father.' To Klaus, his father was not only an unrepentant follower of the Third Reich, but he was 'simply a bad father'.

Karl Otto is the youngest Saur child, born on 14 March 1944. He mostly agrees with his brother's judgement. 'However, as I get older,' he says, 'I think I am becoming more neutral about my father, and not quite as negative as I used to be.'

Karl Otto Saur senior was born on 16 June 1902, in Düsseldorf, the third child in an upper-middle-class Lutheran family, son of a construction engineer. 'His father was strong but nice,' says Klaus. 'He was always described by those who knew him as a good, sympathetic man. But still my father had a very bad relationship with him. And his mother was a terrible person, described as extremely bad. She was very egocentric.'

Saur left this poor family atmosphere to attend high school in Freiburg, then technical university in both Hanover and Karlsruhe, where he received a degree in steel and iron engineering in 1922. He was concerned more with sports than with study, and his grades were the minimum to guarantee his degree. Immediately after graduation he started working at the Thyssen firm, a bitter rival to the prominent Krupp company and one of the largest privately-held industrial conglomerates in Germany. There Saur became a personal favourite of management; he seemed to have a bright career ahead of him when his father died suddenly in 1927.

'His mother and sisters called him and said he had to come home and manage the family company in Freiburg,' says Klaus. 'He later told me he would have preferred selling the company, but his mother and sisters insisted. At the age of twenty-five he was running a company with four hundred employees. And in 1929 it went bankrupt. It was very hard for him since he had taken credit for the company.'

'And to make matters worse, his sisters always blamed him for the closing of the company,' says Karl junior. 'They ignored the terrible economic conditions and that many other companies also closed at this time. They even reminded him of this failure after the war.'

Saur's disappointment with the collapsing firm made him more sympathetic to National Socialism, confirming his feelings that Germany was in dire straits and the Nazis were the only political group advocating workable solutions. He returned to Thyssen that same year. Soon he was promoted to director of the business department and was in constant contact with the family patriarch, Fritz Thyssen. 'And one day he was really shocked,'

Klaus recalls. 'He thought Thyssen was the greatest man in the world, an industrial tycoon, a wonderful man. When Thyssen was on holiday and [my father] was sitting in Thyssen's office, because he held this position when Thyssen was gone, the shock came when he discovered that the office had one of the largest pornographic libraries you could imagine. And my father, who had never had any relationships with women, and was really quite puritanical, was disgusted by these photographs. He stayed at the firm, but he could never get over the fact that Fritz Thyssen should have such a collection.'

While Saur may have been offended by pictures of naked bodies, his morals were not offended by the increasingly harsh language of the NSDAP. He joined the party on 1 October 1931. Klaus believes his father was 'enamoured' of the Nazis, but is not certain of the elder Saur's motivation. 'I think he believed that most German governments had been bad, and that only the Nazis could help in those times, with the unemployment and all.'

'He was basically anti-democratic,' says Karl junior, 'and the Nazis fitted his philosophy very well. He believed things ran better under a totalitarian government.'

However, both brothers know there was family pressure not to join. 'He [Karl senior] was very close to his uncle, my grandfather's brother,' says Klaus. 'He had a very good relationship with him, and his uncle was always telling him, very early in 1923 and 1924, "Don't go to the Nazi party, this will have a bad end." And the director-general of Thyssen, who was my father's great mentor, was completely anti-Nazi.[15] My father had the highest respect for his uncle and the director-general, but he did not accept their warnings. Both his sisters joined the Nazi women's groups, and my father used to joke that he had no problem getting his sisters into Nazi functions, but that for his wife's side of the family he always had to go out of his way to get tickets. His wife never joined the party, and his father-in-law did not like the Nazis.'

Saur was immediately active in the party, becoming the chairman of the Nazi engineering group for the North Rhine. In 1936, he met his wife, Veronica, twelve years his junior, and they married. The following year he moved to Munich where he joined the Technical Institute, a Nazi organization, and worked under Dr Fritz Todt. It was an appointment that altered his career. Todt was a quiet and reserved technician who was the father of Germany's autobahns. He was also an early party member, respected by Hitler and the Nazi inner circle. Hitler rewarded Todt for his loyalty and expertise with one of the Third Reich's most important posts, minister of armaments and production. The armaments ministry was the crucial agency responsible for fuelling the German war effort.

Todt and Saur developed an excellent relationship. 'Todt and my father really liked each other,' says Klaus. 'He was one of the greatest figures and friends in my father's life. In one of his papers Todt wrote that "Saur is thinking, creating and feeling just like myself". This was the greatest compliment for him in his life. And at a famous Nazi rally, Todt began his speech by saying, "Mr Saur and all others". These things set my father apart in the Todt organization.'

Karl junior agrees that Todt was a key figure in his father's life. 'He would have remained loyal to Todt at all costs,' says Karl. 'Maybe the only person who was more important to him was Hitler. But then Hitler was a special case to all men like my father. The Führer held a unique, unassailable position for each of them.'

In 1938, Todt suggested to the prestigious Deutsches Museum that the Nazi presence on the board be increased by the addition of Saur. Although Todt claimed Saur was the best administrative man in the Nazi party, the museum directors first ignored the request and when prodded they rejected the appointment. 'This was really a brave step in 1938, to be so bold against the Nazis,' says Klaus. 'After the war, in 1954, my father was naïve enough to write to the Deutsches Museum and ask permission to start a bookshop in the library's entrance. They ignored his first letter but when he persisted they said no. There was no reason if they did not want him before the war as the Nazi representative, they should want to do business with him afterwards.' Today, Klaus is on the Deutsches Museum's board of trustees, a subsidiary of the executive board to which his father sought appointment fifty years earlier.

But the Deutsches Museum rejection was only a minor setback. Saur's career advanced under Todt's tutelage, and he and his wife began a family. From 1937, Veronica Saur was pregnant each year except 1943. One baby daughter died eight weeks after her birth, and another pregnancy ended unsuccessfully. The Saurs' surviving five children, all born during this period, arrived into a non-religious, very authoritarian household.

But Saur had little time for his family once the war began in September 1939. In Todt's ministry, Saur was appointed director of the technical division, responsible for planning and implementing state-of-the-art weapons production. Together with Xavier Dorsch, another key Todt assistant, Saur was one of the ministry's most respected managers and experts. Todt had a preference for delivering his reports personally to Hitler, and Saur and Dorsch often accompanied him to cover the more technical aspects. This ensured that from an early stage of the war Saur had personal contact with the Führer, contact which gave him prestige in the Nazi party.

'In the war period, every machine-building company came under the direction of the ministry of armaments, so my father became a really big boss and every company had to report to him,' Klaus says. 'And during this time it was not to your benefit if you were a gentle man. So he was pushing them [the companies] very hard for the war effort. While there were times he could be soft and very nice, in his work he was driving them all the time. He was very overbearing in presence. He was only five feet eight inches tall but over two hundred and twenty pounds, and he was extremely loud and often screaming. There was a joke in the Munich Technical Institute: people would say "What is that loud noise?" and the answer was "Mr Saur is talking with Berlin," and then the reply was "Shouldn't he use a telephone?" When I shared a five-room office with him after the war, he would just yell to talk to me and you could hear him from the first office to the last one.'

While the beefy, red-faced Saur may not have made many friends among Germany's industrialists with his brusque behaviour, his performance-driven department was admired in the Nazi hierarchy. Then on 8 February 1942, Saur was stunned by the news that his mentor, Dr Todt, had been killed in a plane crash. That same day Hitler appointed his architect, Albert Speer, as Todt's replacement.

'My father was extremely shocked and very emotional about Todt's death,' says Klaus. 'But he was also impressed that Hitler named a replacement so quickly. He welcomed Speer. He had met him before, but didn't know him well. There was no time for discussion or thinking.'

Karl junior believes his father thought that if anything happened to Todt, he might be named as the replacement. 'Both my father and Dorsch thought they might replace Todt. But my brother is right in that the appointment of Speer was so fast there was little time to think about it. However, for my father, it was the first time in his career that he ever had a chief who was younger than him. This took some getting used to, but eventually he did adjust.'

Speer, unsure of his own qualifications for the new position, relied heavily on Saur and Dorsch, taking them to almost every conference with Hitler. But slowly Hitler became frustrated with the armaments ministry's failure to meet production schedules, which were ever more demanding despite diminishing resources. However, his anger was directed at Speer, not at his two top assistants. As Speer later wrote in his memoirs, he noticed a change in Hitler's attitude by the summer of 1943, and by the autumn Speer said, 'Hitler fell into the habit of calling Saur to ask for the monthly reports.' Speer recognized that Saur was an early party member, on good terms with Hitler's secretary Bormann, and as a result Speer 'gradually began to feel insecure in my own ministry'.

Speer was convinced that Saur and Saur's good friend Dorsch were frustrating his intentions in their departments. The situation worsened from January to May 1944, when Speer was ill. Although he tried to conduct the ministry's business from his hospital room, his sporadic presence allowed Saur and Dorsch to move closer to Hitler. In February, Speer decided that a fighter aircraft staff was necessary to oversee the crisis in aircraft production, and he proposed Karl Hanke, the Gauleiter, or provincial administrator, of Lower Silesia, to become its chief. Hitler brusquely overruled his choice and appointed Saur to the post. By March, Göring was using both Saur and Dorsch in his own presentations to Hitler, hoping to undercut Speer's power with his own associates.

'My father once told me that Hitler said to him in 1944 that if he had known how good Saur was back in 1942, and if he had known him well then, he would have had him, instead of Speer, replace Todt,' says Klaus. 'My father was very proud of this, and I used to think, "What, are you stupid, don't you know you would have then spent twenty years in prison instead of Speer?" It would have been absolutely impossible to tell him this because he would never have spoken to me about it again.

'There was another story he told which showed how Hitler liked him. One time he and Hitler took a walk together, and Hitler said, "Saur, you are only holding a minor rank. Why don't I make you a secretary of state?" And my father said, "Do you think, mein Führer, that I would be put on a level with those other idiots?" And Hitler was laughing and said, "Okay, then, you will be Saur and that is better than a secretary of state."

'There was one other incident he often told us after the war,' Karl junior recalls. 'On Christmas Eve, in either 1942 or 1943, Hitler and my father spoke on the telephone. And at the end of the conversation, Hitler wished him Merry Christmas with a very familiar German saying. It was a very important signal to my father that he was on a personal and close basis to the Führer.'

'My father was never interested in status symbols,' says Klaus. 'He was interested in having power and having the weapons industry production completely under his control, but titles were not important to him.'

Saur was increasingly successful in his acquisition of power. Besides his work with the Luftwaffe, he took sole responsibility for tank production at a time when battlefield losses were mounting. Saur's aggressive and optimistic outlook was welcome in the Führer's headquarters. According to Speer, in June 1944, when quartermaster-general Eduard Wagner painted the bleakest situation on the Eastern front, Saur 'scolded the much older quartermaster-general like a schoolboy, with Hitler joining in'. Hitler appreciated Saur's brusqueness, which was always used in favour of National Socialism.

On 21 July 1944, the day after Colonel Claus von Stauffenberg's failed bomb attack on Hitler, the important Nazi ministers were invited to the Führer's headquarters to present their congratulations. Appended to Speer's invitation was a request to bring Saur and Dorsch. All other ministers were asked to come without their deputies. At the reception, Speer recalled, Hitler 'greeted them with pronounced cordiality, whereas he passed by me with a careless handshake'. Saur and Dorsch were invited to the afternoon tea with the Führer's intimate circle, while Speer was left out. Saur repaid the courtesy. A wave of persecutions and retribution followed the 20 July bombing. Saur denounced two fellow officers, General Schneider and Colonel Fichtner. Saur overheard Schneider complain that Hitler was incapable of judging technical questions; Fichtner had not vigorously supported a new type of tank. Hitler accepted the denunciations and arrested the men. Although Speer intervened to free them from prison, they were dismissed from the army.

While Klaus is convinced his father enjoyed the power he accumulated during the Third Reich, he does not believe that he was driven by ideology. Not even his father's action in turning his colleagues in to the Gestapo changes his mind. 'It was professional ambition that drove him during the war, not ideology. I am sure of it. He was very pragmatic.'

Karl junior agrees that his father was pragmatic, 'but he was also an opportunist. He took advantage of many situations to further his career, and he often did this without any second thoughts about whether his actions were correct or not.'

It was Saur's pragmatism that allowed him to help several Germans 'tainted' by Jewish blood. 'He was not a real anti-Semite,' says Klaus. 'He told me he had a few good Jewish friends. He said a few were good and he accepted them, although in his view many had problems and were not good for Germany. During the war, he helped a young girl he knew from school, Mary Diamond. She was Jewish and he helped her get to Switzerland. Another person he helped was Dr Wilhelm Haspel, the chairman of Daimler-Benz. When Haspel first met my father in 1939 he thought he was too political, and pushy and loud. After many meetings he discovered my father was actually quite soft, and that he would always do the best job on armaments, whether for Hitler or the Kaiser. And in 1944 Haspel came to my father and said he had to resign because he couldn't take any more pressure. And his wife was Jewish and he was not a Nazi party member. Meanwhile, Goebbels was trying to put both Haspel and his wife in the KZ [concentration camp]. My father told him that if he resigned he could no longer help him, and Haspel stayed on. He could never have survived in Germany without this. And after the war, he stayed as chairman of

Daimler-Benz but this time because he was not a Nazi and because he had a Jewish wife.

'The president of the German engineers, Dr Matchoss, was helped in the same way by my father and later told the Allies the same thing. Otto Meyer, another director-general, had a half-Jewish wife, and again my father protected him against Goebbels. He said all these men were critical to the war effort.

'I would like to think my father did this from some humanitarian basis, but for him it was absolute pragmatism,' says Klaus. 'He just believed that whoever replaced these men would not be as good and [would] therefore make his job more difficult. If someone he did not know came to him for help and said, "Please, help me and my Jewish wife," he would have said, "Why?" '

'I have no illusions about his commitment to Germany and the Third Reich,' says Karl junior. 'Since my father was responsible for weapons production, he could come home every night to his family without the guilt of thinking he had personally been responsible for killing someone that day. But even if my father had been ordered to direct the production of something like the mobile gas vans, or the like, I think he would have done it. He would have thought of it as his duty.'

Saur's pragmatism also made it easier for him to become somewhat disillusioned when Hitler ordered unreasonable production quotas in late 1944. By the autumn, the Führer wanted to stop fighter-plane production and increase flak production fivefold almost immediately. Both Saur and Speer thought the proposal unreasonable, and after failing to change Hitler's mind, they decided not to follow the order. It was the first order they had ever refused to carry out. Yet still Hitler continued to rely on Saur more than Speer. This tilt was made explicit in October 1944, at a situation conference. In the presence of all the generals and Speer, Hitler announced, 'We have the good fortune to have a genius in our armaments industry. I mean Saur. All difficulties are being overcome by him.' General Wolfgang Thomale tactfully said, 'Mein Führer, Minister Speer is here.' 'Yes, I know,' Hitler answered irritably, 'but Saur is the genius who will master the situation.' At a conference with Goebbels, Saur and Speer on 4 January 1945, Hitler totally ignored Speer and spoke only to Saur. As the confrontations with Hitler increased, Speer decided to let Saur be responsible for almost all armaments production. In February, Saur humiliated Speer in a series of conference strategies, by presenting much more optimistic projections than those in the ministry's internal reports. Speer watched incredulously at a staff meeting as 'Hitler and Saur went into raptures over the dire psychological effects of an air raid upon the skyscraper canyons of New York'. Through March, under increasing Russian artillery barrage, Saur alone represented the armaments ministry at the Führerbunker meetings.

Klaus's first memories of his father date from this hectic close to the war. He was then three. 'I remember being in the garden of our house; we had a big park there, and a railway station nearby. I recall the rooms and even some of the furniture. My father was living with us during the war, but he was working a lot and usually came home late in the evening. He had a big car with a driver, and one or two assistants, and one or two secretaries with him. I did not know he was important. Although the house was a palace and he had the staff and large car, I thought it was typical.

'And in 1944 and 1945 there was only bad news about the war, and he was always ready to have an explosion. No one was allowed to say anything in the car. And they all hoped that my sister, just one year older than me, would be taken by him in the car, because that made him very happy. He would take her the last mile in the car to the house. None of the rest of the family was ever in the car.

'We did not have much pressure from my father during the war years. And my mother was living a good life in a material way, and she was good to us, very affectionate.'

Although Klaus felt little pressure from his father, he had noticed his frustration over the collapsing German war effort. During the final weeks of the Thousand-Year Reich, Saur tried gently to deflect Hitler's orders for new tanks, rockets, planes, and increased steel production. He was one of the last Nazi officials to visit the Führerbunker during the final days. When Hitler's will was opened within hours of his 30 April 1945 suicide, Saur discovered the degree to which he had earned the Führer's trust.

While Saur helped Hitler at this final stage, his family was sent to the south to avoid the Russian army. 'We went walking,'

Klaus recalls. 'I remember parts of this long walk, the many people on the roads, but I recall it as interesting, not tragic. In the south, a Lutheran priest put us up for three months. It was just my mother, five children, and her sister. I don't remember any bombings during this time, but I heard later they were all around us.

'No one knew where my father was during this time. My mother didn't know if he was alive or dead. We were sent in late 1945 to near Munich and stayed with my mother's brother. Then in 1946 we went to our grandparents' house near Düsseldorf, and in that year we learned my father was alive and held by the Americans.'

Unbeknown to the Saur family, by April 1945 Karl was on US Army Counter Intelligence Corps (CIC) wanted lists as a major Nazi offender. A confidential CIC information sheet noted that according to informants 'Sauer [*sic*] rather than Speer should be at Nürnberg testifying in the trials. . . .' He was finally arrested by the US Seventh Army on 26 May 1945, near Munich. US intelligence officers immediately began interrogating him. By June, he was moved to Chesnay, a small palace in the grounds of Versailles which the US had converted into a temporary prison. Chesnay was the central clearing-house set aside for scientists, technicians, aircraft designers, and agricultural and communication experts. Speer was already detained there when Saur was brought in. British and American intelligence officers arrived early in July. Speer, Saur and others decided to assist their requests for technical information, Speer later recalled, 'I could not contribute much; Saur had by far the better knowledge of details.'

Saur's cooperation at Chesnay may be one of the reasons he was not added to the Allied prosecution list. Several dozen German scientists avoided prosecution by cooperating with the US rocket programme after the war. While Saur's help was much more limited, it certainly did not work against him. The US Army Intelligence and Security Command still refuse to release the 128 pages of interrogation of Saur. They are withheld from responses to Freedom of Information Act requests because the information in them is considered so sensitive that the documents are still classified as secret.

Another factor that probably helped Saur gain his freedom was his pledge to cooperate in a proposed case against

Germany's most prominent industrialist, Alfried Krupp. Saur agreed to testify for the prosecution against the thirty-nine-year-old chairman of Germany's oldest and most distinguished manufacturing empire, a decision he knew would be condemned by Germany's power elite. But to the practical Saur, such a deal was preferable to standing trial himself.

Krupp was supposed to be included with the twenty-two major defendants in the first Nuremberg trial, but the Allies mistakenly indicted his senile seventy-five-year-old father. By the time they realized their mistake, the Nuremberg Tribunal would not delay the trial for Alfried's inclusion. His case was postponed for nearly two years. During that time, the Allies kept Saur under their control.

Karl junior is not surprised by his father's cooperation with the American authorities. 'He respected the technical ability of the US, and had even discussed with Hitler his desire to be appointed as Ambassador to the US after Germany won the war. After the Nazi defeat, which was another great failure in my father's life, he thought the best choice for the future was to work with the United States. I am sure he expected to be invited to the US and put in charge of part of their industrial production. He thought they would want him as they wanted Wernher von Braun.[16] It was disappointing to him that no invitation was ever forthcoming.

'If he had known that German industry would be on the road to recovery within several years, I doubt he would have agreed to testify against Krupp. That was a decision which cost him dearly in his own postwar career. It made many enemies for him inside Germany because Krupp was powerful and had many well-placed friends.'

While waiting to testify against Krupp, Saur was moved to Nuremberg in 1947 and then to a smaller detention centre, Neustadt, near Düsseldorf. Five-year-old Klaus visited his father in Neustadt. 'I had a wonderful time when I went to see him in his camp. No one else from the family was there. I was sent to stay there for a week with him. They had chocolate and everything like that. There were a lot of old Nazis there, and they were all very nice to me.

'Looking back it is interesting because I knew that the Germans had lost the war and this was a big tragedy, but I was

1. Hans Frank, the Governor General of Poland, with his family in 1942. *Courtesy of Niklas Frank*

2. Norman Frank, in his Hitler Youth uniform, receives a ceremonial picture of Adolf Hitler from his father in 1942. *Courtesy of Niklas Frank*

3. Norman Frank poses with his father in 1944. Norman was Hans Frank's favourite child: 'I am torn by the image of a good father and that of a criminal.' *Courtesy of Niklas Frank*

4. Brigitta Frank, together with seven-year-old Niklas and his older sister, Brigitta, entering Nuremberg Prison in September 1946. Less than three weeks after this picture was taken, Frank was hanged. *Courtesy of Niklas Frank*

5. Rudolf and Ilse Hess, together with family, friends and Nazi dignitaries, at the christening for their son Wolf Rüdiger. Ilse holds Wolf up for the admiration of a seated Adolf Hitler, Wolf's godfather. *Courtesy of Wolf Hess*

6. Rudolf Hess playing with Wolf in the garden of their house. This 1941 photograph was taken shortly before Hess's flight to England. *Courtesy of Wolf Hess*

7. Rudolf Hess (front row, second from left) listening to the Nuremberg proceedings. *Courtesy of National Archives*

8. While Rudolf Hess is standing trial at Nuremberg, Ilse Hess helps seven-year-old Wolf with his lessons in their home at Bad Obersdorf. *AP/ Wide World Photos*

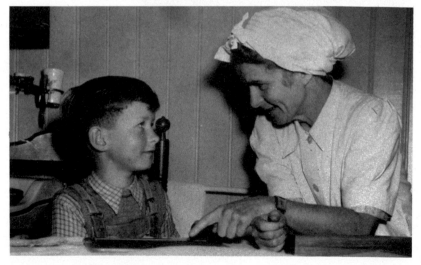

9. On April 26, 1985, Wolf Hess, together with his mother
and his wife, leave the main gate of Spandau Prison
after visiting Rudolf Hess on his ninety-first birthday.
AP/Wide World Photos

10. Wolf Hess staring at the body of his father, shortly after his
mysterious death in 1987. Although the death was deemed a suicide by
Allied officials, Wolf adamantly contends the evidence points to murder.
Bild Zeitung

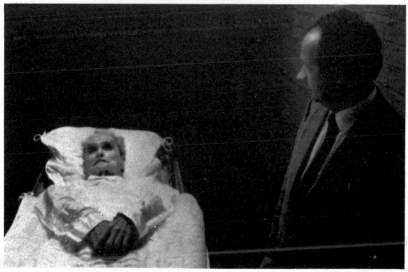

11. Hjalmar Schact, the Nazis' financial genius, joining Hitler for a public rally in the mid-1930s. *Courtesy of National Archives*

12. Manci Schact leads her two daughters, Cordula and Konstanze, to visit their father at Nuremberg. That meeting is Cordula's first memory of her father, 'I liked him very much,' she recalls. *AP/Wide World Photos*

13. Schact, wearing a fur-collared overcoat,
at the tumultous press conference
following his acquittal.
Courtesy of National Archives

14. The Schact family in the library
of their home after the war.
Paul Potter Ltd

15. Josef Mengele, identified by camp survivors as the SS officer at the far right, in an extremely rare photograph of the Auschwitz arrival ramp. *Courtesy of the author*

16. Mengele escaped arrest after the war and settled for four years on an isolated Southern German farm. This is one of two known photographs of three-year-old Rolf Mengele visiting his father. *Courtesy of Rolf Mengele*

never aware at this time of any problem with the Nazis. And I was never thinking, "Why is my father in this camp and always so sad?" '

Karl junior, then only three years old, has patchy memories of his single visit to his father at the Neustadt detention camp. 'I remember the train trip with my mother, and then a jeep ride to the camp with an American GI. The only memory I have of my father is while he took a nap with my mother inside the camp. I remember looking around the barracks and walking among the guards.'

By the time Klaus and Karl saw their father in 1947, Albert Speer had already been tried and convicted in the main Nuremberg trial. Saur was not even called as a witness, although Speer used his name at a crucial point in the testimony. The US prosecutor confronted Speer with an incriminating memo of 17 April 1944. The memo, signed by Speer, was addressed to Himmler and asked for a hundred thousand labourers to be diverted from the Jewish transports being sent from Hungary to Auschwitz. Speer adamantly denied writing the most damning document that tied him to the use of slave labour. 'I did not write this,' he said. 'Saur was the author of this document. It is out of the question that I participated because I was sick at the time.' Saur had the authority to sign his name, Speer said, and moreover, he claimed he did not even know of the Hungarian Jews until several months later. The Allies never called Saur to contradict the Speer claim, and the Speer team did not summon him to verify it.

Klaus is convinced that Speer was angry at his father for avoiding prosecution. 'The major reason Speer is so negative about my father is that it was clear to him that my father was a much more committed Nazi. Also, Speer worked much more intensively than my father to try to help a few things to see that this city would not get bombed, or that this bridge would not get blown up. And my father, up to the last minute, was very close to Hitler. At his own trial, he [Speer] must have asked himself why he should serve twenty years in prison when Saur was free.'[17]

'I think that Speer is harsh on my father,' says Karl junior, 'and very nice to himself. He wrote his memoirs to excuse himself. I used to think that Speer's view of my father was quite unfair. But as time has passed, my opinion changed. While I still believe

Speer is trying to minimize his own actions, I think he is quite right about my father.'

While Speer was being tried at Nuremberg, and Saur was in custody and undergoing de-nazification proceedings, the Saur family tried to adjust to a very different postwar life. They had lost their large home, cars, extensive staff and other privileges. 'From 1945 to 1947 my mother was ill,' recalls Klaus. 'She had some operations on her throat starting in 1946, and they continued up to 1950. Her younger sister was with us, and was very helpful and friendly, but under great pressure. She spoke very good English and got a job with a British officer in Düsseldorf.' That job allowed her to earn a decent salary which supported the family and to obtain goods other Germans could not get. Still, Klaus remembers often eating a 'watery and sickly soup'; he also recalls constant arguments between his mother and her stepmother. 'But it was not terrible for me, not at this time,' he says.

Just before the elder Saur was released to rejoin the family, he made his appearance in the Krupp case. The Allies had prepared for this moment for almost two years. Saur's appearance on 8 June 1948 stunned the courtroom and Krupp's thirty-seven defence attorneys, led by Otto Kranzbühler, the young naval officer who had defended Grand Admiral Dönitz at the first Nuremberg trial. The Krupp defence team was helpless against Saur. He had been too close to Hitler, knew too much, and recalled events in great detail. The most damning evidence he gave was that Alfried, a dues-paying member of the SS, directly intervened with Hitler to use Auschwitz Jews in slave labour. It was Alfried who advanced to the Führer the concept of 'extermination through work'. The only way to counterattack Saur's testimony was to impugn his character, and the Krupp public-relations people went to work with a vengeance. Press reports coordinated by Krupp called him a 'filthy pig' and compared his credibility to that of Josef Goebbels. Kranzbühler said that Saur was 'like a Chinest mandarin, a man who takes all the opportunities available under a dictatorship' and then finds it convenient 'to pretend he was only an errand boy'. A vicious article accused Saur of having 'truly embodied the slave labour programme', reciting examples of his 'boorish manners' and 'racism' and concluding he should have been in the defendant's chair instead of Krupp.

Nevertheless, Krupp was convicted, and Saur's testimony was decisive. The court sentenced Krupp to twelve years in prison and ordered him to forfeit all his real and personal property. But Krupp served only a little more than a year, his sentence commuted by the US High Commissioner, John J. McCloy. The industrialist received a bonus with his early release: his entire fortune was returned to him, McCloy deciding the penalty was too harsh.

Saur had no such luck with the restoration of his wartime glories. Upon his mid-1948 release to his family, the forty-six-year-old engineer was penniless and prohibited by the Allies from holding any management position in industry. The Saurs moved with their five children to a small, single-storey house near Munich. A former maid, no longer working for them, and her child added to the cramped conditions. 'So we were living, nine of us,' recalls Klaus, 'in a space that could really fit at the most four or five, and today would only have two. At first we had enough to subsist, even though I remember we were always extremely short of money. This was very clear. And then we came to the difficult situation.'

Almost immediately after his release, Saur obtained a consulting position to a commercial company. His technical knowledge was not outdated, and it seemed like promising employment. Although the elder Saur never knew it, his sons have since learned that somebody complained to the company about his Nazi past and he lost the position as quickly as he had obtained it.

'And he was unable to get any positions to his liking,' Klaus recalls. 'You see, from 1945 to 1948, a lot of the top Nazis in industry again returned to leading positions in German industry – there was no change. He was expecting that everyone in industry would welcome him again. And he was very surprised and completely shocked that most of them were absolutely no longer interested in even contacting him. As a result, he became increasingly, extremely inflexible. In the Nazi period he was also inflexible, but he could push more then. He became much more rigid now. And my father was such a dictator, and since he had no other people to report to him, he would put us completely under pressure. I think if he had been able to make a commercial success it would have made a difference at home.'

But the financial situation did not improve. Saur suffered a series of bad business breaks. Although he searched for consulting orders from day to day, and organized booths at handicraft fairs, the income was negligible. During this time, Saur published a government report about hydraulics and in 1952 started a small technical publishing firm. In 1954, on the suggestion of a former Nazi aide who had become a millionaire in the postwar iron and steel industry, he decided to consult with the Indian government. Only after Saur had spent four thousand Deutschmarks of his meagre savings in preparation for the trip was the assignment cancelled. Klaus remembers that this put his father into such a 'real bad time that he looked for a way to raise money by even selling his archive of personal wartime papers'.

In 1956, he planned a three-day outing for his family and some employees to celebrate a large contract, but lost the deal at the last moment. 'Again, this was typical,' says Klaus. 'He was very naïve in business, always spending money before an order was final.' In 1957, Daimler-Benz cut back the size of their orders by 60 per cent (Dr Haspel, the Mercedes chairman Saur had saved during the war, died in 1954). This brought another family crisis, with the number of company employees being reduced from thirty to four. At about this time, Saur also lost a consulting contract with a Munich company because his technical knowledge, frozen since World War II, was outdated. This crisis was only alleviated when Saur's anti-Nazi uncle died in 1958. 'His uncle named him in his will,' Klaus recalls. 'It saved him. He died at the right time.'

'When he received the inheritance, he gave my mother two thousand Deutschmarks to buy some clothes for all the children,' recalls Karl junior. 'It was the first time I ever had new clothes instead of hand-me-downs from my brother. But even with this money, the company stayed near bankruptcy for the next several years. If the government authorities had examined the books they would have closed it. Once, I opened one of the bank statements to my father and was pleasantly surprised to see that he had a thirty thousand Deutschmark balance. I thought it was quite good until I realized the account was overdrawn by that amount.

'This inability to make a success of his company was my father's third great failure of his life, following the bankruptcy of his own father's company, and then the Nazi loss in the war. It really brought him to a new low point.'

While their father struggled to support the family, the brothers attended a school near their house. There they heard about the Nazi period. 'We had actually talked about the war for the first time when I was nine years old,' recalls Klaus. 'But the teacher, a woman, liked the period and taught it favourably. And at the school was a boy whose grandfather, a judge, had written the constitution for the Nazis. And my friend's father had been an assistant to him in that. My teacher was always telling him, "You are such a stupid boy, I don't understand it, your grandfather was such a great man and your father was really great also, I don't know what is the matter with you." But this teacher did not know that my father was also a big Nazi.

'Before the lessons in school, I had heard a little about the war from my family. Not my father, never him. He talked a little to my brother, but never to me. But my mother would talk. Although she did not like him [the elder Saur] after the war, she always said he was a genius during the war. And I was very bad at school, and I learned extremely slowly – all the other children were more active and intelligent. It was said that of five children, four are okay and one is a little stupid. That's not a bad ratio. I had absolutely no reputation at home. And my mother would always say, "A genius has stupid sons, and your stupidity is confirmation of what a genius your father is." Even with the bad relationship with him, she still admired his accomplishments. But the maid actually saw things clearer than the rest of us. She knew he was not a genius, just a good wartime manager. But my father thought of himself as brilliant.

'When I was eleven, twelve, thirteen, I always believed my father was a great man. I never realized the problems of the Nazi period. I knew he had been important and had held a high rank. When I would hear about the war I would not go back and discuss it with my father. That was not possible. My father *never* had a discussion about anything, he only gave orders.'

Even later in his education, Klaus never found teachers very critical of National Socialism. 'They never mentioned the excesses in the East,' he recalls. 'Never. I didn't even know they existed as I grew up. Later I heard, "Look, it is a false story, look at Dachau, nothing happened there. Except for a little food shortage at the end, it was not so bad." This was more or less in general from people.'

Karl junior also discovered most of his teachers were quite sympathetic in portraying National Socialism. 'They were older people and since they lived through this period they recalled it somewhat nostalgically. And around the age of ten and eleven I was quite sympathetic to my father and his position. I knew he had been in the war and I felt sorry that he was working so hard to make a living for the family and having such a difficult time. But things started changing for me when I was twelve and thirteen. I read more about the Third Reich and saw it in a very negative light. In part this was a rebellion against the way my teachers presented it.

'But there was also an important event for me around 1955 or 1956. There was a documentary on television about the murder of the Jews and I happened to be at a friend's house and I saw it. It was all new to me and affected much of my thinking about the Reich. Even the next day at school, one of our teachers, a Lutheran priest in his forties, told us he had seen the documentary and was shocked by it. He said he had never known of these murders until he saw them on television. It had a profound effect on anyone who saw it.'

But during the 1950s, Karl and Klaus did not concentrate on judging their father's role during the war. Living in the same house as their father, they were more concerned with his role as a parent. He was not a good father. Part of the household problem was a bad relationship between Saur and his wife. They were very different people. Saur was an early riser, a country man, and sports minded. Veronica was the opposite. 'From 1936 to 1945 it was okay, because he was a powerful man and he had all the money that was possible, and he was young and extremely successful,' says Klaus. 'But after the war there was nothing in their marriage. And all of these things he missed, he found in his secretary. They were very compatible.'

'My father liked having a family,' says Karl, 'but he lived his life as though he was a single man who also happened to have a family. I don't think my parents' relationship was as bad as Klaus describes it, but I know there were real differences between them.'

While part of the problem in the household may have been the bad atmosphere from their parents' marriage, the other part of the difficulty was the elder Saur's dictatorial nature.

'My mother would always tell us, "Go away before he comes so you will have no problems," ' recalls Klaus. 'But she would never say to him, "Please stop this." They would never argue. My father wouldn't argue. He just gave orders. Discussion was never possible. There was always a situation when all of us only had some jam to eat both in the morning and the evening, and my father would have ham and cheese and always some veal. We never had it, only on Sundays. And we always had a big tragedy because we did not have the money to buy a refrigerator, and he liked his beer nearly frozen. So we had to bring it to him every evening, to bring him beer kept cold in a restaurant about five hundred yards away. But on Mondays the restaurant was closed. So he instructed us to put two bottles of beer under very cold water. Most of the time we forgot to do that. And in the end it was always extremely bad for us. And we would sit there without saying a single word. If we did something wrong he would use corporal punishment.

'I remember one time we were sitting in this single room and I asked my second-eldest sister to help me in mathematics and she said, "Oh, I don't know that either." And my father overheard us, and he was very good in mathematics but he was an extremely bad teacher, because he would just say, "It's like this, do you understand? Now repeat it." And I didn't repeat it very well and he slapped me very hard across my face. I remember this well.

'Our upbringing was just very stupid.'

'He was like a dictator,' says Karl. 'And he was nicer to me than to Klaus or my sisters. He treated me the best of all the children. I think I was his closest. But still I found him very difficult.'

At the age of eighteen, in 1959, Klaus was unhappy with the repressive family atmosphere under his father's absolute control. After completing his high school studies and two years at a commercial and business school, he was the first of the five children to leave home. 'My father became a grandfather the next year, and this made him a little more human,' Klaus recalls. 'But regarding the war he was the same. He still only gave lessons or lectures. He never read any books about the period. He once called a newspaper reporter a pig because he worked for the Nazis during the war and now wrote against them.

'It was at this time that I had the first real discussions on this subject, the negative side, at the book-traders' convention at Düsseldorf. Remember, Saur was not such a famous name and people talked to me just like any other person. On my own, I started to see this period much more critically. During this re-analysis I became more and more critical and thought everything in National Socialism was bad.'

In 1960, a Cologne magazine printed a scathing article on Saur. Klaus's first reaction was to defend his father, and he tried unsuccessfully to contact the journalist. He was convinced the author was wrong. 'But he was right,' Klaus says. 'Now I know he was right.'

While Klaus's view of his father was changing, he returned home in 1963, after a three-year absence. He had seen his father only sporadically during the time away. But he still found it impossible to raise the issue of the war with his inflexible sixty-one-year-old parent. Upon his return, he took over the family publishing business. 'I turned down business offers that were three times better,' he recalls, 'to go to work at the family company. I liked the other jobs more, and really had no interest in going back to Munich. It was very difficult for me, leaving all my friends to work with my father. But the company would not have survived otherwise.'

He soon discovered that his father's authoritarian attitude had hurt the business. 'I took some trips to bookshops and libraries, and I am an optimistic man, otherwise I would not have survived because all I heard was negative comments about my father, both on his style and his products. I was pleased that most of the librarians were sixty-five and close to retiring, so it would only take a few years for these people with bad memories of my father to leave the business.'

When Klaus returned to the family business in 1963, Karl junior was already working there. When Klaus had left for Düsseldorf in 1959, Karl had left school at his father's urging to work in the family company. By the time Klaus arrived, Karl had seen the company tottering on the verge of bankruptcy for several years. 'Klaus made a major difference and helped to turn the company around,' says Karl. 'And while my father was happy that the company started to do well, I think he was also a little jealous that his son could succeed where he had failed.'

A year after Klaus's return, Karl junior witnessed the only confrontation in his family over any war-related issue. 'It was between Klaus and my mother. They had seen a discussion on television about the war and a Jewish person had been interviewed. My mother had said a typical German expression, "That is one that should have gone to the gas chambers." And my brother was furious and told her it was stupid to say such things. And she was really shocked that he was so angry. "It's just an expression, it doesn't mean anything," she told him. "You know I don't mean any harm by it." But Klaus was very firm with her. "Those stupid sentences are what eventually led to the types of things that happened in the war," he told her.

'I was quite impressed by him. Those were my sentiments, yet I could not have challenged my parents at this time. I thought it was very good that he could do this. Of course, our father was not present, and I don't think he would have said anything if our father was there.'

David Irving, the right-wing British writer, visited Saur in 1964 and 1965 for a series of interviews. They were the first the former armaments official had granted. Klaus sat in on many of the interviews: 'this was the best information I ever got about my father'. Klaus saw his father was not aware of the historical consequences of his service for the Reich. 'He thought Himmler was an intelligent man,' Klaus recalls. 'He thought [Robert] Ley [director of the National Socialist Labour Front] was a successful and intelligent man. And he greatly admired Hitler. I believe he was very affected by Hitler's personality.

'He never thought about people like Eichmann, Mengele, or [Julius] Streicher [founder of the anti-Semitic Nazi newspaper *Der Stürmer*]. He never defended them. He just thought that in a movement as wonderful and fantastic as National Socialism, you will always have a few bad elements.

'He was not a good judge of his role in history. For instance, near Speer's release from Spandau in 1966, he asked his former secretary, "What should we do when Speer is released, should we meet him right away or wait a while?" Speer would never have accepted a meeting with my father, and this would have shocked him. But he never found this out because he died before Speer was released.'

Klaus remembers that his father also wanted to visit Israel, never realizing that his past activities would subject him to almost immediate arrest. At another point, Saur wanted to publish his memoirs and had discussions with a neo-Nazi publisher. On one occasion they planned a thirteen-part series on the Third Reich's armaments history, and another time a two-volume set, one on armaments and one on Saur's meetings with Hitler. 'Although there was a handshake to publish it plus a two-thousand Deutschmark advance, he never wrote anything before his death,' recalls Klaus, 'much to my relief.'

In July 1966, the diabetic Saur died unexpectedly after an eight-week illness that had not appeared serious. He was sixty-four. 'We still don't know if he had something else, like cancer,' says Klaus. 'No one is quite sure of the actual cause of death, it happened so quickly. He died at home in the middle of the night. Only my mother and I were there. Despite our difficulties, I felt sad.' Although Saur was not a church member, he received a Lutheran funeral service, only after Klaus promised the priest in the middle of the service that his mother would return to the faith. She never did.

'Klaus was more emotional than me at the time of our father's death,' recalls Karl. 'His death was a complete surprise to me, but I did not cry about him. I thought my brother should almost feel relieved by his death, since there had been conflicts inside the business. My father had given the company to my brother and me, but he wanted to remain as president. His death eliminated any problem over this issue.'

Klaus and Karl worked together until 1969. In that year, Karl left to start his own publishing company, but by 1971 he had abandoned his new venture and entered a school of journalism. Klaus, now sole owner of the family company, continued to expand the business.

While pursuing their professional careers, the brothers have not always been free of situations reminding them of their father's unique role in the Third Reich. In 1968 Klaus went to Israel for seven weeks to manage the German exhibit at a bookfair. 'At first I was not sure if I was the right person to do this since my father had been such a high Nazi. Under the Nazi philosophy, if the father was Jewish then the son was also considered bad. I was worried that because my father was a

Nazi, it might be held against me in a similar way. But finally I decided that I was very different from my father, and I should do it.' In Israel, Klaus met important Jewish literary and political figures. He also visited Yad Vashem, the Israeli memorial to the Holocaust. 'I was not surprised by it because I knew about the horrors. But it shocked me even more. The entire trip was very important and good for me. It was extremely impressive.'

In 1974, Klaus was asked to publish the *Journal of the German Society of Documentation and Information*. His father had been a member of the society in 1953, but was expelled in 1954 because 'he was so aggressive in meetings, and they said, "We will not have this old Nazi again and put up with this old Nazi talk," ' says Klaus. 'And I was wondering if it was correct that I should publish the journal of this society. Maybe it would be better to say no; they excluded my father and I will have nothing to do with them. But I said, they are completely different persons and moreover they were not wrong in their earlier decision. Because they were bad to my father, that must not affect the way I deal with them.'

On one occasion, a man in a publishing trade group was shocked to discover that Klaus was the son of the former armaments official. ' "Oh, my God, no!" he said,' Klaus recalls. 'It had been someone my father had pushed down very low during the war.' On another occasion, in 1970, as Klaus was taking over the distribution rights for UNESCO publications, the appointment was temporarily reconsidered due to his family background. But when UNESCO officials realized that Klaus was completely different from his father and had carved out his own individual company, they concluded the deal.

In 1987, at a book fair, Klaus met François Genoud, an elderly Swiss banker who had excellent contacts with old Nazis and was the legal representative for the diaries of Josef Goebbels and the personal letters of Martin Bormann. Genoud told Saur, 'Your father was a great man!' Klaus looked at him, absolutely serious, and said, 'No, he was just a fat man.' Genoud, apparently thinking Klaus must have misunderstood him, repeated the praise. Klaus just shook his head. 'No, he was just fat.' A perplexed Genoud left him alone.

'I have never been confronted with the issue of my father in a professional setting,' says Karl. 'But socially it did arise.' In

1980, as a newspaper reporter, Karl was in contact with Franz Schönhuber, a former Waffen-SS soldier who was a senior executive at Bavarian television. Schönhuber later became the chief of the right-wing Republican political party. 'And Schönhuber was always telling me that my father was a very good person and that I should be proud of him. I always said there is no reason to be proud of him. He never understood my feelings.' In 1983, Karl met the British writer David Irving, who also told him that his father was a great man. Like his brother when meeting François Genoud, Karl left Irving bewildered by his failure to agree that his father was 'a great man in the Third Reich. It's so much the opposite of how I really feel,' he says.

Both brothers seem amused by the admiration some people have for their father. It is alien to them. 'See, I don't feel any love for him, nor do I feel any pride,' says Klaus. 'In Berlin during the war I have a few good memories of my father, and then again for that one week in the detention camp after the war. But after his release in 1948, I don't have any good memories of him. I never had the problem that other children might have of liking my father very much and then learning that he was a very evil Nazi. I never had a positive feeling towards my father, so consequently I never had the problem of thinking, "Oh, he was good to me," or "He was good to the dog," or whatever. He was a loud dictator, and extremely intolerant and unfair.'

'I am not quite as negative about him,' concludes Karl. 'However, I no longer feel sorry for him. I always am trying to put myself into his position and to see how I would have acted. I cannot agree with the choices he made.'

'It is interesting to me,' says Klaus, 'that my brother is negative about my father. It is a little surprising because my father liked him the most. He was extremely friendly to him, much more so than he ever was to me. My eldest sister and my younger brother were my father's favourite children. That was completely clear. He was completely unfair to me and my youngest sister. And normally my brother is more compromising than me, but on this he is extremely strict and says, "No, bad, negative."

'One of my sisters died of cancer and she would have found good things to say about him. And my eldest sister is still like that. She objected once at a company party when I said my father was loud. If you told her, "Your father was an important Nazi, he did produce all the weapons," she would say, "No, he was a good man." And my second sister doesn't think about the problem that he was a Nazi. She says, "Oh, yes, he was a Nazi, but that is very unimportant." '

Yet, despite their criticisms, the brothers are not sure what they would have done if their father had been charged with crimes after the war and fled as a fugitive. 'It would have been much harder for me if my father had been in the SS in the position of a Heydrich or Kaltenbrunner,' says Klaus. (Reinhard Heydrich was chief of the SS Security Service; following Heydrich's 1942 assassination, Ernst Kaltenbrunner replaced him.) 'It is difficult enough without that. But if he had fled, I don't know if I would have turned him in. I cannot give you the answer. I just don't know how it would be. If he was in prison, it is definitely possible I would have felt obliged to help him. I was helping him in the last few years, and it was interesting to try to develop some more with him.'

'I don't think I would have broken with him,' says Karl junior. 'It's a very difficult question to answer.'

In 1987, Klaus noticed that the man sitting next to him in a plane was looking at a brochure for Dorsch, the international engineering firm founded by the man who had served with his father as a key official in the armaments division. ' "Do you work for Dorsch?" I asked him, and he said, "Since I am born." It was Dorsch's son.' Saur and Dorsch promised to meet again and discuss their fathers and their own lives. So far, they have not done so. 'Normally, I am not extremely interested in this field. There are other things very important to me. But I would like to meet him, to see what it was like for him. Our fathers had liked each other when they shared this period together.'

Klaus Saur married for the second time in 1977. The following year he changed the name of the firm to Saur Verlag (Saur Publishing). He has a good marriage and his company's performance has steadily improved each year. Saur Verlag is the vehicle through which he makes an effort to confront his Nazi heritage. His current catalogue shows a broad selection of serious works, including titles on European émigrés, Jewish immigrants, a Hebrew text from Harvard University, and a selection of anti-Nazi books. 'I have published dozens of these books and made a profit on only two or three,' he says. 'But the decisions for these books are made completely independent of the decisions for other titles. Profit is not the motivation. These books are difficult and complicated, but it is my way of doing something because my family had a Nazi past. It is my personal tribute to compensate for what my father did.'

Karl has been married for twenty-five years and has raised three children. His journalistic career has been very successful, and he was recently appointed the cultural editor at Germany's leading weekly news magazine, *Der Spiegel*. 'I have tried to raise my children very different from the way my father raised us. My entire life is lived differently.

'In my career I have tried to emphasize the need to have programmes and articles about the war and what happened. It is important that people understand the truth. Too many people in Germany talk about the "good" things that Hitler did, and then they speak about the bad things as though only a few criminals were responsible. Their feeling is that the Third Reich gave off all this light and it is only natural that there be some shadows. This is wrong. They do not understand that the entire régime, in its everyday operation, was dark. My father was responsible for helping to create those shadows. He must be held accountable for his own actions.'

CHAPTER 5

The Old Wizard

Tuesday, 1 October 1946. The Nuremberg courtroom was packed, the international press jammed ten deep next to Allied representatives and members of the defence teams. It was the day for the tribunal's verdicts. The judges arrived in black bullet-proof cars escorted by siren-blaring jeeps with machine guns mounted on them. An extra contingent of armed guards were on alert throughout the building. Most of the defendants had had difficulty sleeping the night before: Göring, Frank, Dönitz and Schirach hid behind dark glasses as the twenty-one men filed into the dock together for the last time.

At ninety-thirty sharp, the reading of the judgements began with the front row of the defendants' box. Göring was first, guilty on all four counts. Each judge took a turn in reading a verdict. The next nine defendants joined Göring: 'Guilty'. After each verdict the courtroom remained absolutely silent, the defendants staring straight ahead and avoiding contact with one another. Then Francis Biddle, the American judge, shuffled a new set of papers in front of him and directed his attention to the final defendant in the first row, Dr Hjalmar Schacht. The tall, sixty-eight-year-old, bespectacled Schacht was the monetary wizard who had single-handedly saved Germany from financial ruin during the early 1930s. The former president of the Reichsbank was absolutely still as Biddle addressed him. 'The tribunal finds that Schacht is not guilty on this indictment,' Biddle continued as a murmur swept through the courtroom, 'and directs that he shall be discharged by the marshal when the tribunal presently adjourns.' Everyone stared at Schacht, and Speer leaned forward to congratulate him. Schacht just gazed staight ahead to the judges' panel, maintaining, as he called it, an 'iron composure'.

Schacht was one of three men who walked free from Nuremberg that October. They were out of the prison when Göring committed suicide, the ten others were hanged, and the seven remaining prisoners were transferred to Spandau. Of all the defendants at Nuremberg, Schacht was the only one who was supremely confident of his acquittal. 'He never doubted for a single moment that he would be set free,' says Cordula Schacht, the younger of his two daughters by his second wife. 'He had great confidence God would help him. He had some self-doubts during his life, but he always had a great assurance about his actions.'

Cordula is a successful attorney in Munich. She was born on 25 February 1943, when Schacht was already sixty-six years old, but he lived to be ninety-three, and Cordula had an opportunity to know her father unavailable to the children who lost their parents to a life sentence or to the hangman. Over several decades she studied him closely. What she discovered was a fascinating man who seemingly played contradictory roles during the Third Reich, but a man she very much loved.

Hjalmar Horace Greeley Schacht was born in North Schleswig on 22 January 1877, the second child in a poor Lutheran family. His parents had just moved back to Germany after five years in America. His father, a teacher and journalist, had become an American citizen and his parents were married in New York in 1872. Schacht missed being an American only because his parents were homesick and moved back while his mother was pregnant. However, while in the States his father so admired New York *Herald Tribune* owner Horace Greeley that he vowed to name his next son after him. Only at the insistence of his grandmother was 'Hjalmar' tacked on at the last minute.

The Schacht family moved to several towns, ending in Hamburg for most of Hjalmar's early education. His father, sometimes unemployed or working at odd jobs, supported the family, but it was a very frugal existence. Schacht was an excellent student, studying in five universities, at different times, medicine, German literature and political economy. He also studied economics and commerce in Paris and London, and finally earned his PhD in philosophy, since economics was not yet an established doctorate.

In 1903, he joined one of Germany's leading banks, the

Dresdner, and quickly moved up the hierarchy to become its general manager at the end of World War I, at the age of forty-one. It was there that Schacht met some of Germany's leading bankers and industrialists. It was also at the beginning of his banking career, when he was financially secure, that he married his first wife, Luise Sowa, whom he had known for seven years. He had two children by her, and they remained married until her death in 1940. Cordula Schacht has learned that they lived separate lives during the last part of their thirty-seven-year marriage. But no strains showed early in the marriage. The Schachts travelled on holidays to many countries, including the United States, and Hjalmar's career was successful enough for them to build a small villa in a Berlin suburb, Gühlen.

At the end of World War I, at the age of forty-one, Schacht entered politics by co-founding the right-wing German Democratic Party, an anti-Bolshevist group of industrialists and financiers. He was soon consumed with the time's most pressing problem, hyperinflation which crippled the nation's currency and destroyed the capital of millions of German families. Within five years the Deutschmark had sunk to five hundred billionths of its original value. At this stage, Schacht was appointed Reich currency commissioner and then president of the Reichsbank. Few in Germany wanted these positions, considered untenable since the economy was careening out of control. But Schacht showed a genius for economics. He arranged critical loans from Britain and instituted a series of policies which stabilized the mark remarkably.

While many Germans sang his praises, Schacht never thought he was given enough credit. He was called a superegotist, often rebuking opponents with biting sarcasm. 'He was definitely not a superegotist,' says Cordula. 'The individual person did not interest him, apart from family members and friends. He was accustomed to thinking in huge quantities. He was even unable to count in small numbers.'

In 1930 he resigned his position, in protest at government economic policies he disliked. That same year Schacht also first took notice of Hitler's National Socialists, when they zoomed from twelve to 119 seats in the September Reichstag elections. As he studied the National Socialist platforms, he discovered he shared many of their views on rearmament, curbing leftist tendencies, eliminating the onerous reparations schedule of Versailles, and the need for totalitarian government control. In December 1930, Schacht attended a dinner party given by a former director of Deutsche Bank: Hermann Göring was the guest of honour. Schacht found the Luftwaffe chief 'pleasant and urbane' and accepted a Göring invitation to have dinner with Hitler that January. In his memoirs, Schacht recalled he was 'impressed' by Hitler's eloquence and absolute conviction. Within several weeks, Schacht telephoned politicians, urging that the National Socialists be incorporated into a coalition government. In the Nazis he saw a tool to help destroy the weak Weimar Republic, which he despised. But his efforts at a coalition government were rebuffed. However, his general approval of the Nazis was a major propaganda coup for Hitler. The fifty-three-year-old Schacht was one of Germany's most prestigious bankers and had excellent contacts with monied industrialists and financiers to whom Hitler had no access.

'If my father had a weakness, it was not a professional one but rather a human one,' says Cordula. 'It was his lack of perception in judging people. My father not only underestimated Hitler, but he overestimated his power to control Hitler. It was both. He thought he was clever and could manage Hitler, and perhaps in this way, because I know from several people that Hitler had professional respect for my father, he might have had some influence. But his influence was not strong enough, and he realized this too late.'

In January 1933, Hitler was appointed to a figurehead chancellorship; Schacht and some of his colleagues believed they had gained Hitler's cooperation while rendering him powerless. To their surprise, they watched this Austrian peasant display the same talent in power politics that Schacht had in economics. Instead of being shunted aside, Hitler was soon the most powerful member of the new government. 'It is not surprising to me,' says Cordula. 'My father was mainly interested in economics, and not politics. He was convinced that economics should govern politics, not vice versa. He was not that well versed in political intrigue.'

Schacht continued to help Hitler. In early 1933 he introduced Hitler to a group of Germany's elite businessmen. Impressed with his anti-communist fervour, they contributed more than three million marks to the Nazi coffers. Although Schacht was given the Nazi party's gold badge of honour, awarded to all ministers, he never joined the NSDAP, instead staying on the periphery.

In March 1933, Hitler rewarded Schacht for his work by giving him back his old position as president of the Reichsbank. Less than a year and a half later, in August 1934, Schacht was also named minister of economics. In these roles he obtained foreign investment and credit, again stabilized the economy, and arranged for secret financing to assist the rearmament programme. While Schacht controlled runaway inflation, he also tripled the German government debt from 1932 to 1937. More than a third of that debt was incurred in rebuilding the military, a fact which would be used against Schacht by the Nuremberg prosecution. 'I remember my father telling me that at Nuremberg he had been blamed for having financed rearmament,' says Cordula. 'He told me he could prove he had actually decreased the money used for that purpose.'

In his memoirs, Schacht argues that he tried to limit the money siphoned from the budget for the military, that he wanted to rearm Germany only for defensive purposes and was never privy to Hitler's plans for aggressive war. But by 1937 Schacht was proving troublesome to Hitler for other reasons. While he tolerated legislation towards Jews that provided separate but equal treatment, he was adamantly against the anti-Semitic violence which had become part of Nazi policy. He obtained apologies from the virulent *Der Stürmer* when it attacked several members of the Reichsbank for their 'Jewish connections'. He closed a branch of the bank in a highly public dispute over purchasing goods from Jewish tradesmen. 'My father was certainly no anti-Semite,' says Cordula. 'He helped many Jews; this is documented. But, on the other hand, my sister told me once that a Jewish woman asked for help for her and her family, and he did not give it to her. You cannot help everyone. I think in the end it was ambivalence. I just learned to accept that both sides were part of my father. I do not allow myself to judge him on every point because I know too little. I did not live that period. I must just accept that he did some things I liked, and some things I do not like. But unless I know why he acted, I do not judge him.'

Concerned that party excesses were hurting Germany's foreign image, Schacht repeatedly urged the Nazis to moderate their policies. He was not a mere yes-man, and this did not sit well with Hitler. 'Remember, my father was first attracted to National Socialism because of financial policies,' says Cordula. 'He was not enamoured of Hitler. My father spoke his mind, and this was not always appreciated.'

In April 1938, Schacht complained to Göring that the economy would be out of control within six months unless rearmament was curtailed. Göring ignored him. Frustrated at government infighting, Schacht tendered his resignation as minister of economics to avoid the blame for what he thought was an inevitable economic crisis. After delaying three months, Hitler accepted the resignation in November. Schacht was still, temporarily, president of the Reichsbank.

Kristallnacht, the 9 November 1938 Nazi rampage against Germany's Jews, prompted outrage from Schacht. He approached Hitler, condemning Goebbels's orchestrated violence, and offered a plan to solve Germany's 'Jewish question'. He proposed that all German Jewish property be placed in trust, and international bonds floated against it. Jews in other countries would be encouraged to buy the bonds, which would pay 5 per cent interest, and the money would be used to pay for the emigration of every Jew who wanted to leave Germany. Hitler professed to like the idea and ordered Schacht to begin discussions with prominent Jews in England. There Schacht received a lukewarm reception, with most Jewish groups rejecting the plan out of hand. His negotiations on behalf of the Nazis ended when Hitler dismissed him as president of the Reichsbank in January 1939. In a meeting at the old Chancellery building, the Führer abruptly informed him that 'you don't fit into the general National Socialist scheme of things'.

Schacht was left an unpaid minister without portfolio until 1943; this was also used against him at Nuremberg. It appears likely that Hitler left Schacht a minister to hide from the public the extent of the rift between them. 'I think my father believed it [keeping the title of minister] was more effective to serve his purpose, to remain minister without portfolio,' says Cordula. 'By keeping this title he could act more like he wanted and perhaps still have some influence on events. He would have no influence if he quit all his positions.'

Returning to private life, Schacht left Germany on extended foreign travel. During his trip, he maintained a daily diary which contained so many negative references to Hitler that he had to hide it on his return, lest it be used against him in a prosecution.

When the war broke out in 1939, Schacht did not keep his opposition a secret. He continued to alienate himself further from the Nazi hierarchy, who thought him a very intelligent but pompous man, too timid to be a true National Socialist. The extent of his disfavour in the régime was clear by 9 January 1941, when a Nazi newspaper, the *Völkischer Beobachter*, devoted several pages to every accomplishment in the first eight years of the Thousand-Year Reich. The tiniest details were mentioned. The propaganda machine ensured that not a single word was printed about Schacht.

The last time Schacht saw Hitler was in February 1941, when he informed the Führer of his forthcoming marriage plans. The next month Schacht married Manci Vogler, thirty years his junior, and tried, through his life with her in their Gühlen country house, to forget about the Nazi government. But he was not silent for long. In September 1941, he wrote Hitler urging him to make a peace treaty and stop the war. The Führer had an adjutant dismiss the suggestion. By early 1942, Schacht asked to be relieved of his powerless ministerial title. Hitler at first refused. In November 1942, Schacht wrote a long letter to Göring castigating the war effort. The letter caused a complete break with the Nazi hierarchy. First Hitler dismissed him from his ministerial position. Then Göring wrote, chiding Schacht for his 'defeatist letter' and expelling him from the Prussian State Council. Finally Bormann wrote, demanding the return of Schacht's Nazi party gold badge of honour. As Schacht recalled in his memoirs, 'It gave me peculiar satisfaction to comply with this request.'

But the harassment did not stop there. After being stripped of his titles, he noticed he was under Gestapo surveillance. Schacht was in contact with some members of the conspiracy against Hitler, but they never took him into their full confidence. Most of them thought that while Schacht was no friend to Hitler, he was an opportunist who could not be trusted with their secrets. When Schacht was approached shortly before the 20 July 1944 bomb attack on Hitler, and asked if he would join a new government, he hedged his answer, saying he would have to know more about the new government's policies. The conspirators were infuriated by his lack of commitment.

'I do not view my father's lack of enthusiasm for the conspiracy as lack of commitment, but rather as caution,' says Cordula. 'I do not view my father as an opportunist. I believe he had the goodwill to use his position to serve his ideals, and not those of Hitler. The conspirators may have been sceptical of my father, but that is only because they did not really know him. I believe he agreed with their goal, but not their method. He thought it was too unprofessional, too dangerous. He wanted Hitler killed, but he thought they were dilettantes.'

While the conspiracy against Hitler was gaining ground, Schacht and his new wife had two children. His first daughter, Konstanze, was born in December 1941 and Cordula was born on 25 February 1943. By this time, Schacht's eldest daughter from his first marriage was forty years old.

Schacht did not have much time to enjoy life with his new daughters. On 20 July Colonel Claus von Stauffenberg placed the bomb that almost killed Hitler. That prompted a broad sweep to crush the resistance; Schacht's earlier dissension made him suspect. That suspicion was enough in Nazi Germany. Three days later, at seven o'clock in the morning, the Gestapo arrested a pyjama-clad Schacht and drove him to Ravensbrück concentration camp. Most of the time he was kept in solitary confinement. Interrogations started within days of his internment. By August, he was transferred to No. 9 Prinz-Albrecht-Strasse, the principal Berlin headquarters of the National Security Service. For the next four months, the sixty-seven-year-old Schacht was confined to a small basement cell. In December his wife visited him for the first time, just prior to his return to the Ravensbrück camp. There he remained until February 1945, when Russian troops drew near. He was moved to the Flossenbürg extermination centre, then to Dachau, and finally, in early April, farther south where American troops finally liberated him.

Unknown to Schacht, the Allies had convened in London to finalize plans for the Nuremberg war crimes trial. From an initial roster of 122 major criminals, the British and American delegations narrowed the list through the summer. The

Americans proposed the name of Hjalmar Schacht, together with those of Walther Funk, who had replaced Schacht at the Reichsbank, and Albert Speer, the armaments minister. The US team wanted to emphasize the economic aspects of Nazi aggression. There were no objections from the British, French or Russians.

Meanwhile Schacht, expecting an immediate release, was astonished to be detained. Until September he was kept with other prominent members of the Third Reich in a former Göring headquarters, Kransberg Castle. During this time he had no idea of what had happened to his wife or children, as the Allies barred all family contact.

At the end of August, Schacht heard his name in a radio report about the twenty-two defendants scheduled to appear before the International Military Tribunal. He was stunned. Worried for his life in Nazi concentration camps for nine months, he was now charged as a leading Third Reich conspirator. Before being moved to Nuremberg prison, he was confined for three weeks in a small cage in a camp near Oberursel. In his memoirs, Schacht said this incarceration was worse than any of the Nazi concentration camps.

During his imprisonment in Nuremberg, Schacht acted as though his arrest was a mistake. Upon his arrival he told the prison psychiatrist that he 'hoped the trial would take a short time so they could hang those other criminals and let me go home'. He was contemptuous of his accusers and adamantly believed he was innocent of any wrongdoing. 'My father was always following his ideals,' says Cordula. 'He would admit that he might have committed some error, but he never behaved in a way that he could not accept. He thought it was very important always to be honest, and he thought he *had* always been honest. And that belief gave him strength through the KZ and the Nuremberg trial. In his view, he could not be found guilty for having misjudged some people or having made a mistake and not realized it at the time.'

On 20 October 1945, Schacht was given a copy of the indictment. He was charged under counts one and two, conspiracy and waging aggressive war. Incredulous at being formally arraigned, Schacht was aloof and disdainful of most of his fellow defendants. When the defendants were given IQ tests by prison authorities, Schacht scored the highest, 143. The result reinforced his superior attitude towards his colleagues. He was blunt in his opinion of them: Göring while of 'superior intelligence' was still 'egocentric, immoral and criminal', the 'worst' of the accused; Streicher was 'a pathological mono-maniac'; Kaltenbrunner was a 'callous fanatic'; von Ribbentrop 'should be hanged for extraordinary stupidity'; Hess had 'fifty-one per cent retarded intelligence'; and Keitel was an 'unthink-ing and irresponsible yes-man'. While sitting in the front row of the defendants' box Schacht often glanced at his former colleagues with undisguised hostility. During his direct examination he blamed the Nazis for most of Germany's economic problems and for leading the nation into an unneces-sary war. Of Hitler, he admitted the Führer was 'a mass psychologist of really diabolical genius' but condemned him in harsh language for betraying the German people and being a 'perjurer a hundredfold'.

'I think a major character flaw of my father was his overbearance, or the presumptuousness of his mental prowess,' says Cordula. 'He viewed others, more often than not, as his intellectual inferiors. In most of the cases he *was* intellectually superior. He had a great intellect, was very well educated, ingenious and witty. But I think it is important to be humble. Although my father was a religious man, he was proud of his intelligence in a pretentious way.'

The brunt of the case against Schacht was that he was an early advocate of Nazism and had brought about Hitler's rise to power by winning over bankers and industrialists. The prosecu-tion also claimed that Schacht was instrumental in financing German rearmament and that he must have known its purpose was to wage aggressive war. While they acknowledged that he resigned from most posts in 1937, they argued that the resignation was the result of conflicts in professional opinion and not a matter of principle. As for Schacht's contacts with the resistance, they emphasized the view that he 'attempted to play both sides of the fence'.

During Schacht's cross-examination, most of the other defendants were rooting for the American prosecutor, Robert Jackson. They were infuriated by Schacht's personal denuncia-tions and arrogant behaviour and hoped he would be cut down to size in the witness chair. They were disappointed. Schacht was so confident that he was the only witness to answer questions in English. When Jackson tried to invade the territory of finance and economics, Schacht totally outmatched him, and the cross-examination seemed only to strengthen his defence.

It was while waiting for a verdict, after the conclusion of the trial, that Cordula and her sister saw their father for the first time in over two years. Cordula, who was only one and a half when the Gestapo arrested him, had no recollection of him.

'My earliest memory of my father was in Nuremberg. I remember the fence and the watchtower at the prison, and my mother told us not to walk on the side with the fence but instead on the other side of the street. I saw him in the visitors' section behind a mesh screen. Next to him I remember an American soldier in a white helmet, and behind him was an open water closet. I remember it very clearly. It was the first time I saw my father knowing he was my father, and I looked at him a very long time. I remember that I then said, "I do like you."[18] This is how I first remember him.

'I remember the feelings of sympathy and warmth I had for my father seeing him in prison, and when he was looking at me very intensely that is when I knew I really liked him. He sat the whole time, and he seemed very mild to me.

'I don't remember seeing my father any other time in prison or in court. I only have small pieces of memory from this period, and this is the one time I clearly recall.'

While Schacht was confident of acquittal, he and his family were unaware that the tribunal was almost evenly split during deliberations. Some thought Schacht's courtroom performance was evasive, although it gave the appearance of frankness. Initially the English and Americans wanted to acquit him, while the French thought he deserved ten years and the Russians wanted to execute him. After hours of hard bargaining the judges compromised on a guilty verdict and a sentence of eight years.

Then, in a most unusual twist, the following day Schacht became the only defendant to have a judgement reversed by the tribunal. In the case of Franz von Papen, who had preceded Hitler as chancellor, the Americans and the British voted for acquittal and the Russians and French for conviction. Neither side would compromise. It was the first deadlocked vote, and after a severe argument with the Russian delegates, it was decided a tie vote meant acquittal. Von Papen was not guilty. Within several days the French judge had decided Schacht was not worse than von Papen, and if von Papen was acquitted Schacht should be freed as well. He switched his vote, creating a tie, and Schacht was added to the acquittal list.

Schacht never learned of the intrigue during the deliberations. 'He wouldn't have believed you,' says Cordula. 'He was so certain he would be acquitted, I don't think he thought it was even a close vote.'

After his acquittal, Schacht left the Nuremberg prison and went to the house his wife had stayed at during the trial. There, two German policemen were waiting; they arrested him for denazification proceedings. Schacht did not think he needed denazification since he had never joined the party and had ended up in a Nazi concentration camp. When he was returned to his home under house arrest, he left for a quick holiday, but was again arrested, in Württemberg, and sentenced by a Stuttgart court to eight years in a labour camp as a major offender. Though his appeal was successful and he was released on 2 September 1948, he was retried and acquitted again by a German jury in 1950.

The seventy-three-year-old Schacht had been in jail for more than four years and had spent seven years fighting the charges against him. 'It was normal for me when I was young that my father was not living with us,' recalls Cordula.

When released from prison, he had two and a half marks in his pocket and was virtually destitute. All his bank accounts and stock securities had been lost by the Reichsbank. His Gühlen property was in East German hands, while three small Berlin properties had been bombed and requisitioned. He was heavily in debt to his lawyers. His first income came from the publication of a book, *Settlement with Hitler*, written while he was in prison. It sold very well, giving the Schachts a financial foundation. Soon his publisher let him use an apartment in Bleckede, in Lower Saxony, and there Schacht lived with his wife and two daughters.

'Those two years in Bleckede were very happy ones,' Cordula recalls. 'This was our first home after the war where all four of us lived together. We never succeeded in doing so again. My father was writing economic papers, called Schacht briefs. We lived on top of the editor's office, which we had to cross to get to our apartment. It may be that my love of books was initiated by those wonderful scents of paper and freshly sharpened pencils.'

Cordula remembers her father as affectionate but strict. 'He did not show his affection very much. North Germans don't use many words and use even fewer gestures. Still, there was a clear understanding that we loved each other. While he could be very strict, he was also soft. He did have a temper. When he was young he was quite hot-tempered. But when I knew him, he raised his voice very seldom, but when he did it had quite an impact. I was never afraid of my father.'

After two years, the Indonesian government asked Schacht to advise them on a new economic plan. He accepted the invitation and left Germany for an extended trip that also involved advice to the Indian, Syrian, Egyptian and Iranian governments. Cordula and her sister Konstanze were left with a cousin in a small Tyrolean village. There the Schacht daughters attended school, waiting for the return of their parents.

'I liked my cousin very much, and she did me,' says Cordula. 'And she was the first person to tell me I was smart, sweet and even beautiful. Up to that time I had always thought my sister was much more clever, reliable and intelligent.'

After a year Schacht was back in Germany, buying an apartment in Munich. While the apartment was under construction, Cordula and her sister lived in a nearby children's camp. Soon her sister left for boarding school, and Cordula was alone, 'feeling very lonely as my sister had been very important to me. I moved so much from school to school it was very difficult to make friends during this time. My sister was my only real friend.'

When the apartment was completed, nine-year-old Cordula moved to Munich and her sixth school. During this time, her father had finished his memoirs and founded his own Düsseldorf-based bank, Aussenhandelsbank Schacht & Company. His work required him to stay in Düsseldorf during the week, so he saw his family only at weekends.

'I don't remember the weekends with my father during that period. A little later I remember them because my mother had difficulty with me and when my father came to visit she would tell him to correct me, and it would create family friction. He would have to correct me, which he didn't like at all, nor did I.'

After Cordula had attended one year of the German equivalent of high school, she was sent to a boarding school. She hated the repressive atmosphere and tried to come home, but her mother insisted she stay. So Cordula deliberately failed some courses and was allowed to return to a public school in Munich, her ninth. It was here that she learned that Edda Göring was also a student, a couple of years ahead of her. 'She had only one close friend, and whenever her friend wasn't there, she would stand alone in the hallways and everyone would say, "Oh, there is Edda Göring." Everyone knew who she was.' Cordula stayed at this school until she was twenty, in 1963.

'From a very young age I knew my family was different. We had moved a lot, did not live together, and I also knew that my father had been a famous person. I knew it from my parents, and all the people that visited our house would act as though my father was still very important. Even on the street people would approach him. You could walk with him and hear, "That is Schacht passing", or something like that. People treated him with great deference. You must remember he was very tall [six feet three inches], stood very erect, had narrow shoulders and a long neck and all this gave the impression he was even taller. Together with his mind and strong will he gave the impression of being straight and honest.'

At the age of sixteen, Cordula was taught about the war, at school. 'I knew it already from my family. I knew he had been on trial, he had held high positions, he ended the war in German concentration camps. My father's name came up of course, but nothing in the presentation was different or a surprise to me from all I had already been told. I felt the teacher did not really feel at ease knowing I was the Schacht daughter. Everybody knew who my father was.

'I had learned what this meant, to be his daughter, around the age of eleven. My father would talk to me about those things. Or visitors would come over and ask him about the past and he would answer and then I heard and learned about it. My father talked very freely about the war. He never made a mystery of that time.'

Cordula knew her father was considerably older than the

parents of most of her friends. Yet she found him so vigorous that his age never mattered to her. 'I didn't have the impression of an old man. He never had the feeling that his time in the German KZ or at Nuremberg had adversely affected his health after the war. I mean, of course, on his eightieth birthday he complained that it had taken seven years of his life. It was time he couldn't live, but it wasn't time that had ruined him. His health was good although he did have a double inguinal hernia, three times, from poor treatment and lack of food in the camps.'

During her teenage years, Cordula grew closer to her father. 'I always admired his intelligence and his culture. On Sundays at breakfast he would quiz me to identify passages of poetry. And since he wrote his own poems, if I knew it was a real Schacht instead of Goethe or Schiller, he was very happy. I could really understand my father, because in many ways I felt like him, and that pleased him.

'We talked a lot when we were together. I went to him for advice. There was a turning-point for me when I wanted to become a translator and go to a fine school in Munich. But he told me, "Just learning languages makes a secretary out of you." At the time I was furious but too weak to oppose him, as I had no money and couldn't do it without his support. So I went back to school and actually became a much better student.'

In 1963, upon graduating from high school, Cordula spent a semester at the Sorbonne in Paris, undecided about her career. The following year her sister married, 'but my father had such difficulty in letting her go from the family that he developed shingles from nerves and wasn't able to attend the church or the reception'.

That same spring, Cordula accompanied her father on a trip to America. Schacht had been invited on a lecture tour in several states, and for Cordula the trip brought a revelation. 'It was the first time I realized my father had some fear of failure. That was really something for me, since I never thought he was afraid of anything.' He was afraid of giving speeches in English and of the reception he would receive. His first talk in Chicago was disastrous, with Schacht merely stopping halfway through an hour-long lecture when he was abruptly informed his limit was thirty minutes. After that he put away his notes and spoke extemporaneously; the reception improved in each city. In

Washington, DC, Cordula particularly remembers a television programme with her father as a guest. 'He was on with the mother of the Kennedy assassin, Oswald, and the author of a book I remember as *Sex and the College Girl*. It was very American. It was also very funny because all of a sudden they would say, "And now we have to stop for a break," and they would do this right in the middle of thoughts and sentences. I thought it was quite bizarre and at the time so did my father. But he was happy because he was paid; dollars were quite expensive at the time, and he could use the money.'

Upon her return to Germany, Cordula decided to study law, something that made her father 'very pleased'. The two of them had long philosophical discussions that Cordula found 'a good, exciting give-and-take of intellects'.

It was also during this time, her early twenties, that she heard the first negative comments about her father. 'Not everything was positive,' she recalls. 'I heard people say he had his positions in the 1930s because he merely wanted to get ahead, that he was an opportunist. They would say it to me, or in front of me so I could hear it.

'When I heard these criticisms, I had an open mind. It wasn't as though I said they were true and let them upset me. If I heard something that raised a real question, it was a catalyst to question my father directly and he would explain it. Otherwise, I had studied my father closely and thought I had found out how he really was, and I had made up my own mind about him. I realized he had character pluses as well as faults. Yet I always saw the positive outweighing the negative in him.'

Cordula studied three law-school semesters in Hamburg, before her mother implored her to return to Munich for the remainder of her studies. 'I wanted to stay in Hamburg and develop in the way I wanted. My father encouraged me to stay, but my mother said, "You'd better come back, you don't know when your father will die." So I came back and I stayed until my father died.'

Schacht was alert during his final years. He still entertained visitors at their house, but Cordula was not always pleased with his guests. 'There were some people who came and flattered him and he liked it. He did not realize that they were dishonest and just wanted to be associated with him. This was very disappointing to witness.'

Cordula was in Munich with him during his final four years. Then, one day in May 1970, he fell when putting on his trousers, breaking his hip. The ninety-three-year-old patient was presented with two possibilities, a natural cure that would take at least eight weeks or surgery that could cut the time in half. Schacht, as impatient as ever, opted for the surgery. 'My mother and I had to accept his decision,' Cordula recalls. 'He would have been in a very bad mood if we had forced him to take the longer cure.'

The doctors were pleased with the operation and had given him a release date when he developed an aneurysm in his leg. From the time the nurse first saw the condition, it was only a few hours until he died. Cordula and her mother were there.

'I was not surprised by his death,' says Cordula. 'I accepted it. It was the right time for him to die. He did not suffer from any illness, but he was always short of breath even when taking a few steps. He was quite hard of hearing and would not wear a hearing aid. I believe it is not so easy to become old.'

Hundreds came to mourn at Schacht's funeral, including many from the banking world, but not one representative of the German government. 'That would have bothered him,' Cordula says. 'He was bitter that the politicians of his time didn't ask for his help. He was very upset that the West German government abandoned him.'

Cordula says that as her father aged he was also increasingly upset over his Nuremberg ordeal. 'He didn't have any bitterness towards the Americans or British, just the idea of being on trial. Once he had a problem with Israel: on one of his travels to the Middle East he stopped in an airport there. Later he read in the newspapers that if they had known it, they would have arrested and imprisoned him. He was angry that the Israelis would think of him like that, but he was also happy not to have been arrested.'

Cordula considers it an advantage to be the daughter of Hjalmar Schacht, but says it 'was also hard to bear. I had the impression no one ever accepted me for myself, but only as his daughter, and for some years I hated it. Once I even said that he wasn't my father, but only once. I felt terrible afterwards. It was difficult to become my own personality. Even when I was dating, the boys would ask me, "What does your father know or think about this and that?"

'If my father had been convicted at Nuremberg, it would have changed things. I suppose I would have had much more interest in history, and I would have tried to defend my father, that's a child's natural feeling. I had no incentive to do this because it was unnecessary.

'It's harder for me to understand a child who condemns his or her parent. Niklas Frank, for instance: I cannot approve of him. But he must have had a terrible youth, a terrible time after the war.

'When I grew up, I learned that people would always continue to ask me about my father. I have worked very hard to establish my own independence and I have started to feel successful in moving away from his shadow. It has taken a long time, but I am very pleased that I can confidently say I am Cordula Schacht, the daughter of Hjalmar Schacht. Now it is an enrichment to have had this father, and no longer a burden.'

CHAPTER 6

'No Justice, Only Avengers'

Although it was springtime in Brazil on 14 October 1977, by midday it was hot and humid. Rolf Mengele, the thirty-three-year-old only child of Josef Mengele, the fugitive Auschwitz doctor, was soaked in perspiration. He was 'tired and suffering from nervous exhaustion' as he weaved a rickety Volkswagen bus through crowded city streets. Rolf had arrived in Brazil two days earlier from West Germany. His trip had a single purpose. For the first time in his adult life, he was about to visit his father, the world's most hunted Nazi. 'I had to learn more about him,' Rolf recalls. 'I had to see him face to face, to discuss all the questions I had. I thought I would get more out of him in person.'

The bus pulled into Alvarenga, a duty street in a rundown São Paulo neighbourhood, and Rolf stopped in front of a yellow stucco house. A swirl of dust blew away, revealing an old man, stooped by age, his grey hair carefully combed, standing near the front gate. Josef Mengele walked forward to embrace his son.

It was twenty-one years since they had met. Then, in the Swiss Alps, Rolf was introduced to his father as a long-lost uncle who told spellbinding wartime tales. During those twenty-one years Mengele had been revealed as one of the most vicious war criminals. But the man who stood before Rolf was a shadow of the SS officer who terrorized Auschwitz inmates, earning the nickname 'Angel of Death'. His pride and self-assurance had vanished. He seemed pathetically eager as he awkwardly raised his arms. 'The man who stood before me,' recalls Rolf, 'was a broken man, a scared creature.'

Josef Mengele trembled from excitement. Rolf saw tears in his eyes. 'For him there was a lot of emotion,' Rolf remembers. 'It was a very high moment for him, the only time his son was arriving. I felt bad that I could not reciprocate and return his emotions. He was a stranger to me. I knew this was my real father, but we did not have the natural relationship of a father and son. But that's when I made a few gestures to overcome the unfamiliarity and the emotion,' he said, and he responded to his father's embrace.

Josef Mengele was sixty-six years old when they met in 1977. He was born on 16 March 1911, the eldest of three sons in a prosperous Catholic family in Günzburg, a picturesque Bavarian village. Mengele & Sons, a farm-machinery company founded by Josef's father, dominated the town as its largest employer. Josef Mengele grew up in a privileged but emotionally austere household. At school he excelled. He was an apolitical nineteen-year-old in 1930 when he decided to become a doctor instead of joining the family company. 'He had wonderful conditions,' says Rolf Mengele. 'He had so many possibilities before him. It is one of the things that make it so difficult for me, that he wasted these opportunities. Wasted his life.'

Rolf views his father's initial years of medical study as the start of his corruption. Mengele attended the university in Munich, a city intoxicated with Hitler's fiery National Socialism. The university faculty was heavily influenced by Nazism, and taught the half-baked theories of the 'Aryan master race'.

Mengele studied under Ernst Rudin, an architect of the compulsory sterilization laws, and a leading advocate that doctors should destroy 'life devoid of value'. While pursuing a medical degree, Mengele also obtained a PhD under Professor T. Mollinson, who claimed he could tell if a person had Jewish ancestors simply by looking at a photograph. In 1937, Mollinson recommended the twenty-six-year-old intern for an appointment that changed his life. He became a research assistant at the prestigious Third Reich Institute for Heredity, Biology and Racial Purity at the University of Frankfurt, joining the staff of one of Europe's foremost geneticists, Professor Otmar Freiherr von Verschuer.

Von Verschuer, who devoted much of his time to research on twins, was an outspoken Hitler enthusiast. Mengele became the professor's favourite student. Together they were at the epi-centre of Nazi philosophical and scientific thinking. In May

1937, Mengele joined the Nazi party, and one year later the SS, guardian of the nation's racial purity. With von Verschuer's assistance he quickly moved up the Nazi academic hierarchy, embracing the idea that through appropriate selection a race's heritage could be improved. He also accepted the Nazi propaganda about Jews. 'When I visited him,' Rolf recalls, 'he alleged he had evidence that Jews were different or abnormal. But he couldn't furnish any convincing proof.'

While Mengele was strictly dedicatd to his Nazi-tainted studies, he did take time in 1939 to celebrate his marriage to a businessman's daughter, Irene Schoenbein. Finally, in August 1940, eager to join the battle, he left von Verschuer and joined Hitler's most fanatical fighting troops, the Waffen SS. For a year, serving with the SS Race and Resettlement Office, he examined the racial suitability of conquered Poles. By mid-1941 he was posted to the Ukraine, and the following year was wounded, earning an Iron Cross First Class and a reassignment back to Berlin and Verschuer. His mentor encouraged him to work in a concentration camp, holding out the inducement that such an assignment was in the interest of science. As wartime director of the Kaiser Wilhelm Institute for Anthropology, Human Hereditary Teaching and Eugenics in Berlin, Verschuer secured funds for Mengele's concentration-camp experiments. In turn, Mengele sent him his lab results, skeletons and body parts, wrapped in thick brown paper and marked 'Urgent – War Matériel'. After the war, Verschuer returned to teaching while Mengele was a fugitive for his crimes. Although that does not engender any sympathy for his father, it still angers Rolf: 'I am not happy that the man who sent my father to Auschwitz, the man who gave the order to go there and conduct the studies, was never punished. For those who were behind desks during the war, in my view, it was easier than if they were there. At the minimum, Verchuer had a moral responsibility.'

Shortly after a promotion to Haupsturmführer (captain), Mengele received his new posting. In May 1943, he was on his way to Auschwitz. The camp was located in an isolated part of south-west Poland that many Poles considered too inhospitable to live in. During the summer the sun scorched the earth and the stagnant air was heavy with the smell of burning flesh. In winter, ice storms swept off the Vistula river and ravaged the inmates.

At its most productive in 1943 and 1944, it contained five crematoria and gas chambers which could gas and burn 9000 victims daily. On clear days, flames and black smoke spewing from the crematoria chimneys could be seen for thirty miles. While mass extermination was Auschwitz's primary purpose, it also provided slave labour for thirty-four German companies with work stations at the camp's perimeter. Corporations, many of which are household names like Bayer, AEG Telefunken, Krupp, Siemens and I. G. Farben, used the tortured labour of inmates. Auschwitz was packed with more than a hundred thousand prisoners at a time, and most worked until they dropped dead.

This was the setting that greeted Mengele upon his arrival. During the next twenty months he established his dubious place in history. Whereas many of the SS doctors viewed their camp work as a difficult and distasteful assignment, Mengele relished his duties. His enthusiasm was most evident in selections of incoming prisoners. An SS doctor was required to meet the hundreds of thousands of prisoners who arrived in miserable conditions, crammed into cattle cars. The new inmates marched before the doctor who sent them to the right or left. Those sent to the right went into Auschwitz's work sections. Most were sent to the left, to the gas chambers.

His fellow doctors found the selections the most stressful part of their duties. Yet he did not wait for his weekly assignment to the train ramps. Instead he volunteered for extra duty. Survivors have provided vivid accounts of their first sight at Auschwitz. Mengele's SS uniform was immaculate, his black boots glistened, and his soft cap was angled rakishly across his forehead. He was young and good-looking, his white-gloved hands often fiddling with a polished cane or smoking a filtreless cigarette. He occasionally smiled or whistled one of his favourite operatic tunes. While the crowds were pushed into separate sections for men and women, he walked among the inmates searching for twins, his speciality in medical experiments. Josef Mengele sent four hundred thousand people to their deaths through his ramp-head selections.

'For me that is enough for him to be guilty of everything,' says Rolf Mengele. 'Just to be at a place like Auschwitz is a crime. But the selections are all I need to know to say he is guilty as charged, that he is responsible for murder. I have tried so many times to understand how he could have ended up there, doing the things he did. I cannot. It is so foreign to me. He is like an alien to me. Auschwitz seems like another planet.'

In this strange camp setting, Josef Mengele went far beyond his role of playing God in choosing those who would live and those who would die. Soon after his arrival, his zeal earned him an appointment as chief of the women's, children's, and gypsies' camp. In that role he conducted numerous surprise selections in both sub-camps, as well as the sick bays, at all hours of the day and night. The mere sight of Mengele was enough to inspire terror.

Adding to his camp reputation was a special pathology laboratory built to his specifications in Crematorium Two at Birkenau, where newly gassed victims were dissected. Fitted with the most modern equipment available and a red concrete floor, the lab was dominated by a polished marble dissecting table, surrounded by several sinks. The funds for the lab were obtained by Mengele's Berlin mentor, Professor von Verschuer. It was there that Mengele conducted 'research' to unlock the secrets of perfecting the 'Aryan race'. To guarantee the racial purity of future German generations, he gathered thousands of twins. One child in each pair was used as a scientific control. His guinea-pigs were housed in a special barracks nicknamed the 'zoo'.

His research involved crude surgery and painful tests, almost invariably without anaesthetics. There were needless amputations, lumbar punctures, typhus injections, and wounds deliberately infected to compare reactions. Solvents were placed under the scalp to turn dark hair blond, and dyes into the eyes to turn brown to blue. If one twin died, Mengele had the other killed immediately so their autopsies were simultaneous. He used electric-shock equipment to test the endurance of prisoners, leaving many of the guinea-pigs either dead or comatose. X-ray machines were used to sterilize women. On a whim, he taped a mother's breasts to see how long her newborn baby could survive without nourishment. She mercy-killed her own child after a compassionate nurse gave her morphine and a syringe.

Eye-witness survivors provide hundreds of examples of Mengele's cruelty, all quite unrivalled at Auschwitz. At times he showed kindness to his guinea-pigs, most of them children under the age of twelve, but would then subject them to horrendous experiments in the name of science.

To his colleagues, he was the epitome of the dedicated SS officer. He never discussed his personal life, even though his wife, Irene, visited Auschwitz twice. She kept a diary while she stayed at the SS barracks on the camp's perimeter. Irene saw the incoming trains, but thought Auschwitz was a massive detention centre for political and wartime prisoners. Her diary has no indication she knew of the conditions inside the camp or the experiments controlled by her husband. He refused to answer any of her questions, and when she pinpointed a 'sweet stench' he told her, 'Don't ask me about this.' Irene claims Auschwitz changed her husband and that he was depressed because he felt trapped by his orders. 'His ambition was his undoing,' she later commented.

'It was the beginning of the end for their marriage,' Rolf recalls. 'They never had a proper marriage with the war, and she noticed changes in him at the camp. These were her first doubts about him, although there is no question she loved him, and saw a much more human side of him than I did.'

On 16 March 1944, Mengele's thirty-third birthday, Rolf was born in Günzburg. The reticent Mengele made no mention of the birth to any of his SS colleagues, and instead of taking leave to visit his son, he stayed at Auschwitz between April and August performing thirty-nine railhead selections of ever larger shipments of Hungarian Jews. He did not see his son until six months after his birth, while on a one-week pass from the camp.

After the war, some of Mengele's friends and family suggested that the stories about him were exaggerated and that, although he was at Auschwitz, it was a terrible assignment and he did the best he could under the most difficult conditions. Rolf heard the same defence directly from his father: 'My father felt that Auschwitz existed before he arrived and that he was merely a little cog in a big machine. When I told him that I considered Auschwitz one of the most horrible examples of inhumanity and brutality, he said I didn't understand. He said he went there, had to do his duty, and carried out orders. Everybody had to in order to survive, the basic instinct of self-preservation. He said he wasn't able to think about it. He didn't feel personally responsible for what happened at the camp.

'He claimed he wanted to help people but there was a limit to what he could do. The analogy he used was of a wartime field hospital. If ten critically wounded soldiers are brought in at once, a doctor must instantly decide whom to operate on first. By choosing one, another necessarily dies. My father asked me, "When people arrived at the railhead, what was I supposed to do? People were arriving infected with disease, half dead." He said it was beyond anyone's imagination to describe the conditions there. His job had been to classify only those "able to work". He told me he tried to grade as many people as "able to work" as possible.

'My father tried to persuade me that in this way he saved thousands of people from certain death. He said that he did not order and was not responsible for gassings. And he claimed that twins in the camp owed their lives to him. He swore he had personally never harmed anyone in his life.' Despite his father's protestations, Rolf, alone of the Mengele family, does not accept his claim of innocence.

As the Russian army moved closer to Auschwitz during early January 1945, Mengele did not act like an innocent man. Colleagues and inmates recall that he was severely depressed because his work would soon fall into Russian hands. He was often seen pacing in the SS doctors' office, silent, morose, his head in his hands. Although he had continued his experiments until 5 December 1944, he also took steps to disguise his work. His pathology lab was dismantled while the crematoria and gas chambers were dynamited. He packed as many of his personal and medical papers as possible and destroyed the rest. On 17 January 1945, as Russian artillery pounded in the distance, Josef Mengele fled the madness of Auschwitz.

He ran westwards for Günzburg and the safety of his family. But before he arrived on his wife's doorstep in September 1945, he was twice arrested by the American Army and placed in US detention camps under his own name. Although he was on a dozen wanted lists as a 'principal war criminal', the Allied administration was so chaotic that no one realized Mengele had been captured. After his second release he finally reached his family. They arranged for him to work under an alias on a farm in Rosenheim. There, in the middle of the American occupation zone, he spent the next four years. Despite the risk of being followed, Irene visited him from Günzburg. His morale was so low that she believed the importance of her visits outweighed the danger. Their meetings were often stormy events, with Mengele's moods fluctuating wildly. He vacillated between turning himself in to prove his innocence; being afraid the Americans might catch him; and being angry at having to be a farmhand, separated from his normal life and family. He often argued with Irene over her friendships, especially with other men. 'He was insanely jealous,' Rolf says. 'During their short meetings in the forest he made scenes that really embittered her. He told her to separate from her acquaintances and not to see her friends. She shouldn't leave the house. He did not appreciate the danger she undertook every time she visited him.'

On some of the trips, Irene took Rolf.[19] Mengele was happy to see his son, but Rolf does not have any memory of the visits. 'Nothing,' he says. 'I look at the pictures from the time and really try to jog my memory, but I can't.'

During the late 1940s, Mengele was consumed by the war crimes trials. He was mentioned in the main Nuremberg proceeding, and some doctors who had conducted similar experiments were tried and executed. These developments so unsettled Mengele that he decided to leave Germany. With financial assistance from his family and organizational support from ex-SS members, he purchased false travel documents and was guided across the Alps into Italy for a journey to South America. Irene Mengele decided not to join her husband. Rolf describes the predicament his mother faced: 'My mother simply did not want to go into hiding with him. She loved Germany and Europe, the culture was dear to her, and she was close to her parents. Also, in 1948 she had met Alfons Hackenjos, who was to become her second husband. Still, it was a very difficult decision for her because she still had feelings for him. With this decision, she made a conscious effort to erase his picture from her mind and terminate her feelings for him.'

Spurned by his wife and wanted by the Allies, Mengele fled Germany, alone and bitter that his service at Auschwitz had been thus rewarded. Once in Genoa, he was arrested by Italian police when they noticed that his Red Cross passport was a rank forgery. Incarcerated for the third time since the war's end, Mengele was freed just two days before his scheduled departure for South America when his father dispatched a company executive with a five-hundred-dollar bribe. In mid-July he sailed for Argentina.

In South America, he began a diary. It reveals that while upset by his fugitive existence, he adapted to Buenos Aires much more easily than he or his family had anticipated. Arriving under an alias, Mengele unobtrusively melted into a large and powerful German community. Fascist dictator Juan Perón was unabashedly pro-Nazi and had provided ten thousand blank Argentine passports to the collapsing Nazi Reich in the closing days of the war. With anti-Semitism institutionalized throughout Argentinian life, Mengele found the climate more agreeable than postwar Germany. Soon he met other leading Nazis, including a key figure in the Nazi escape network, Colonel Hans-Ulrich Rudel, Hitler's most decorated pilot, as well as Adolf Eichmann, the SS colonel in charge of shipping Europe's Jews to the extermination centres. Although Rudel became a good friend and helped Mengele throughout his fugitive years, Mengele considered Eichmann a pathetic loser. They met several times at a downtown Buenos Aires café, but never developed a close bond. Eichmann, burdened with his wife and three sons, was a foreman at the Mercedes factory. He had a downtrodden aura that Mengele disliked.

In contrast to Eichmann, Mengele had very different ideas for establishing his new life. After making important contacts in the Nazi underground, he started his first business, selling the family firm's farm equipment in Argentina and Paraguay. Soon he owned a carpentry shop, and then invested in a pharmaceutical company.

While he successfully adapted to South America, Irene had decided to end their marriage. She asked for a divorce, and he consented, executing a power of attorney which finalized the divorce in March 1954. Alienating herself from the Günzburg Mengele family, Irene proudly announced she did not want a penny from them. Shortly after the divorce, she married Alfons Hackenjos, the owner of a Freiburg shoe store. To ten-year-old Rolf this new man became his real father: 'Hacki [Rolf's nickname for him] was a true father to me. He was really a special man, and he raised me as a son. When I think of a father, it is Hacki I consider, even though I know he is not.'

It was easy for Rolf to develop a deep attachment to his stepfather, because as far as he knew his biological father was dead. 'My mother and the rest of the family had always told me that Josef Mengele, my father, was missing in action. He had been a hero on the Eastern front. I heard stories that he was a cultured man who knew Greek and Latin and had fought bravely for Germany. That was the image I had of my father. They just thought it was best that I did not know he was alive, until I was older and might understand better.'

In 1956 Mengele made his first and last return trip to Europe. At the urging of his family, he flew to Switzerland. They wanted him to remarry, and the proposed bride was his sister-in-law, Martha, widow of Mengele's younger brother, Karl. This was considered the best way to keep control of the family company, and the secret of Josef Mengele's South American life, among trusted people. Greeting him at Engelberg, Switzerland, were Irene and Rolf as well as Martha and her son, Karl Heinz, who was the same age as Rolf, twelve. Rolf remembers his aunt Martha as 'ravishingly beautiful' and he liked Karl Heinz, 'although we were not especially close; [he was] just a cousin I saw on holiday gatherings.'

The charade of his father's death was continued during this meeting, the first time that Josef Mengele had seen Rolf in over seven years. Rolf was told the dashing visitor from South America was 'Uncle Fritz'. 'I really didn't give it too much thought,' he recalls. 'I was only twelve years old, and it didn't seem unusual to me that there was another family member who lived away from Germany. I thought he was an uncle on my father's side of the family. I mean, he wasn't a stranger to me. In prior years I had received several letters from "Uncle Fritz". They were nice but nothing very special. Mainly I remembered him for sending me stamps from Argentina.'

Mengele spent a lot of time with Rolf and Karl Heinz, regaling the boys with adventure stories about South American gauchos and his supposed experiences fighting partisans in World War II. 'He was very interesting,' Rolf says, 'and very sympathetic to us, always joking. He liked to ski, and was very good at it. He dressed very well, formally, for dinner. And he always gave Karl Heinz and me pocket money, the first I ever had. When we went to the restaurant we would order from the waiter whatever we wanted to drink or eat. This was also a new experience, because my mother and stepfather had told us it was not allowed for children to order.

'He was also, I remember, the first man I ever heard speak about the war. At that time, no one spoke about the war. It was taboo. And of course as young boys we were excited to hear about all the fighting and the action. I liked him very much – as an uncle.'

Although Rolf noticed that 'Uncle Fritz' was especially attentive to Martha, he thought it was ordinary family affection. Following a week in Switzerland, Mengele visited his hometown of Günzburg for another week and then drove to Munich, where he was involved in a car accident. The police questioned his South American identity papers and told him not to leave the city until they checked him further. 'My grandfather went to Munich and paid the police some money to forget about the accident,' Rolf says. For the fourth time since the war's end, Josef Mengele avoided capture either through a bureaucratic snafu or a bribe.

Upon his return to South America, Mengele decided to abandon his fugitive life and prepare for the arrival of Martha and Karl Heinz. By 1956 he felt confident enough to relaunch himself under his real name. Although he was on wanted lists, there still had been no formal indictment. He obtained a certificate with his true name from the West German embassy in Buenos Aires. No one at the embassy asked the forty-five-year-old visitor why he had lived under an alias for his first seven years in Argentina. He applied to the Argentine courts for a change of name, and no one raised a single question. He even obtained a West German passport in his own name, at the time when he was on a dozen wanted lists.

In October 1956, Martha and Karl Heinz moved to Buenos Aires and joined him. For the next four years Mengele acted as Karl Heinz's father and the two developed a close bond. It was a much firmer relationship than the one with his own son Rolf, whom he had seen on only a few occasions. 'Years later he would berate me for not being as good as Karl Heinz,' Rolf says. 'He would always compare me to Karl Heinz and ask why I couldn't do this or that as well as my cousin.'

Mengele felt secure in his new life. He listed the shares of his company, took out a mortgage and got married, all under his true name. In 1958 he was even listed in the phone book. A Nazi-hunter could have found the fugitive doctor by calling directory assistance, but no one was looking in Buenos Aires.

Just as it appeared that the worst part of his life on the run was over, major efforts to bring him to justice began in earnest in both West Germany and Israel. And in August 1958 he was detained by the Buenos Aires federal police, under suspicion of practising medicine without a licence. The chief detective on the case later admitted accepting a five-hundred-dollar bribe to free him and close the file.

But Mengele was scared by his first encounter with the Argentine police, believing that his Auschwitz past might be uncovered. He established a business over the border, in General Alfredo Stoessner's right-wing haven, Paraguay. By May 1959, he moved to Paraguay and only occasionally returned to Argentina to visit Martha and Karl Heinz. This proved a stroke of good fortune: on 5 June 1959, a German federal court, prompted by the chilling facts compiled by a single camp survivor, finally issued an arrest warrant and a seventeen-count indictment of premeditated murder. The Germans concentrated their effort in Argentina, not knowing that Mengele had already moved. He was also fortunate the following year, when an Israeli secret-service team kidnapped Adolf Eichmann in front of his Buenos Aires home and smuggled him back to Israel, where he was tried and hanged. The Israelis also searched for Mengele, checking his former addresses. They found Martha, but no fugitive.

The West German indictment, coupled with the Eichmann abduction, meant his crimes were now publicized. The press became interested and Mengele was in the news.

The family could no longer hide the truth from sixteen-year-old Rolf. 'It was my stepfather, Hackenjos, who sat down to tell me,' Rolf recalls. 'He assumed the responsibility and told me that my father was really alive, and that it was Uncle Fritz, and there were these charges against him. It was very strange for me. Hacki felt like my father, but now I learned that my biological father was alive, and I knew him only a little from his few letters and our meeting in Switzerland. He didn't feel like my father. Now that I knew the truth, I wished I had another.'

Rolf's family tried to soften the impact of the disclosure by minimizing the charges against his father. 'They told me that it was not the truth. He was not a murderer in the camps, not personally murdering by his own hand. We knew it was Auschwitz, a concentration camp, and all those things, but that he was just a small part in the machinery. And I blocked out the rest, any questions or any thoughts.

'But still it affected me very strongly. At the time, I thought I had a father who was a soldier fighting in Russia, and who had been a hero. Now I understood that he had been at Auschwitz, and although I was told he wasn't really killing there, he had still been a part of it. It was not easy for me. People talked about it. I got teased about it at school. Other children at the school teased me, "Oh, here is Mengele's son, your father is a criminal", "little Nazi", or "SS Mengele", things like this. I was never abused by the teachers, only by the students. This went on for some time and it bothered me. I told my family, and they said I should not take it so badly and they tried to get me through it. After high school I never encountered this type of prejudice as directly. Never again as directly.'

While Rolf tried to adjust to the news that his father was not only alive but a wanted war criminal, Martha and Karl Heinz decided to return to Germany. Although she loved Mengele, Martha did not want to be a fugitive's wife. In November 1960, she left him in his new hide-out, Brazil. Their return added to Rolf's confusion about his real father: 'Karl Heinz had lived with my father. He really liked him and told me how wonderful he was, and I thought, "That's not his father, it's my father." ' At school, Rolf's teachers complained he was lazy. They ascribed it to 'father trauma'.

Unaware of his son's difficulty in accepting him, Josef Mengele settled into new Brazilian hide-outs, supported by Hungarian and then Austrian neo-fascist families. He increasingly turned his attention to his diaries and letters. He started an autobiographical novel so that 'my sons, R and K [Rolf and Karl Heinz], will get to know about the family'. Until his death, he sent hundreds of long letters to his family. Many were addressed to Rolf. They were contact with his father that he did not want. 'I would get these letters,' Rolf recalls, 'and it was always the same. It would take me a long time before I even thought about answering them, and then only because my mother or someone would tell me, "He is down there and it is really hard for him, so you must send him something." I would write to him like you would write to a prisoner. I didn't like answering those letters.'

Father and son did not agree in their political or historical discussions, and often the letters became a lecture from Josef Mengele and a vigorous dissent from Rolf. 'We did have some normal discussions between father and son, between the generations. But as for the political or historical discussions, we had opposite views. We had discussions and debates through the letters, but in the end I knew it was futile, because he would always turn everything around and not move from his positions.'

Rolf's politics were quite left of centre and he ws shocked by many of his father's opinions, which seemed to be in a National Socialist time-warp from the 1930s. In one letter, his father referred to Hitler as the 'Man of the Century', and compared his régime to 'those of Alexander the Great, Charles XII of Sweden, Frederick the Great (of Prussia) or Napoleon'.

'I had nothing at all in common with my father's views. On the contrary, my opinions were diametrically opposed. I didn't even bother to listen to him or think of his ideas. I simply rejected everything he presented. My personal attitude to politics and history was never in doubt.'

Josef Mengele did not enjoy these discussions with his son, but rather viewed them as evidence that Rolf had not developed as fully as the more agreeeable Karl Heinz. It was rare that a letter to Rolf did not mention his cousin, and in the most praiseworthy terms. After Mengele's younger brother died, Karl Heinz took charge of the company. Rolf had no share or role in the business. This further enhanced Karl Heinz's prestige in Josef Mengele's eyes. He constantly harangued Rolf by comparing any failure to Karl Heinz's success and by taunting him for a supposed lack of academic ambition. All of this only pushed his son farther away.

Rolf entered college in 1964 at the age of twenty. From there he attended universities in Freiburg, Hamburg, Munich and Geneva. During that time, he still received letters from his father. 'He wasn't on my mind, not somebody I thought about, until I received a letter from him. There wasn't much media attention at this time about him, and therefore I was never really confronted with having to deal with him. He was so much like a stranger to me that I just didn't think about him too much. I was very busy with my studies.' By 1969, Rolf took his first series of law exams, and after a three-year apprenticeship he became a full member of the German bar. Although he had sworn to uphold the law, he did not feel pressured by the issue of whether to turn his father in to authorities searching for him on two continents.

'It was not even an issue. It was basically decided for me by my uncle, grandfather and mother. So I grew up with the understanding that it was not a question for me. Of course, from the view of the victims, a public trial would have been the best solution. But I knew that his capture and a trial would not be the best thing for the family, and it was best avoided. It would have been very difficult for the family to hear every day the testimony, the witnesses, the charges against him. If he was caught without my help, that was different. But I have thought a lot about it since he has been in the news so much, and even now, with all I know of his crimes, I still would not do anything different. He was still my father and you could never expect me to turn him in.'

If his father were captured, Rolf realized he might have to defend him in a trial. 'I would have been a very poor aid to him, but he has a right to a defence, and if no one would defend him, I would have done so. But you should know that I have seen the statements of the witnesses, and I think if he was healthy enough to stand trial he would have been found guilty of murder and given a lifetime in prison.'

But Josef Mengele's plight was not on Rolf's mind in 1972. He was concerned with establishing his career as well as with plans for his first marriage. Yet even in this instance, his father found reasons for criticism. In commenting on wedding photos Rolf had sent, Mengele said, 'Unfortunately I hardly know her, or rather I only know her as much as the few photographs reveal. But do I know the son better? . . . The description accompanying the photos – you really could have tried a little harder. I myself would have realized that these were your friends and not your enemies that accompany you to the registry office!' Then Mengele could not resist reminding Rolf of his own dire predicament: 'One more little contribution I do nevertheless want to make to your new start: I will forget the pain and bitterness of not being informed of anything for years.' Rolf ignored the complaints. He was accustomed to them.

One of the few things they did agree on was Rolf's decision to inform his new wife of his father's fugitive life. 'I felt I knew her very well, we were getting married and all, so I just trusted her,' Rolf recalls. 'She had a right to know before she settled with me.' He was right in trusting her. Even though they divorced within the year, she steadfastly kept the secret of Josef Mengele's whereabouts.

However, Mengele found the divorce reason for further castigating his son: 'When it finally finished it did not of course surprise me. The speed with which you ruined your marriage can only be considered in a favourable light in that the liquidation of a marriage without children is much less complicated than one with children. . . . I do personally lose a mail partner with Irmi [Rolf's wife], who connected me indirectly with you. It wasn't so much, but one who has so little suffers any loss.'

Then he turned his attention to Rolf's decision not to pursue a doctorate. The doctorate had been a sore point for more than a year, and now he was convinced that Rolf's 'laziness' was at the root of the problem. 'You let me down. It is the only thing I asked of you in my whole life. I doubt that being an attorney would satisfy me. If I compare it to being a medical doctor or any kind of PhD, then I must draw a negative conclusion.'

Their relationship worsened when Rolf told his father, shortly after establishing his legal practice, that he could not support him financially. Mengele retorted angrily: 'I can relieve you of your worries about me. Let us keep things as they are. In any case I haven't been a financial burden to you up to now. I am sure however you will manage one or two letters a year.'

Mengele's letters to his son almost always contained a barb or a complaint. He continued to belittle him for his failure to obtain a PhD. When the company Rolf worked with went bankrupt, his father found new reasons for reproach. For Rolf, communicating through the letters was increasingly disappointing. Disputes and differences seemed exaggerated instead of being resolved.

This frustration made him realize that only a personal meeting might dissolve the wall which had risen between him and his father. 'It was actually quite natural,' says Rolf. 'The letters were futile. I wanted to speak to him face to face. I thought I would get more out of him in person. It was the major reason I wanted the visit. At first, my family was not so anxious that I should go. We had an understanding not to take any risks, never to contact him directly. We did not know how tough the Germans and others might be looking for him. Also I had to convince my family that I was not a stupid little boy, that everything was done well and prepared, and that I could go there and the risks were minimal.'

It took more than three years to make the final arrangements. During that time Rolf continued his legal career in southern Germany while his father moved to São Paulo and the protection of a new Austrian family. In occasional letters, Rolf tried to set the trip's agenda. In one letter he criticized his father for his racist views, prompting his father to ridicule Rolf's 'didactic explanations about the lack of racial differences among the human species. I had worked out a long exposé on the subject for you.' But Mengele changed his mind because 'it seems to me rather silly that I of all people should have to enlighten my son about something the Jews have known for 4000 years'.

Besides objecting to Rolf's agenda, Mengele set forth conditions for the trip which resembled a set of military orders, including that Rolf obtain a false passport and a 'watertight alibi'. While he waited for his son to arrange the visit, Mengele occupied his time watching soap operas and the *Wonderful World of Disney* with a sixteen-year-old Brazilian gardener. Few of his South American friends wanted to be near him, since his extreme moodiness made him intolerable. Tired of a life on the run, he fell deeper into depression. 'He was so unhappy living in South America,' Rolf recalls. 'It was very hard for him to be cut off from his family and country. It was no luxury for him. It was not a life he would have chosen for himself, that is, to live in São Paulo. For him there was no civilization, of having to live with so many different cultures in this melting-pot of different races. This was a punishment for him. Not a punishment where he was executed, but rather a personal one, one that was quite serious for him. It was as though he was spending a useless life, without any family, or culture, or research. Thirty years on the run damaged him.'

Mengele ended 1975 with a letter to a German friend, Hans Sedlmeier, in which he noted, 'Nothing can improve my mood.' He spoke of suicide, saying it would be a blessed relief from his aches and pains and from a world that did not care for him. By May of the following year, his growing tension led to a stroke. Although it was a mild attack, his father's illness convinced Rolf that he could no longer postpone the trip: 'He was sick and it did not seem to me he was going to get much better. He had not had an easy life, and it was important for him to see me, and I thought this might be the last chance. So I thought I should do it. I was fed up with the written arguments. I wanted to confront him personally.'

The possibility that Rolf would visit after a twenty-one-year absence gave Mengele the strength to recover. He was so anxious to see his son that he was even willing to have the discussions that Rolf sought – with certain restrictions. Mengele told him in a letter: 'You wish to have a dialogue. Very well. On the one hand I cannot hope for your understanding and compassion for my life's course; on the other I do not have the minutest inner desire to justify or even excuse any decisions, actions or behaviour regarding my life. . . . When it comes to indisputable traditional values, where I sense danger to those close to me or to the unity of people, my tolerance has its limits.' Yet, while he feared a confrontation with his son, Mengele also hoped that the visit would be a lengthy one: 'It is not going to be easy for me to express how much I look forward to that meeting. Perhaps with the confession that it represents the next goal in my life. Therefore I want you to reflect on not making the stay too short.'

Despite his earnest plea, Mengele could not resist taunting Rolf in the same letter. Although Rolf had sent greetings for the fugitive's sixty-sixth birthday, his father chided him for 'caring more about your mother's birthday than mine'. He also complained that he had not been informed of a recent car accident involving Irene. To Rolf, it was merely evidence that his father had not fundamentally changed, despite the appearance of desperately wanting to see him.

Although the eventual trip was planned with great secrecy and precision, the family did not have to take such precautions. The West German authorities had not placed any Mengele family members under surveillance. Rolf left Frankfurt for Brazil on 12 October 1977. He travelled on a passport he had stolen from a friend who greatly resembled him. An hour or so into the flight he began to have second thoughts: 'I remember thinking to myself, "Should I really be going? It won't change anything." But these misgivings were just nerves. I knew that I wouldn't turn back once I got to Brazil. It was something I had to do. I'd been thinking about it for too long.'

Mengele was also nervously anticipating his son's arrival. His friend Hans Sedlmeier had written warning that in Rolf he would find a representative of a new German generation, whose ideology and values were wholly different from his own. Sedlmeier's words seemed harsh to Mengele: 'The world, especially here with us, has changed tremendously and these changes have passed you by. . . . You have not been through these times with us. You have no right to criticize from afar. The preconditions that you take as a basis for all actions and thoughts simply no longer exist. You have stood still in the concepts of the old days, which unfortunately, yes, I use the word unfortunately, are no longer valid.'

The warning was accurate, but for Mengele, set in his ways after half a lifetime on the run, it came too late. He could not change his feelings only days before his son's arrival. Rolf discovered this once he settled in to his father's small house. Their discussions began cautiously. Rolf remembers these days very clearly. 'I told my father I was interested in hearing about his time in Auschwitz. What was Auschwitz according to his version of events? What did he do there? Did he have a role in the things he was charged with? For tactical and psychological reasons I very cautiously touched upon this subject, trying to analyse it and separate out the more obscure and complex arguments my father was trying to inject.'

The questioning continued nightly. Mengele strayed from the essential points, justified his racist theories, filled his arguments with philosophical and pseudo-scientific verbiage, and even gave Rolf a detailed critique of evolution. 'There were many things he could not answer,' says Rolf. 'His arguments for why he thought some races were superior to others were quite unscientific. He waffled on and on when I asked him why many crippled and deformed people had brilliant minds. He was so sure he was right in all respects, I asked him why he had not turned himself in. My father replied, "There are no judges, only avengers." '

Mengele became angry as the exchanges continued. At one

point, sensing Rolf's incredulity, he screamed: 'Don't tell me you, my only son, believe what they write about me? On my mother's life I have never hurt anyone!' It was at this moment that father and son agreed there was no useful point in pursuing the debate. As Rolf explained: 'I realized that this man, my father, was just too rigid. Despite all his knowledge and intellect, he just did not want to see the basis and rules for the simplest humanity in Auschwitz. He didn't understand that his presence alone had made him an accessory within the deepest meaning of inhumanity. There was no point in going on. I had to resign myself to that fact. He did promise to write everything down. He kept saying that if I had time to study what he meant, I might see his point. But unfortunately he never did.'

In the end it was impossible to discuss the concepts of evil or guilt because his father felt no guilt: 'I tried. These allegations, these facts left me speechless. I was hoping he'd say, "I tried to get a transfer to the front. I did this, I did that." But it didn't even come to this preliminary agreement. Unfortunately, I realized that he would never express any remorse or feeling of guilt in my presence.'

Although the two of them spent time visiting Mengele's friends as well as his father's two previous homes in the Brazilian interior, Rolf knew the wall he encountered around the subject of Auschwitz would never be breached. After two weeks, he decided it was time to go. The farewell at São Paulo airport was a brief, formal affair. Mengele was too preoccupied with his fear that someone might be watching him. ' "We shall try to meet again very soon, all of us," were his last words,' Rolf recalls. 'But I knew I would never see him again.'

Upon returning to Germany, Rolf was kept busy with marriage plans with a new bride, Almuth. Again his father wrote to him, but this time there was none of the criticism that had been directed at the first marriage. Rolf's trip had changed Mengele's opinion of his son. Even though Rolf was not subject to his influence, Mengele justified it as poor education, postwar propaganda, and the influence of a weak stepfather. He no longer blamed his son. He was proud of him, thinking of him as a soldier who completed a successful reconnaissance patrol. He summed up his feelings in the letter's closing line: 'Now I can die in peace.'

While the relationship had improved for Josef Mengele, it was not any better for Rolf. Although the visit had satisfied his blood ties as a son, it did not resolve any of the conflicts which had developed during twenty years of difficult letters. 'I wanted to find out the charges were not true or that there was a human side of him I had not seen. No, he left me nothing. He was unrepentant.'

Sixteen months later, on a holiday with his Austrian friends, Mengele had another stroke while swimming in gentle waves at Bertioga Beach, south of São Paulo. Although he was pulled from the water and given mouth-to-mouth resuscitation, it was too late. The world's most wanted Nazi died at the age of sixty-seven. Rolf's reaction to his father's death was one of enormous relief. 'I basically had a conflict that could never be resolved,' he said. 'On the one hand he was my father; on the other hand there were these charges, these horrific pictures of Auschwitz. I was very relieved that this solution came about and not another, like maybe a trial, important though that might have been.'

Josef Mengele was buried in Our Lady of the Rosary Cemetery in Embu, Brazil, under the name of one of his former protectors, Wolfgang Gerhard. Nine months after his father's death, Rolf again returned to Brazil. He spent Christmas with his father's friends, giving them the run-down house where his father lived his final years. He took with him his father's gold watch, letters, diaries, and pictures. Before returning to Germany he stopped in Rio at the posh Othon Palace Hotel, where two years earlier he had checked in under a false name. There he had one of his most uncomfortable moments. On this trip he travelled under his true name. When he checked in, the concierge said, 'Ah, Mengele. Do you know you have a very famous name around here?' Rolf smiled weakly, but inside he was in turmoil. He hid the duffel bag crammed with his father's personal papers inside the dropped ceiling of his hotel room. 'Any professional search would have found the material in less than a minute,' Rolf said, 'but it was the best I could do.'

Since Mengele's death remained a family secret, the hunt for him continued unabated. During the next six years a slow-burning fuse on the case finally resulted in worldwide media attention. From 1984 to 1986, he was the subject of dozens of magazine cover stories and television specials. The extent to which he became notorious was that he even made the cover of *People* magazine, and was listed in the annual edition as one of the 'twenty-five most interesting people of the year'. Mengele sightings became a popular sport, with *Life* magazine and the New York *Post* reporting he lived in a private house near a *yeshiva* (a Jewish seminary or day school) in Bedford Hills, thirty miles north of New York City. Even internal CIA reports added to his mythology, speculating that Mengele had become a key figure in the international narcotics trade. On a more serious note, the governments of West Germany, Israel and the United States launched their first joint effort to capture a Nazi. Rewards for information leading to Mengele, alive or dead, were posted by governments and private organizations and totalled more than $3.5 million. It is ironic that the manhunt did not pick up such enthusiasm and concerted effort until he was already dead.

By now the story seemed to have a life of its own. But the public focus created problems for Rolf and the rest of the family. Karl Heinz worried that the negative publicity would hurt the family business, still operating under the name Mengele & Sons. The family had decided in 1979 not to disclose the death, in order to protect the South American families who had helped Mengele. But now that profits were threatened by the unabated negative publicity attached to the name, Karl Heinz had second thoughts. On 23 March 1985, Karl Heinz summoned Rolf to Günzburg. There, in the presence of another cousin, Dieter Mengele, Karl Heinz proposed leaking word of Josef's death, so long as the family were not incriminated. He was convinced that unless the death was made public, the hunt would continue indefinitely. Dieter had a farfetched scheme. He wanted to collect the bones from São Paulo and dump them on the doorstep of the German prosecutor, with a note saying 'These are the remains of Josef Mengele'. Rolf immediately ruled that out. 'I said, "And who's going to go and get the bones? Me, I suppose, because it was my father. No, thanks." ' Rolf was opposed to any leak, arguing that protecting the security of those who helped his father was paramount. 'After they are dead, then we can disclose it,' he told his cousins.

However, even without the help of the Mengele family, government authorities made progress in their investigation. On 31 May 1985, they raided the home of Mengele's long-time friend Hans Sedlmeier and after an hours-long search found copies of some Mengele letters hidden in the false bottom of a wardrobe. The letters led to São Paulo and Mengele's protectors. By 6 June, the investigators, together with a small circus of media hounds, surrounded the Embu gravesite. Once the bones were uncovered, a great debate broke out between the governments and private Nazi hunters as to whether the bones belonged to Josef Mengele. Several teams of forensic experts were assembled to fly to Brazil and test the remains.

The one person who could provide proof of Mengele's death was his son. But Rolf had no idea what had happened, since he was on holiday with his wife and child, touring Spain in a caravan, cut off from newspapers and television for nearly two weeks. He had no set itinerary, so the family could not reach him.

On Friday evening, 7 June 1986, Rolf returned to his Freiburg home, switched on the television, and saw the late news. He immediately knew the secret was out. 'I knew it was serious,' Rolf recalls. 'I thought Dieter must have leaked it and it all went wrong.' But a telephone call established that Dieter was not the source of the break in the case. Soon, an NBC camera crew camped in front of Rolf's house, and newspaper reporters were knocking on his door and telephoning his office non-stop. 'It was all coming out,' Rolf says. 'Everyone was talking in South America. Since it would all come out sooner or later, I proposed that the family make a statement. But Dieter and Karl Heinz refused. Everyone in Günzburg was paralysed.'

Rolf decided to go public. 'I had waited long enough,' he says. 'Even after my father's death there had been conflict about staying quiet. While I felt my first duty was to those who had protected him, I was also aware that the victims were still looking for him and I felt bad that they were wasting their efforts since he was dead. It was not easy, but I kept quiet. Now it was too much, it was time to speak.'

Rolf issued a brief public statement admitting he had visited Brazil in 1979 to 'confirm the circumstances of my father's death'. He also arranged to donate his father's personal letters and diaries to Munich-based *Bunte* magazine, on the condition that they could do a series of articles if they donated the profits from their increased circulation to concentration camp victims.[20] 'Dieter and Karl Heinz were totally opposed to any announcement, particularly to my going public with *Bunte*,' Rolf says. 'Their position was that the family should not be tied to this in any way. They haven't spoken to me since. On the 1985 announcement of the birth of our daughter, Dieter returned it unopened. He had seen our name on the envelope. My aunt Martha obeys her son's wishes and has no contact with me. I have been totally rejected by them for talking about my father. I don't like the split, it's never good when you are estranged. But they do not like it if you go your own way. They have tried to punish me by cutting me off.'

Rolf is the only one in the family who has tried to confront the magnitude of what his father did. While the rest of the Günzburg clan rationalizes Mengele's role in Auschwitz, convinced that some of the charges are exaggerated, Rolf completely condemns him. He is the only family member to have publicly apologized for his father's crimes and to have admitted that he is 'ashamed' to be his son. The fundamental differences in judging Mengele's crimes have left the family little room for reconciliation.

Rolf does not share the 'pity' that some other children of prominent Nazis feel for their parents: 'I don't feel sorry for him. I feel he got the package he deserved. I don't pity him as my father, only that he wasted his life. He wasted it because he was so blinded, or because . . . I don't know what happened to him. I can't understand him. He didn't learn to be a father, to have a son, and really to know this experience. And I know from his letters to me that he wanted this extremely and suffered from not having it.'

But Rolf will not bring himself to the position of Niklas Frank who hates his father. 'This seems too final for me. Hate is such a strong word. Maybe he feels that way, but for me at least, it's a little too much. I am more indifferent to my father. I don't feel strongly enough about him to hate him.'

In sharp contrast to the children of Hess, Dönitz, and others who consider it an advantage to grow up as the child of a prominent National Socialist, Rolf views it as 'a definite disadvantage. It's different to be the son or daughter of a famous Nazi military figure, this is not so bad, not such a disadvantage,' Rolf says. 'After the rearmament of Germany, the military was all right, but the SS were always on the outside. It is worse if you are the child of a lower party member, at least it's better if your father was important. But the worst is a party member who was like my father, to be involved in the extermination and the camps. You see, after the war, a vast majority of the German population who were involved with the Nazi party found an easy way to draw back from their participation. They said, "Yes, we elected Hitler, but only to improve the motorways, and it might have been very bad for the Jewish people, but the people who did it were Mengele and Eichmann and they were just a few, and these were the bad people." So even in Germany the buden is put on a few of us.

'From my perspective, it was a great disadvantage being the son of Mengele. The only advantage I could see is that, having this legacy on my shoulders, I had always to think about the essence of life, and the conflict between good and bad. But I am sure I don't know 80 per cent of what happened to my life and my professsion as a result of this. For instance, I was always interested in politics, but I always stayed out of it because I didn't want people to shout at me to shut up because of my father. There are many negative aspects to being such a son. I feel it was my destiny to be Josef Mengele's son, just like another might have had the fate of illness or being handicapped. So advantage-disadvantage in a common sense, economically, professionally, I don't know exactly. You don't always know if someone avoids you or does not come to you for business because they say, "Oh, that is Mengele's son, we must stay away from him." Sometimes I may be dealing with Jewish businessmen or other victims of the war, and I may never hear the objection or the reason I do not get the work. Maybe I am looking for excuses for myself when I didn't reach some goal in my career. Maybe I just say it must be because of my father. Maybe it is my psychological escape.'

Rolf does not only have to cope for himself with his father's legacy. With three children, he must now pass the information to a new generation. 'It is hard,' he says. 'It's very hard for us. My eldest daughter [twelve years old] has already asked us. But they understand it when we explain we were also children. We were in their position, just one generation removed. We weren't involved. It would be nicer to say he was a great scientist or soldier, but instead we must tell them the truth. They must hear it from us instead of from friends or school. It is my obligation to them.'

In 1987 Rolf changed his surname for the sake of his children. 'They deserve to grow up without having to answer for what their grandfather did,' he says. He does not have any fear that whatever drove his father to such crimes might also be in him or his children. 'We are different. We have established our own lives in a very different way. Whatever it was that drove my father, it wasn't genetic. Our environment is totally different.'

Because he has made such a strong effort to create a new life for himself, he is disappointed that so many people think of him only in relation to his notorious father. He cannot break the legacy left to him by a man who was more a stranger than a father. 'We, the children of these parents, must deal with it,' Rolf says. 'More than any other German group, until now, we are faced with these issues. The other Germans say, "Okay, it happened, and it is too bad, but it's done and let's get on with life." They don't get involved as much as we, the children of the direct participants. I must always seem to have an answer for what he did. He is gone, but he has left me here to answer the questions of what he did and why he did it. He is gone but I must bear the burden.'

CHAPTER 7

The Last Führer

In the final hours of his life, at 4 a.m. on Sunday, 29 April 1945, Adolf Hitler finished his last will and testament. Russian soldiers were only five hundred yards away and the sound of artillery penetrated the Führerbunker's thick walls as he summoned Josef Goebbels and Martin Bormann as witnesses. The will was a rambling document brimming with hatred for 'international Jewry', blaming the Allies for starting the war, and castigating the German army for losing the conflict. While he exhorted the German people to continue fighting, he prepared to abandon the struggle. On the next day, resolved not to be captured alive, not to be a 'spectacle, presented by the Jews, to divert their hysterical masses', he placed the barrel of a Walther pistol in his mouth and killed himself with a single shot.

The Third Reich was on the verge of collapsing, but Hitler's will established a new government. He stripped his most likely successors, Himmler and Göring, of their ranks, titles, and positions. Then he created a new cabinet of fourteen veteran Nazi hacks. But the section that named his successor shocked his Berlin aides – it proclaimed as the next Führer the reserved chief of the navy, Grand Admiral Karl Dönitz, who was not even a Nazi party member, but who was the only officer of the Reich whom Hitler trusted to lead Germany in its final battle.

While many thought Hitler's death would instantly end the war, it initially appeared Dönitz had different ideas. Upon his appointment, he hailed Hitler's 'hero's death', demanded loyalty from the armed forces, and seemed unequivocal in exhorting more battle. But behind the scenes, he was a realist who knew the war was over. He quietly countermanded Hitler's standing orders for the destruction of Germany, ordered military evacuations instead of final battles, and tried to buy enough time so that millions of German troops and civilians could move westward, avoiding the closing Soviet pincer in the east. Dönitz's government lasted only a week, until General Alfred Jodl signed the armistice on 8 May, although the British did not arrest Dönitz until 23 May.

The man who was Hitler's successor had three children. His two sons, Peter and Klaus, died at twenty-one and twenty-four years of age, both killed in action while serving in their father's navy. His daughter, Ursula, was born on 3 April 1917. She is the oldest person interviewed for this book. She was also her father's favourite. 'I had a very loving relationship with my father,' she recalls. Ursula was sixty-three years old when her father died in 1980. During those six decades she studied him and came to understand his nature and motivation.

Karl Dönitz was born on 16 September 1891, in Grünau-bei-Berlin, a small town eighty miles outside the German capital. He was the second son in a middle-class Lutheran family. His father was an optical engineer, and when his mother died in 1895, the elder Dönitz ran a strictly Prussian household; he never re-married. Dönitz became a disciple of this harsh philosophy, and was instilled with an absolute sense of duty and obedience to the state and to authority.

'He did not talk much about his family,' Ursula recalls. 'He was very private. I don't think he had much love in his own family. He was only three when his mother died. It affected him, and I think he suppressed certain things. He couldn't show his emotions. I know he had them but it was never a public show. He cared for his father very much, keeping a picture that he drew of his father on his desk always. It was stolen at the end of the war.'

After completing a semi-classical education, Dönitz graduated at eighteen and joined the navy. Like many early-twentieth-century Germans, he was convinced that his landlocked country could rival Britain as a world power only if it developed a strong navy. At the naval academy, a single philosophy was drilled into the cadets: fulfilment of duty was the highest moral value. Dönitz finished second in the cadet class.

His father died in 1912, as Karl first set sail for a two-year baptism of fire as a member of a multinational force intervening for Turkey in the Balkan Wars. He served courageously and was highly decorated and quickly promoted. His superior officers thought he was a model sailor. In 1915 he met Ingeborg Weber, twenty-one-year-old daughter of an army general, and they married the following year. During the same period, Dönitz was assigned to the vessel which became his personal favourite for the remainder of his career, the U-boat. The early models were cramped steel cylinders which afforded no privacy and virtually no comfort. Fifty men shared a single bath and toilet. Each U-boat carried a large supply of cheap cologne to mask the body odours of men who seldom changed clothes during an entire voyage. Dönitz's vessel, the *U-39*, quickly gained a reputation for close-range ambushes of Allied shipping. He obtained leave only once, to return home for the April 1917 birth of Ursula. But he soon left again for open warfare raging in the Mediterranean. This time it nearly cost him his life.

In October 1918, Dönitz was commander of *U-68* when it came under heavy British attack off Sicily and he and his crew were captured. British interrogators described the twenty-seven-year-old first lieutenant as 'moody and almost violent', crushed by the news of the humiliating terms of German defeat. He remained a British prisoner until he appeared to go mad, which prompted a short stay in the Manchester Lunatic Asylum and then a release to Germany. Ursula Dönitz says her father later confided that he fooled his British captors by drinking a combination of oil and tobacco to make himself ill and then feigning mental problems. 'He never talked about World War I, but once when he was older he told me about the way he fooled the British to win his early freedom back to Germany. He knew he had to pretend to have this illness to come home. There was not a real breakdown.'

Upon his return to Germany he re-enlisted in the new Reichsmarine. Although the Versailles Treaty had stripped Germany of most of its military power, Dönitz hoped the military restrictions would be short-lived. By the summer of 1920 he was with the torpedo-boat fleet at Swinemünde, where he moved with his wife and Ursula, now three and a half, and his newborn son, Klaus. Ursula's first fleeting images of her father date from this time.

'I have very good memories of Swinemünde. It was a nice sea resort where Berliners vacationed. I shared a room with my brother at this time. We lived in a comfortable apartment. I liked it very much.

'And the first memories of my parents are also very positive. Later, I saw they had a good marriage and it was reflected in the house, although I also realized later that my mother let my father dominate her a little too much. He tried to instil very strong values in all his children. My father was strict, but not too much with me. Only once do I remember him striking me. And it is interesting because he never yelled or raised his voice – he was extremely controlled. But around the age of five, I remember I got a terrible spanking. I had taken a cake from a plate and when I was later asked if I had, I said no. But I had crumbs around my mouth and I received this spanking both because I stole the cake and because I had lied. This was a special lesson for me all my life, very important for me. My father's upbringing was to tell the truth and it meant a great deal to him. Ever since that event, I have had difficulty in telling a lie.'

Ursula felt very close to her father, even at a young age. 'I got along best with him. Whenever he was in a bad mood, my mother would send me to talk to him. Not my mother, but me. I could speak to him when he was in a bad temper and bring him out of it. No one else in the family could do this.'

Yet, despite this special bond, she does not recall much affection from her father. 'It was very difficult for him to show affection.' She pauses, almost melancholy. 'I don't remember that he ever gave me a kiss. But he would take my hand and hold it. He never once said, "Ursula, I love you," but I knew he did. His entire nature tended towards silence. He always seemed reserved to me, and later I learned that his strong inner discipline precluded any rash remarks or emotional displays.'

Even his navy colleagues found Dönitz a quiet man. Not an amusing or witty talker, he concentrated on his naval career. His superior officers appreciated his single-mindedness. In 1921 he was appointed Kapitänleutnant (lieutenant), and in 1923 was transferred to Kiel and placed in charge of submarine hunting techniques. His Kiel assignment coincided with a period of hyperinflation in Germany. The Dönitz family was one of many whose capital was destroyed. His military salary barely covered family expenses.

'He had taste for good things,' Ursula remembers. 'He had a

very good collection of Oriental carpets. They were important to him. He had purchased several in Constantinople [now Istanbul], and a dealer told him that one of the rugs was hundreds of years old and was museum quality. "It should be on a wall," the dealer said. "Don't walk on it." My father did not have the money to put another rug over it. You must know that an officer in the navy did not earn a lot of money – he had three children and we were happy when his pay arrived each month. But then, we were not nearly as badly off as many other families.'

By 1924 Dönitz was transferred higher up the naval ladder, this time to Berlin and the Marineleitung (general staff command), where he was chief of general military affairs.

'Berlin was my third school in three years,' Ursula says. 'Actually I think I went to eight different schools altogether. We were always being transferred, but always to naval communities within the cities. My father often went on ships as part of his duties and he was away a lot when I was young. Sometimes he was gone months at a time. For me it seemed normal. I was too young to understand this and miss him. My friends were all from navy families so it seemed normal for all of us.'

Their life in Berlin was simple. 'It was a very good time, with visits to museums, sailing on Lake Wannsee or all of us going for walks,' she remembers. Ursula's parents spent most of their time at home. 'Sometimes he played the flute at night. We had a gramophone but he did not stay and listen to it for hours. I don't remember him reading too much. For him, the evening was a time to relax from his work. When we prepared to go to sleep, he would read us books of poetry. We lay in bed and he would read ballads to us, with much vehemence and emotion and, in conjunction with the pictures in the book, the impression was so deep that even today I can recite particular verses.'

By 1927, Dönitz was transferred to an assignment closer to his desire for active sea service. He became the navigator aboard a cruiser. To celebrate his new position he took his family on a holiday. 'It was the first holiday we ever had together,' says Ursula. 'We never really felt we had to go anywhere since we almost always lived by the sea, but at ten I was taken to the islands in the North Sea. We travelled fourth class on the railway, which meant wooden seats to sleep on during the trip.'

While the vacation may be a good memory, a split in the

family that same year left a bad impression on ten-year-old Ursula. 'My father and his only brother had a falling-out. It was too bad because I liked my uncle, who was two years older than my father, very much. But after this argument they never spoke again. I never saw my uncle or discovered what caused the break-up. My father never told me and I would never ask him. If he wanted to tell me he would have done so. His brother was killed in a bombing raid near the end of the war and then my father took his wife into our house. But no one mentioned the problem between the brothers.'

Within a year Dönitz was again promoted, given his own torpedo-boat command with some twenty officers and six hundred men. To hold such a position at the age of thirty-seven was a considerable achievement in a navy with one of Europe's oldest officer corps.

By the autumn of 1928 the family moved once again, this time to the high command of the North Sea station in Wilhelms-haven. 'This was the first time we lived somewhere for a long time,' Ursula recalls. 'Before this we moved every year or two. I liked it there very much, my favourite time of all as a youngster. I don't think my father had a favourite place since his work was his favourite thing, the place didn't matter much. But for me, it was good all around. It was my finest time in school. I didn't have to change friends from year to year. It was very good.'

Although these were years of great upheaval in Germany, Ursula insists that National Socialism did not influence her father during this period. 'Remember, we were always in naval sections of the cities, and the Nazis had very little presence in the navy towns. We never saw the Nazi rallies. The party was very small and fairly inactive in our area. It might be difficult for you to believe, but we had *nothing* to do with the party or politics. You know my father never joined the party. And during this time when I was twelve, thirteen, and fourteen, I don't remember his ever talking about politics. He was a navy man – it didn't matter who made the politics.

'Looking back, all these changes were taking place in Germany, but to me we were just a normal and quiet family. I didn't realize the times were unusual. If he did talk about politics, I don't remember it because I wasn't interested. As a young girl, I had no ears for this. I mean I knew that some things

17. In 1956, Rolf Mengele accompanied his cousin, Karl-Heinz, for a skiing holiday in the Swiss Alps. There, he was introduced to an 'Uncle Gregor', a family visitor from Argentina. Unknown to Rolf, Gregor was actually Josef Mengele. *Courtesy of Rolf Mengele*

18. The first page of a children's fable, complete with crayon drawings, made for Rolf by Josef Mengele while he was on the run in South America. *Courtesy of Rolf Mengele*

19. Karl Dönitz greets Hitler before a strategy meeting. *Courtesy of National Archives*

20. Dönitz (seated, centre) speaking to his fellow defendants during a break at Nuremberg. Göring is holding his head in his hands with Hess (front, right) appearing to be listening intently. *Courtesy of National Archives*

21. Ursula Dönitz (second to right) celebrating her father's release from Spandau Prison on October 1, 1956. She is standing between her husband, Günther Hessler, a decorated U-boat commander, and her mother. Ursula's children surround the grand admiral. *Ullstein*

22. Claus von Stauffenberg in 1942 at German army headquarters in the Ukraine. *Ullstein*

23. Stauffenberg recovering from his nearly fatal wounds received in North Africa. He is surrounded by his children as well as some nephews and nieces. Franz Ludwig is at the far right. *Ullstein*

24. Karl Saur (right) during a private stroll with Hitler at Obersalsberg, Hitler's summer retreat. *Courtesy of Karl Saur Jr*

25. Four of the five Saur children in 1948, with Klaus (second from left) and Karl Jr (to his left). . *Courtesy of Karl Saur Jr*

26. Karl Saur with nine-year-old Karl Jr, in 1953. *Courtesy of Karl Saur Jr*

27. The 1937 church christening of Edda Göring angered many
in the Nazi hierarchy, but it did not stop Hitler from attending.
AP/Wide World Photos

28. Hitler holding Edda after the ceremony. *Voak Collection, Hoffman
Archives, Vienna*

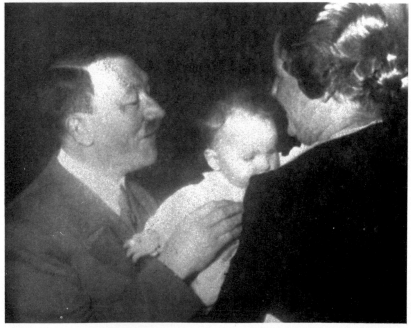

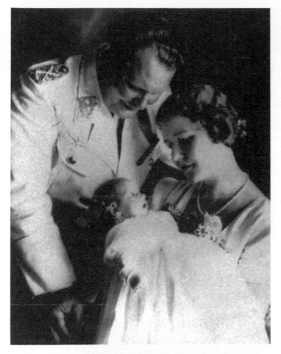

29. The official Nazi party photograph of the Görings and their new baby. *AP/Wide World Photos*

30. An American soldier snapped this picture at Fishhorn castle of Emmy and Edda at the moment Göring was driven away to prison. *Courtesy of the Keith Wilson Collection*

31. Göring, to the left and Hess, hold their heads in dejection as they listen to the Nuremberg verdict on September 30, 1946. Dönitz sits rigidly in the rear. *AP/Wide World Photos*

32. Emmy and Edda visiting Göring at Nuremberg prison on September 26, 1946. Edda fondly recalls that final meeting with her father. *AP/Wide World Photos*

were not good in Germany, especially around the Depression. I knew that Versailles was a bad treaty, not just from my father, but everyone knew that Versailles was bad.'

His colleagues and reports from superiors support Ursula's recollection. During the fundamental German transformation to Nazism, Dönitz was particularly apolitical. As a soldier, he was prepared to follow the dictates established by any political leader who controlled the state. However, National Socialism's strong anti-communist and Versailles-bashing platforms must have appealed to him. Hitler promised to expand Germany's borders and build a military machine that rivalled Britain's. Although Dönitz exhibited no signs of anti-Semitism during this time, he later seemed to accept the Nazi theory that Jews were an internal threat to Germany. Ursula never recalls any discussion with her father 'about Jews'. She claims that after Kristallnacht he officially complained to the highest ranks. There is no record of any such protest.

By 1933, Dönitz's superiors thought he was such a promising officer that they awarded him a travel grant which allowed him to stay abroad for six months. It meant he was out of Germany when the Nazis took power in 1933 and brutally settled their scores with enemies. By the time he returned home that summer, a national revival was under way. Increased confidence was widespread. The navy was particularly pleased with Hitler, who had established a five-year plan for rebuilding the entire fleet. That autumn Dönitz was made a commander and received a brilliant evaluation. For a middle-ranking forty-two-year-old officer, the future looked promising.

As her father's career advanced steadily, an important event happened in sixteen-year-old Ursula's life: she met her future husband, Günther Hessler. 'He was eight years older than me, and I liked him right away. He was in the navy, and my father knew and liked him. We were together six months but I was too young to marry. We married four years later. It was an advantage that my father liked him, although if he did not approve, I still would have dated [Günther]. I was quite independent.'

While Ursula continued her studies, the following summer her father's naval dedication was rewarded: he was given his own command. On 2 November 1934, as was customary on the eve of departure for foreign-going naval commanders, Dönitz met Hitler for the first time. Ursula does not remember if her father discussed the meeting with his family. Years later he told a British historian that his initial impression of the Führer was that he was 'honest and worthy'.

His tour of duty lasted nearly a year. He travelled throughout Asia and India, and around Africa. When he returned in July 1935, Grand Admiral Erich Raeder, chief of the navy, appointed him commander of the navy's small U-boat fleet (he was soon given the title 'Führer der U-boote'.) 'My father was very young [forty-three] when he was put in charge of the submarines,' Ursula says. 'He was only a commander then, and it was a major position. I was a little bit proud.'

However, U-boats were initially overlooked in German rearmament. At the start of World War II Germany had only twenty-two submarines for all the Atlantic, while Dönitz wanted three hundred. Yet, even with such a minuscule fleet, his U-boats were highly effective, claiming more than 21.5 million tons of Allied shipping before advanced radar limited their effectiveness. Dönitz fundamentally changed the nature of submarine warfare by organizing U-boats into deadly packs whose sole mission was to ambush enemy ships.

During this time, his two sons had joined the Hitler Youth. Ursula was required to join the girl's equivalent, the Bund Deutscher Mädchen (League of German Girls), but left in 1936 during her final year of high school. 'I found it rather silly,' she says, 'since neither of my parents was in the party. We liked being non-political. As for our feelings towards the National Socialist party, we were fairly average for that time in Germany.'

Ursula had more on her mind in 1937 than the League of German Girls. She finally married her young naval fiancé, Günther Hessler, that November. Although he was a committed navy man he was not a Nazi party member. Her father heartily approved. 'My father came home to Kiel for the wedding. My husband and I lived there until 1939. It was the first time I lived away from my family. I was very excited to be married, but I missed my parents. They lived very near us so I still saw them about three times a week.

'I was a young wife, soon to be a mother, and was very happy. With the merging of Sudetenland, and Germany being strong again, we were all very proud. These were very good times for me.'

The following year Ursula and her husband joined Dönitz on a skiing holiday. Despite his command of the U-boat fleet, his relatively junior rank kept him far removed from the inner Nazi circle. He was skiing when Hitler annexed Austria. 'It was an annual holiday for us and at this time he was like many other Germans in that he learned of events as they took place. It certainly did not interfere with our trip. My father was a good skier, and I was the only other one in the family who skied. So I used to go with him alone, without my mother or brothers. These were very good holidays for us; it was the one time my father had a real opportunity to relax.'

But as events led inexorably to full-scale war, Dönitz eschewed his winter holiday in 1939. Instead he published a book called *Die U-Bootswaffe* (The U-Boat Arm), a primer on how he intended to use his fleet during war. Unfortunately, British intelligence did not obtain a copy until 1942. By that time the Allies had experienced Dönitz's tactics on the open seas.

Just before the outbreak of the war, Ursula had her first child, a son, Peter. Dönitz 'was extremely proud to become a grandfather at only forty-seven,' Ursula says. She also remembers it was near this time that her father warned her of the coming conflict. 'It was one time when my father drove me home in the evening after I had visited my parents. My husband was away at sea and my father said to me, for the first and only time, "There will be a war and it will be a long one. The British will not allow Germany to get too powerful." It surprised me a little because I had not thought it was that certain.'

When the war started, in September 1939, Ursula never feared for the life of either her father or husband. 'I was never nervous for my father. Never. I was convinced he would come back. It was the same for my husband, with one exception. One night, I remember very clearly, I woke up and had a panic, thinking, "Oh, what if he doesn't come back?" But that was the only time I worried.'

In the first months of the war, Dönitz's U-boat fleet followed the Prize Law, a treaty which mandated warnings before firing torpedoes. However, as the war rapidly intensified, Raeder and Hitler prodded him to flout the Prize Law. Unrestricted U-boat warfare was waged by mid-1940. The results were impressive. The British lost aircraft-carriers and destroyers, and tons of Allied merchant shipping were sent to the ocean bottom. Hitler was ecstatic about this elite and dangerous naval fleet which mirrored Dönitz's pride and enthusiasm.

In June 1940, France fell. That convinced many in the navy that world domination was within Germany's grasp. Ursula is not certain her father shared the enthusiasm for eventual victory. 'I remember a conversation during the war, when he said very earnestly, "It will be a long, long and very hard war." And I was shocked, for it seemed to me at that time that all was well and we were winning. Perhaps he already had doubts, but he would never utter them.'

Ursula was the only one to hear any doubt from her father. To his colleagues, Dönitz typified the military optimist. During 1940 and 1941 he pushed his U-boat fleet to its physical limit. Turnaround time in port was slashed to a minimum and intense pressure was exerted to sink ever larger Allied ships. But his fighting men adored him. They felt Dönitz ws one of them, and in return they pledged unwavering loyalty. The staggering U-boat successes, combined with his immense popularity, favourably impressed the Nazi hierarchy and the Führer.

During the summer of 1942, Dönitz took an extended holiday in Badenweiler, a hillside resort in the Black Forest, with his wife and Ursula. 'The summer trip was for three weeks. Since I had not seen him much recently in Kiel, it was good to have some time with him. He was very serious as he had a lot on his mind. So I took my son along and this really pleased him.'

Ursula's husband had by this time earned a reputation as an ace U-boat commander. He held the wartime record for a single voyage, sinking fourteen ships totalling 87,000 tons. Following their holiday, Hessler joined Dönitz's command staff at U-boat headquarters in France, leaving Ursula alone in Germany with her son. Now working under his father-in-law, Hessler witnessed the same absolute drive and commitment to the war that all Dönitz's colleagues already knew.

In September 1942, as Dönitz prepared a status report for Hitler, an incident took place which later became a key part of the Nuremberg case against him. A U-boat sank a British troop transport, the *Laconia*, with over two thousand men aboard.

Four U-boats arrived at the scene to save survivors, and, their decks crammed with Allied troops, they steamed along on the surface towards a safe port. All the vessels flew large Red Cross flags. Three days into their rescue mission, in clear and visible weather, American planes circled for an hour and then bombed the submarines. One U-boat was badly damaged. Against the advice of his staff, Dönitz did not call off the rescue operation. When Hitler learned of the Allied bombing, he telephoned in a rage. He screamed that German lives should never be at jeopardy because of rescuing enemy soldiers. Dönitz responded by issuing a directive, later dubbed the *Laconia* order, to cease all attempts to save survivors at sea. He proclaimed: 'Rescue contradicts the most fundamental demands of war for the annihilation of ships and crews.' He ended by urging his troops to 'be hard. Think of the fact that the enemy in his bombing attacks on German towns has no regard for women and children.'

Although not an order to shoot survivors, the *Laconia* directive could be so interpreted by individual commanders. The Allies charged that Dönitz left the language ambiguous, hoping his fleet would resolve the question in favour of murder. Ursula later spoke to her husband about the order, and is adamant that it was never intended as permission to kill survivors.

What is indisputable is that the *Laconia* order kept Dönitz on a favourable footing with Hitler. The Führer liked his enthusiasm and absolute willingness to follow orders. As the war turned against the Nazis, Dönitz's personality suited Hitler more than Grand Admiral Raeder's formal and somewhat depressing reserve. When Raeder resigned in January 1943, after a significant loss in an Arctic convoy, fifty-one-year-old Dönitz reached the zenith of his career as Hitler appointed him grand admiral and supreme commander of the German navy. 'He was young and of lower rank than expected when he was given this appointment,' Ursula recalls. 'I was not surprised. He never surprised me with what he could accomplish. I was happy and very proud even though I had never been interested in ranks or promotions. When I was a young girl all the other girls would always talk about the boys in terms of one stripe or two. One day I particularly remember, my husband came back and said, "Don't you see anything different?" and finally he held out his arm and said, "Here is another stripe." It didn't matter to me.'

In his role as commander-in-chief, Dönitz began regularly attending conferences with Hitler. This close contact bolstered the embattled Führer's faith in him. His positive response to almost any inquiry was exactly what Hitler needed to boost his flagging energies.

As grand admiral, Dönitz moved into a large, turn-of-the-century house in Dahlem, a Berlin suburb. With his promotion he received a grant of three hundred thousand Reichsmarks, which he used to furnish his new house lavishly. Now guarded by a full-time SS contingent, Dönitz issued his first staff directive. It showed his Prussian upbringing still in absolute control: 'Our life belongs to the state. Our honour lies in our duty-fulfilment and readiness for action. No one has the right to private life. The question for us is winning the war. We have to pursue this goal with fanatical devotion and the most ruthless determination to win.'

He applied that same single-minded devotion to his role as commander-in-chief. His work habits were strenuous despite his new rank, with visits to Ursula reduced to only several a year. He was quickly under pressure in the Atlantic war. Although the Germans did not yet know it, the British had cracked the Enigma code used by U-boats for communication. Naval losses skyrocketed. U-boat sinkings spiralled to more than twenty a month throughout 1943. Eventually, more than twenty-five thousand of the forty thousand Germans who served in U-boats were killed. One of those who died in May 1943 was Dönitz's son, Peter. The grand admiral showed no emotion when he learned of Peter's death. 'How can one feel when a son is killed in war?' says Ursula.

Dönitz lost himself further in the war effort. Throughout 1943 and 1944 the grand admiral spent days at a time at the Führer's headquarters. He was not a mere sycophant under Hitler's spell, but instead a leader who took control of discussions and wrested many concessions from the Führer.

During his military service, Dönitz had virtually no contact with the SS extermination programme for Jews. Although he gave some anti-Semitic speeches condemning the 'Jewish poison in the Reich', he later claimed that the more virulent ones were written for him by Goebbels's propaganda ministry, and that in some cases he did not even deliver them. He was unconnected with the physical excesses in the East, although at Nuremberg he was charged with utilizing twelve thousand concentration-camp labourers in the navy's crash building programmes. But the use of slave labour does not establish that Dönitz knew the details of the Final Solution. Although he was at a conference in Posen in the autumn of 1943, when Himmler informed senior party members of the extermination programme, some ministers claim Dönitz had left by the time of the Reichsführer's talk. Ursula never remembers her father being anti-Semitic and does not believe her father knew the details of the Final Solution until the Nuremberg trial. 'Although my father's rank was high, his work, even with Hitler, was concerned only with the navy,' she says. 'I think my father was also shocked by what happened in the East.'

At Nuremberg, after watching a film of the concentration camps with his head in his hands, he excitedly told the prison psychiatrist, 'How can they accuse me of knowing such things? They ask why I didn't go to Himmler to find out about the concentration camps; why, that's preposterous! He would have kicked me out just as I would have kicked him out if he'd come to investigate the navy! What in God's name did I have to do with these things? It was only by chance that I rose to a high position, and I never had a thing to do with the party.' What seems probable is that Dönitz was willing to follow Nazi policies against any enemy of the state, whether external ones like Britain or the United States or internal ones like communists and Jews. Whatever he heard about the extermination programme during the last years of the war, he did not consider it his duty to investigate.

By late 1943 Dönitz had more on his mind than internal enemies of the Reich. He was committed to Hitler's idea of defending 'fortress Europe' from an Allied invasion. Consumed with stopping the imminent assault, he issued 'reckless attack' orders, the equivalent of suicide directives, to the U-boats. He urged them to stop Allied landing ships at all costs, even if it meant losing their own ships.

In May 1944, just before the Allied invasion, Dönitz suffered another personal tragedy. His son Klaus was killed off the south coast of England when a reconnaissance ship, on which he was a guest of the commander, suffered a direct hit from a French destroyer. After several days his body washed ashore on the French coast.

When Dönitz received the news on 14 May, his aides remember, he showed no emotion and continued to work. After the morning U-boat briefing he left to tell his wife, but was back at headquarters, together with his wife, in time for a one o'clock luncheon with the Japanese ambassador. The luncheon went off without a hint that the Dönitzes had just lost their second son. When the Japanese contingent left, Ingeborg Dönitz collapsed.

Two weeks later, Dönitz met Ursula and her family for a holiday in Badenweiler. Again he did not talk about his son's death. 'During this holiday, the hotel we went to had a firm policy not to accept children,' Ursula recalls. 'My father told them, "I am the grandfather, and if you don't take my grandchildren, then you don't take me." They changed the policy for us. He needed this holiday because of his worries and problems. We avoided talking about the war because we realized the purpose was to give my father a break from his pressing work.'

But he did not relax. Four days into the holiday he was awakened in the middle of the night: the Allies had invaded and achieved complete tactical and strategic surprise. To Ursula it was a sign the war was lost. 'Even though all the radio reports were quite positive, they were all propaganda. When the Normandy landings took place I could tell from my father's reaction that it was very serious.'

The invasion news infuriated Dönitz. His U-boats had played no role. Although the invasion shattered his concept of 'fortress Europe', it strengthened his resolve for battle. Dönitz's 1944 speeches are among his most inflexible. As the war worsened he echoed the Führer's calls for resistance to the bitter end. His Prussian upbringing never faltered. The more adverse the situation, the more polished his armour-plated confidence. His enthusiasm was infectious at the Führerbunker. Even the acid-tongued Goebbels noted that Dönitz constantly made a 'fine, imposing impression' and that Hitler thought him the 'best man in his arm of the service'. As Dönitz's importance increased, Hitler protected him with a five-ton armoured Mercedes, and forbade him to fly since the risk was too great.

Dönitz earned Hitler's trust. Even in February 1945, when

Albert Speer pulled him aside during a conference and pleaded that something must be done since the war situation was disastrous, Dönitz refused. He told Speer, 'The Führer knows what he is doing.'

That same month, Ursula moved north of Berlin with her children. 'I went to my parents' house,' Ursula recalls. 'I was there when a housemaid rushed into my room in the morning and said the Russians were very close and their tanks were advancing. My father then sent me and the children to Schleswig Holstein. No one wanted to be captured by the Russians. We had all heard the stories of the Russian atrocities.

'I arrived in Schleswig-Holstein with four pieces of luggage and two and three-quarter children [Ursula gave birth to a second son the following month]. Then my mother arrived and helped as a nurse in the hospital. She came with nothing. Although my father had sent some silver, carpets and personal goods, they were not much, and they were all stolen anyway. When I gave birth, on the way to the hospital, enemy planes flew overhead and forced us to hide in a trench. The war was everywhere by this time. My only comfort was that my father and husband were together. I felt better that their fate was linked in this way.'

What Ursula did not know was that, by April, her father was the only ranking officer bringing optimistic reports to Hitler. By the middle of the month Dönitz issued a stinging proclamation supporting Hitler and rallied his troops with the ultimate battle cry, 'It is, then, victory or death!' He rejected all efforts at peace negotiations and echoed Hitler's view that the German people and nation should be destroyed if they capitulated. Boundless optimism certainly affected Hitler's decision to appoint Dönitz his successor.

At 6.35 p.m. on 30 April, Bormann sent Dönitz an urgent message. It made no mention of Hitler's death, but said in full: 'Grossadmiral Dönitz. In place of the former Reichsmarschall Göring, the Führer appoints you, Grossadmiral, as his successor. Written authority on the way. You should immediately take all measures which the current situation requires. Bormann.'

Dönitz was stunned. Ursula was not so surprised when she heard the news a day later. 'I don't remember how I heard of my father's appointment as chief of the Riech. It was not impossible to talk to my father during this time, but it had become much more difficult. The news of that appointment, it's hard to explain, but I thought he could do almost anything, and now he was just in another position, just higher up. At that time everything was upside down, and the death of Hitler was one of many events.'

Although aware the war was lost, Dönitz tried to postpone the surrender so Germans could evacuate westward ahead of the Russians. His government went through the motions until 23 May, when he personally surrendered. Convinced that he had fought a fierce but fair war, he hoped for a quick release so he could return to rebuilding postwar Germany. 'Neither I nor my father ever expected him to be charged with any crimes,' Ursula says. 'This was just not something we thought of.' They both soon realized the Allies had different ideas. He was initially moved to Bad Mondorf, where Göring and the rest of the party and SS hierarchy were detained. By late summer he was moved with some of the other prisoners to Nuremberg. There he waited for news of his fate, furious that he was not accorded the special prisoner-of-war treatment called for by his high rank.

Unknown to Dönitz and his family, a heated debate between the Allies had taken place over his inclusion in the list of major Nuremberg war criminals. The British admiralty had issued a long opinion arguing that while Raeder, the navy's first chief, could be indicted, Dönitz had merely conducted a naval war in accord with accepted international rules. The British viewed his conduct as no different from that of any of the Allied navies. The French and Russians were ambivalent about Dönitz's inclusion. Only because of the insistence of the Americans was he named as a defendant. He was charged under three of the four counts: conspiracy to wage aggressive war, crimes against peace, and war crimes. When he was informed of the charges he scoffed, 'None of these indictments concerns me in the least; typical American humour.'

Ursula learned of the indictment on the radio and was 'shocked. I didn't know what to think or to say or do. It was all so abnormal.' She tried to understand the charges against him as she settled into postwar life in occupied Germany. 'We were in the British zone. It was good there. No one ever came to ask us a single question. But I know that in the American zone all the wives and children were thrown into the camps. The Americans were much worse. There was a story widely told at the time that a general music director was put into a camp by the Americans because he had the title "general".

'There were many changes for all of us. My home and my parents' home in the north, we never saw those again. They were just taken from us intact. Our personal belongings were all looted. It was impossible to complain about that. But I was still happy. The war was over and my father and husband were still alive.'

Ursula's worries were over the charges against her father. But the prosecution did not have an easy case against Dönitz. Not only was he represented by one of the trial's best defence lawyers, a young naval officer named Otto Kranzbühler, but the prosecution had difficulty in finding facts to use against him. It was hard to establish crimes against peace since the war had been raging for three and a half years before he achieved real power. As a result, the bulk of the case went into proving war crimes.

Here difficulties abounded. The laws of naval warfare are ambiguous. The indictment charged 'murder and ill treatment . . . of prisoners on the high seas' but did not include a single incident. The crux of the case became the 1942 *Laconia* order. But the order's ambiguity was to Dönitz's advantage.

Kranzbühler presented an aggressive defence. But Dönitz did not help his own case. As a witness he was stiff and appeared arrogant, often arguing with the prosecutors. The facts behind the navy's use of twelve thousand concentration-camp labourers incensed the tribunal. Dönitz's defence of a wartime speech in which he condemned the 'spreading poison of Jewry' was to say that 'the spreading poison might have had a disintegrating effect on people's power of endurance'. These sentiments generated little sympathy for him. Fortunately for Dönitz, the tribunal did not have a copy of another wartime speech in which he said he would rather eat dirt than allow his grandson to grow up in 'the Jewish spirit and filth'. Of the fifty-two copies made for distribution, fifty-one had been destroyed. The one that escaped detection was not discovered until after Nuremberg.

During this time, Ursula listened to daily radio reports. 'I would get news summaries of the trials. The German broadcasts were controlled by the British and Americans. There was one correspondent I specifically remember because he was very mean-spirited and it was very hard for me. For the first time I heard about the excesses in the East, the killings. I was shocked, the same as I believe my father must have been at the trial.'

Ursula was heartened when Kranzbühler called several effective witnesses, including her husband, Günther. 'My husband went to the trial under the protection of the British. And after he testified, the Americans arrested him for no reason! They kept him over a year and never told us where he was or why he was in prison. Every one or two months I would get a letter from him and when I would write back he would already be in another camp.'

While her husband was detained, her father's case was bolstered from an unexpected source – Admiral Chester Nimitz, the highly respected wartime commander of the US Pacific fleet. His views on naval law were considered authoritative. Sent written questions by Kranzbühler, Nimitz responded with reassuring news for Dönitz. Nimitz said that from the date of Pearl Harbor, 7 December 1941, the Americans had practised 'unrestricted warfare' throughout the Pacific. US submarines had orders almost identical to German U-boats: not to help survivors if such action placed them at any risk. The Nimitz statement dealt the prosecution a major blow. It appeared the tribunal would either have to decide that both navies had acted criminally and both their commanders should stand trial, or that each side had reasonably interpreted existing law and no war crimes had been committed.

During this time, Ursula visited her father in Nuremberg. 'It was the first time I saw him after the war. We already knew we could not go to the trial, so this was our opportunity to see him.

'When I saw him there was a cage between us and guards all around. There was a row of seats on each side of me for the other families of the men charged as war criminals. The visit was short, less than an hour. They would not let me come more than once. I wanted to go more often to see him. I remember we took Göring's daughter back with us. She was a child, but very excited about riding in our car.

'I also met Kranzbühler at this time. He was young and seemed very earnest. Defending my father was a most important assignment for him. He instilled confidence in me.'

Ursula hoped the Nimitz testimony would exonerate her father. This quandary split the judges. The American judge, Francis Biddle, argued that Dönitz must be acquitted because of the Nimitz affidavit. Biddle said, 'Germany waged a much cleaner war than we did.' But the other judges were persuaded by the British argument that even if both sides broke the law, that did not clear Dönitz. Of the judges who voted him guilty of waging aggressive war and of war crimes, a majority carried the day with a ten-year sentence.

Ursula was deeply disappointed by the verdict. 'I heard it on the radio,' she recalls. 'It was a shock for me. It was hard to say, but I had hoped he would be free. I did not think they had proven he did anything wrong. It seemed like a nightmare, not at all real. But I later learned that he actually thought they would condemn him to death.'

In an interesting twist, the tribunal allowed Biddle, who voted for acquittal, to write the Dönitz verdict. It is the most poorly conceived of the trial, creating considerable confusion because it does not set forth the basis of the conviction, probably since Biddle himself did not know it. When Dönitz was sentenced by the tribunal his eyes blazed at the judges. After hearing his sentence he banged the earphones against the podium and angrily stormed out of the courtroom. Kranzbühler used the poorly worded verdict to appeal against his client's sentence, but to no avail.

During this time, Ursula was adapting to postwar life. 'My family was better off than most. We had shelter, firewood and over seven hundred pounds of potatoes. The children were healthy, and we lived in a beautiful landscape, not in a damaged town.' But her father had been sentenced as a war criminal and her husband was still missing in the American prison camps. 'My mother was working as an assistant at the local hospital,' Ursula recalls. 'The men were gone from the family. It was also a hard time.'

After the executions of the condemned, seven prisoners remained at Nuremberg. In his postwar memoirs Albert Speer recalled conversations with Dönitz in the prison yard; the admiral complained bitterly about the lack of Nuremberg justice, convinced the Germans had not acted differently from the victors.

By mid-1947, Ursula was finally reunited with her husband. 'Kranzbühler went to the English and said, "He came freely to testify and then you allowed him to be arrested." So an English officer went to the American zone and went from camp to camp looking for my husband. I lived in the countryside at this time, not even a town or village, and one night I was woken from a deep sleep by the sound of a car engine, actually a jeep. When I looked out of the window, it was my husband. The English officer had brought him back to me after a year. My husband told me the treatment in the American camps was not very good.'

In July 1947, the Nuremberg prisoners were transferred to Spandau and Dönitz became Prisoner Number 2. 'At Spandau, he looked terrible,' Ursula remembers. 'On the first trip to visit him I went on my own. Later I would go with my son or daughter. My son found it quite exciting with the guards and all. He was only seven and when I told him he would visit his grandfather in jail he said, "So, if you lose the war you must go to jail." He thought this was normal.

'[My father] had on wooden shoes and his clothes were terrible. When the Russians controlled the prison the men went hungry. It hurt me to see him like that. I could never reach over and touch him. In the beginning we could only stay for half an hour. There was always a guard nearby and we could only talk about the family or general matters, no politics of any kind. I did not want him in that prison. It was very emotional for me.' Ursula so disliked seeing her father in prison that she visited infrequently. She saw him only eleven times in seven years.

Although angered by his imprisonment and cut off from his family, Dönitz adapted quickly to the hard Spandau régime. He had the shortest sentence and was more accustomed than the other prisoners to a Spartan existence and disciplined work. And his spirits were bolstered by the smuggled news that an organization of ex-naval officers had organized a massive publicity campaign to erase the stigma of his conviction and make him a national hero. Dönitz liked the public effort, and actually contemplated a return to politics, even as head of state.

Yet, with Dönitz still far removed from a release date, his family barely kept abreast of their monthly bills. 'My mother's salary was not much from her hospital work. I had some savings. The British never came and asked what we had.'

Ursula's mother, Ingeborg, was upset that the government only gave her a pension appropriate to a captain's rank. The authorities claimed that Dönitz owed his promotions above that rank to Hitler. When the news reached him in Spandau, he was infuriated. Mixed with his anger towards the government treatment of his family was evidence that he had not wavered in his attitude to Hitler. Repeatedly, Dönitz told his fellow prisoners he would do it all over again, in exactly the same way. One day he chastised Speer when he heard him talk negatively about the Führer. In his prison diary for that day, Speer noted: 'To this day Hitler is his Commander-in-Chief.'

Dönitz maintained his equilibrium in Spandau by involving himself in hard work and disciplined tasks. His letters to his family showed continuing disappointment at his postwar treatment. During the Cold War tension, the Berlin blockade and the rearming of West Germany by the Allies, Dönitz and some other prisoners thought their release was imminent. Appeals to the Americans for an early release were quashed in 1952 by the Russians, who demanded he serve his full sentence. 'I never thought my father's sentence would be commuted,' Ursula says.

The following year there were rumours of a neo-fascist attempt to obtain Dönitz's freedom and make him Germany's new leader. When Speer asked him about the rumour, Dönitz announced, 'I am and will remain the legal head of state, until I die.' When Speer protested that there was a new West German president, Dönitz said, 'He was installed under pressure from the occupying powers.' Another prisoner, Konstantin von Neurath, said of him that the idea of leading Germany had become 'an obsession with him'.

In mid-1953 Dönitz's spirits were lifted when a German opinion poll showed that 46 per cent of the public had a good opinion of him and only 7 per cent a bad one. (Surpisingly, 24 per cent still thought favourably of Hitler.)

Dönitz did not have a good relationship with most of the other prisoners. Instead, he spent much of his time alone, occupied by voluminous reading and contemplating his own memoirs. On the final day of his imprisonment, 30 September 1956, he attacked Speer, accusing him of recommending his appointment as Hitler's replacement. 'What did I have to do with politics? But for you, Hitler would never have had the idea of making me head of state. All my men have commands again. But look at me! My career is wrecked!' Speer yelled back, accusing Dönitz of being more concerned with his career than with the fifty million killed during the war. Only during that final night did Speer feel any sympathy for the former admiral. Dönitz went from cell to cell to shake hands with the remaining prisoners; Speer says he later heard him crying in the adjoining cell. Only at that moment did Speer realize that the prison pressures were so great that even the 'strong-nerved Dönitz' quietly wept during his last hours of confinement.

It is impossible to check Speer's story against Dönitz's version of their conversations, because in later years the former grand admiral refused to read Speer's books or be drawn into a discussion about him. Ursula has not read the Speer account, either, but views all of it with 'scepticism'.

On the stroke of midnight, Donitz was released. 'My mother went to pick him up and then I met him shortly after,' Ursula recalls. 'I felt fantastic! It was one of the happiest days of my life.' But it did not take Ursula long to realize that the ten years in prison had made changes in her father. 'A curtain had fallen,' she said. 'After Spandau he was more withdrawn, less able to show any feelings.'

After his release, he moved into two rented rooms in a villa outside Hamburg. While it was not very grand, he enjoyed the surrounding countryside, and it was convenient for reunions with his U-boat comrades. His pension had been raised to the amount designated for the rank of admiral, only two ranks below his last post, and while the family did not have a lot of money, they were comfortable. He had barely been released from prison when he began his memoirs. In 1958 they were published as *10 Jahre und 20 Tage* (Ten Years and Twenty Days) and was exclusively about his actions as a naval officer. The book's discussion of the Third Reich was designed to separate the German navy from the criminal side of the Nazi régime and to reinforce Dönitz's emerging reputation as an honourable but hard officer. The positive reviews showered on the book in Britain and America indicated that he largely succeeded in those goals.

One of his major critics who criticized the book was Speer, who read a smuggled copy in Spandau. He felt it was 'the book of a man without insight. For him, the tragedy of the recent past is reduced to the miserable question of what mistakes led to the loss of the war. But should this surprise me?'

During the early 1960s, as Dönitz slowly realized that he was part of a past which modern-day Germany no longer wanted to embrace, he abandoned his idea of entering political life. Instead, he attended many U-boat gatherings, visited old comrades, and gave interviews to numerous historians. Ursula remembers that her father had a reason for helping historians. He hoped that some of them would see the past as he saw it.

In May 1962 his beloved Ingeborg died. 'If he was withdrawn before my mother's death,' Ursula says, 'he was much worse afterwards. Looking back, I now realize he was happy when he was first released from prison, happy to be free. But later the Federal Republic ignored him and the navy wanted nothing to do with him. This made him very bitter. They acted as though he didn't exist. His whole life had been dedicated to the navy. Even today under Kohl it would be the same. The politicians ordered no one to deal with him because of his Nuremberg conviction. This really hurt him.'

The seventy-one-year-old Dönitz, now alone except for three or four visits annually from Ursula, concentrated on his grand years during the war. 'He dwelt on this subject,' Ursula remembers, 'but it was hard for him to talk about it. Instead, he read many books on the period and thought they were mostly horrible. When they were like that it made him more bitter and closed him off even more.' His frustration prompted him to work on a new volume of memoirs. *Mein wechselvolles Leben* (My Changing Life), a diatribe against the Nuremberg proceedings, was published in 1968. In yet another volume, *40 Fragen an Karl Dönitz* (Forty Questions to Karl Dönitz), he quoted from some of the hundreds of unsolicited letters he had received from former enemies. They typically expressed great sympathy at his sentence, which most considered a travesty of justice. He also revelled in the opinion of British and American naval authorities that he was the most dangerous enemy they ever faced.

However, during the early 1970s several books reconsidering the navy's role in waging aggressive war upset Dönitz's political rehabilitation. They exposed the grand admiral's total identification with Hitler. When the BBC interviewed him in 1973 for a documentary on U-boats, they found him suspicious of any questions about National Socialism or Hitler. He refused to answer most questions without checking the books that lined his walls.

That does not surprise Ursula, who had watched his spiritual deterioration since Spandau. In addition to his intolerant nature, there was worsening deafness. His visits to the Hesslers were infrequent. Ursula even felt that he liked being alone when they left him after their occasional visits.

A highlight came in 1976 when two American authors published a book entitled *Dönitz at Nuremberg: A Reappraisal*. The highly favourable book prompted a brief effort to clear the eighty-five-year-old grand admiral's name. Dönitz and his former colleagues thought the book was vital to his rehabilitation. But as had happened many times before, the Federal Republic refused to hear any of it. They refused to allow him to have any official contact with the West German navy. They ignored all attempts to clear his name. Again, he was embittered at their rejection. By the autumn of 1980 his health was failing. After several weeks in a hospital, the nearly blind, nearly deaf eighty-nine-year-old man was taken back to his house. Each morning his loyal comrades from the U-boat service visited and fed him, read him the newspapers, and typed out his letters. At Christmas, they attended in groups, singing carols and sea songs.

Ursula was there on Christmas Eve, in the early evening, when his heart finally failed. 'I was sitting by his side, stroking his head. And then after some time he rested his head back and slept and I knew he was gone.' She is choked with emotion at the memory of his death. 'He had a good life, but a hard life.'

Dönitz and his former colleagues had fervently hoped for a state funeral. He had often told his pastor that he prayed every Sunday that the government would place the black, red, and gold flag of West Germany over his coffin. The flag was draped over the coffin, but no government representative attended. Wearing any World War II uniform at the funeral was prohibited. 'All the men who knew him and were still alive loved him,' says Ursula. 'His funeral was so crowded, with over a thousand people, but not a single member of the German government.' The mourners, from all branches of the German military and the Nazi party, packed the local Lutheran church for the service early in January. Wolf Hess was the only child of another prominent National Socialist to attend. He had come to pay tribute to a 'true soldier' in the German war effort.

'I must say in looking back on my life, it was never a disadvantage to be the daughter of the grand admiral,' Ursula says. 'I never had anyone say anything critical to me. On the contrary, people often have very kind things to say once they know who I am. Countless people have come to tell me what a great man my father was. My eldest son, whose name of course was Hessler, began using the name Dönitz-Hessler from the age of fourteen. Never in his life did he have any problem with this, not even a slight word in the negative about his grandfather. It would have been different if my father had been in the SS, although not all SS were bad, but he was in the navy and well respected.

'I am proud of my father. No one can change my mind on this. I am not happy that my father has the title "war criminal" but there is nothing I can do about it. But it is not important to me because I know he is not a criminal, and that is all that matters.'

The daughter of the last Führer lives next door to a Turkish family; some observers say Turks are Germany's new Jews. 'Many things have changed since the time of my father,' she told me. When I last left her, I noticed the concrete underpass outside her home had been sprayed with large black painted letters, 'Auslander Raus!' (Foreigners Out!). Maybe things have not changed as much as Ursula Dönitz thought.

CHAPTER 8

Operation Valkyrie

A coup against the Nazi leadership was planned by the German resistance for March 1943. Details of the revolt were set by two German generals; after Hitler's assassination, the army was prepared to smash any Nazi resistance, take the reins of government and strike a peace deal with the Allies. The key was killing Hitler. It was no easy task. Surrounded by an elite SS bodyguard, Hitler changed his schedule constantly to avoid any potential trap. He had not made a public appearance since 1942, and access was restricted to the most trusted and ranking officers. Even his oversized cap was lined with three and a half pounds of steel plating.

The conspirators decided to bomb the Führer's plane. The advantage was that the explosion might look like an accident, eliminating resistance from Hitler supporters. The decision was finalized after the plotters obtained several state-of-the-art British bombs. One was used in 1942 to kill Reinhard Heydrich, the SS officer in charge of implementing the Final Solution. The English explosives were considered superior because their fuses did not make the low hissing sound that gave away the German devices.

Two explosive packets were disguised as a couple of brandy bottles, and an unsuspecting colonel took them aboard the Führer's plane on 13 March 1943. As the bomb was given to the colonel, one of the conspirators reached inside the small parcel and started the timing mechanism. There was no clock. The ingenious design held a small bottle, which when broken released a corrosive chemical which ate away a wire and then released the critical spring to the detonator. The explosion was expected thirty minutes after take-off. Two hours later the conspirators were stunned to learn that Hitler had landed safely at Rastenburg. The bomb was not discovered, and two days later one of the plotters retrieved it at great personal risk. The wire had dissolved but the denonator had not fired.

The conspirators, fearful that Himmler's SS was close to exposing their multi-year effort, immediately reorganized for another attempt on Hitler. Eight days later the opportunity presented itself when Hitler, Göring, and Himmler were present at a ceremony for German war heroes. After a speech, Hitler was scheduled for a thirty-minute tour of captured Russian war trophies. A colonel in the conspiracy vowed a suicide mission: He planned to place two bombs in his overcoat, then stay close to the Führer until they exploded. The bomb fuses were set for ten minutes, but the cold weather on the scheduled day meant they would corrode for fifteen to twenty minutes before exploding. Hitler changed his plans at the last moment to an eight-minute review. The bombs could not be set.

There were three further 'overcoat operations' in 1943, and each was similarly frustrated. Attempts to bomb the Führer at staff meetings were missed on another three occasions due to last-minute schedule changes.

By the late spring of 1943, the conspiracy was on the defensive, with several plotters in the inner circle arrested by the Gestapo. Two prominent field-marshals who had been courted by the resistance further demoralized the movement by reaffirming their faith and loyalty to Hitler. The conspirators had lost much of their commitment and heart. They seemed disorganized and unable to mount a successful attempt to remove the stain of National Socialism.

By the autumn of 1943 one man almost single-handedly reversed the dismal situation – Colonel Claus von Stauffenberg. A thirty-six-year-old army officer of astonishing gifts, he used his dynamic personality, the sharpness of his mind and his considerable talents as an organizer to breathe new life into the movement against Hitler. Not only did he revive the flagging effort to remove him, but less than a year later it was Stauffenberg who made the physical assassination attempt. His name has justifiably come to symbolize the movement against Hitler.

Stauffenberg had five children. Franz Ludwig Schenk was the

third child, born on 4 May 1938. As are his brothers and was his father, he is a German count.[21] At the age of thirty-four he was elected to the Bundestag, and today he is a member of the European parliament and chairman of its legal committee. He remembers wartime events distinctly and has carefully analysed his father's role in the movement against Hitler, as well as his own feelings as the son of a German officer who earned fame not for what he did for the Third Reich but for what he did to bring it to an end. His experience is in marked contrast to those children whose fathers' careers revolved around allegiance to the Führer.

Claus Philip Schenk von Stauffenberg was born on 15 November 1907, the youngest of three sons of one of the oldest and most distinguished South German families. Through his mother, Countess von Uxküll-Gyllenband, he was a great-grandson of Neithardt von Gneisenau, one of the heroes of the war of liberation against Napoleon and a co-founder of the Prussian general staff. Through her, he was also related to Yorck von Wartenburg, another celebrated general of the Bonaparte era. Claus's father had been Oberhofmarschall – privy chamberlain – to the late king of Württemburg. The family was solidly Catholic and highly cultivated.

Stauffenberg grew up in a massive, turreted Renaissance château which had been the ancient seat of counts and dukes. Strikingly handsome and with a fine physique, he excelled both academically and in sports. Developing a passion for horses which qualified him for a place in the German Olympic team, he also exhibited an inquisitive and intelligent mind that pursued literature and the arts; he spoke fluent Greek and Latin.

'My father was raised in an environment in which humanitarian liberal ideas were very strong,' says Franz Ludwig. 'I do not mean "liberal" in the American sense, but in the continental European way. It was the Stuttgart environment of many professors and literates, and philosophers and the like. It gave my father a very specific mix which I think was quite important for his ideas and also his relation to the Catholic Church.

'It is true, definitely true, that my father was influenced by Stefan George [a German poet of the late nineteenth and early twentieth centuries]. He was greatly influenced by him, and his early experiences in growing up were affected by the writings of George. But I also think that in many accounts of my father the extent to which George was an influence has been exaggerated. It was an important part of his life, but it is not the explanation for everything he did. It was not the main influence in his life, but an important one.'

For a while, young Stauffenberg considered a musical career, then architecture; but at the age of nineteen, in 1926, he entered the army as an officer cadet in the famed Bamberg Cavalry Regiment.

During the hectic years of German economic unrest and the Nazi rise to power, Stauffenberg remained an apolitical military officer. In 1930, he met seventeen-year-old Nina von Lerchenfeld, descended from a line of the Bavarian nobility. They married after a three-year betrothal. 'There is no question and no doubt they had a very good marriage,' says Franz Ludwig. 'She also came from a fine family, similar to my father's lineage and background. One item to note: my father was Catholic and my mother was Lutheran. On the other hand, my father's mother was already Lutheran, so it was not totally strange or unknown to him. The children were brought up as Catholics. In these families like mine, that was the traditional way. The religion went with the father's side, the name, the family's tradition.'

By 1936, when Stauffenberg was posted to the war academy in Berlin, he and his wife had started a family; their first son was born in 1934. In Berlin, his all-round brilliance attracted the attention of ranking German officers and in two years he emerged as a twenty-nine-year-old officer of the high command. He was a dedicated patriot, and according to Franz Ludwig, 'basically a monarchist. He was not dogmatic. He saw in the monarchy a better type of constitution than the one that existed in the Weimar Republic.

'He was not an early addict of Hitler, and I have seen this information published. I would not have much of a problem if it were so. It would be very decent for a young man to be quite enthusiastic and then to change his mind as he discerned and saw new facts which brought him to a new conclusion. But it was not like this. My father was not a definite opponent from the very beginning, but he was not a disciple or an addict in any way. It was not in his character or his personality. This report of my father is simply not true.'

Franz Ludwig is correct. His father, while not opposed to National Socialism in the mid-1930s, was certainly far from a slavish follower of Hitler. Stauffenberg's first doubts about the Nazi programmes came during the virulent anti-Jewish campaigns of 1938, the year Franz Ludwig was born. But when the war started in September 1939, Stauffenberg was willing to perform his duty. He did so with characteristic energy and talent, earning a solid reputation as an officer in the Sixth Panzer Division's campaigns in both Poland and France. In early June 1940, just before the Dunkirk assault, he was transferred to the army high command. And for the first eighteen months of Operation Barbarossa, the Russian campaign, he spent most of his time in Soviet territory. There he witnessed first-hand the brutality of the SS. His Russian service disillusioned him with the Third Reich.

During his service at the front, Stauffenberg obtained leave for major holidays, especially Christmas. Franz Ludwig's first recollections of his father date from these brief visits to the family when he was three, in 1941. 'I recall quite well my father because it was always a very important and special occasion when he came home for a short holiday or Christmas. My earliest memories go back to Wuppertal, where the family lived until 1942. My family fled from there when there was a real danger of bombing raids. It came within the range of British bombers by 1942, so since it was safer in southern Germany, we went to my grandmother's home [father's side]. It was a nice but not extraordinary estate, but it was the first place I considered my home. It has very good memories for me, and I am more attached to it than to any other place in my childhood. After the war we stayed there until 1953.

'The gatherings at my grandmother's house were quite large family affairs. We all adored my father. He was *the* important person in our family, in our opinion, because it was always a rare occasion, always some type of holiday when he came and, as far as I remember, he paid quite some attention to his children – going for a walk, or playing in a sand-pit with us, or explaining different toys to us, and that sort of thing. I have very positive memories of my father at that time.'

Stauffenberg's visits to his family were welcome respites from the deteriorating situation on the Russian front. The unnecessary disaster at Stalingrad in February 1943 further alienated him from Hitler's strategy. As soon as the battle for Stalingrad finished, he asked for a transfer to a new front, and he was sent to the Tenth Panzer Division in Tunisia, just in time to join the last days of the fierce battle for the Kasserine Pass.

On 7 April 1943, his car drove into a minefield and he was seriously wounded. He lost his left eye and suffered injuries to his left ear and knee. He also lost his right hand, and the surgeons had to amputate part of that arm as well as the ring and little fingers of his left hand. The doctors doubted that he would survive; if he did, they thought, he would not regain his sight. 'And I remember very well when he was wounded, with his eyepatch and the stump of his arm, and the two fingers on the other hand also gone, and I remember quite well his firm objections when someone tried to help him with his bandages and dressings,' recalls Franz Ludwig. 'For a very long time he was in a hospital, and not at home, but he came back to us in the early autumn of 1943 for recovery and convalescence. He had been in a military hospital in Munich for most of the time. For quite some time he was not recovering very well. And that was the time he made his most important contacts with the people preparing the plot. And when he agreed to take on staff duties in Berlin, it became important for them.

'I was too young [five years old] to realize how really critical his condition was. We knew that he was badly wounded and that he was in a hospital, but I only learned much later how truly serious it was, and that it was life-threatening. At the time we didn't know that. We just expected his return some day and we waited for him. None of us, my older brothers or me, ever visited my father in the military hospital. It was a very long way away.

'The family reunions with my father were only long when he was recovering in the late summer of 1943. That was a good part of his recuperation. I remember he came to us for Christmas 1943 when we were in Bamberg. He came on the holy eve as a surprise. My mother knew but we didn't know, and it was a great excitement and joy, which I remember quite well.'

Any other man, almost dead from his wounds, would probably have retired from the military and the conspiracy. Stauffenberg did neither. By midsummer, after much practice with the three fingers of his bandaged left hand, he wrote letters to his superiors notifying them of his intention to resume his duties within three months. He also confided to his wife that he felt compelled to act to save Germany. 'We general staff officers must all accept our share of the responsibility,' he told her.

By September 1943 Stauffenberg was back in Berlin as a lieutenant-colonel and chief of staff to General Friedrich Olbricht at the army administrative office. Now with a black eyepatch, the heavily decorated six-foot-three Stauffenberg had become a legendary soldier in the Berlin command. While he settled into his new assignments, he also quickly achieved political control of the disheartened conspirators. He insisted that the new government have an anti-Nazi cabinet, and he recommended a list of potential leaders. Recognizing that the conspiracy needed younger military men ready to mobilize their commands, he persuaded some of the most important German officers to support the coming putsch.

In early 1944, a senior officer let it be known that he would be available to the conspirators: Field-Marshal Erwin Rommel, the celebrated 'Desert Fox'. Stauffenberg and many of the other conspirators did not trust Rommel, considering him a Nazi who was adandoning Hitler only because the war was being lost. Whatever his motivation, Rommel differed from the conspirators on a major point. He was against assassinating Hitler, believing it would make him a martyr. Instead, he thought, Hitler should be tried before a German court for his crimes, while a separate peace was signed with the West and the war continued against the Russians.

However, Stauffenberg and many of his friends realized the West would never accept a separate peace. As the war situation worsened, they speeded up their plans to remove Hitler and take control of the government. The new effort was code-named Valkyrie, after the beautiful maidens in Norse mythology who hovered over the battlefield to select those who would die. In this case, Hitler was to die.

In June 1944, Stauffenberg and many of his colleagues were surprised by the successful Allied landing on the beaches of Normandy. Some of the conspirators thought they should abandon the assassination plans since the end was inevitable, and they did not want to be blamed for bringing about Germany's defeat. But in heated discussions, Stauffenberg convinced the plotters it was critical to kill Hitler to stop needless loss of lives, and to prove to the world that the men of the German resistance dared to take the decisive step against the Nazi dictator, despite incredible personal risks.

By July, he had been promoted to full colonel as chief of staff to the commander-in-chief of the home army. This was a stroke of good luck for the conspirators since it gave him frequent personal contact with Hitler. Stauffenberg was now the key man in the conspiracy. Any chance of success rested on his ability to kill Hitler. He approached his new assignment with the same zeal and determination that marked his entire career. He practised setting off the English-made bombs with his three remaining fingers.

It was during this hectic preparation for the assault against the Nazi machinery that Stauffenberg had his final reunion with his family. 'I distinctly remember a weekend trip to a place where an old great-uncle of mine lived, near Bamberg. It must have been around Pentecost [the seventh Sunday after Easter], perhaps a little earlier. He was home for a short leave and we were able to take this prolonged weekend trip. Motorcars were very rare around this time, so one had to go by rail and then by a little cart with a horse, up the mountain. It was quite a long expedition, and I remember him being with us. It must have been the last time.'

On 11 July, Stauffenberg took a bomb to Berchtesgaden, and although he was with Hitler and Göring for half an hour, he did not release the bomb because Himmler was not present. The conspirators had decided it would be best to kill the three top Nazis simultaneously. A second chance came on 15 July, this time at Rastenburg. Himmler and Göring were not present. Stauffenberg left the room and telephoned his conspirators in Berlin to inform them that though only Hitler was present he was about to plant the bomb anyway. When he returned to the conference room, Hitler had left.

On 20 July, he was again scheduled to meet Hitler, this time at the Wolf's Lair, his East Prussian headquarters. This time, the plotters decided to kill Hitler no matter who was present. Instead of being held in the underground bunker, where the closed area would magnify the blast, the meeting was held in the conference barracks, with all ten windows open because of the hot weather. Walking to the conference with Field-Marshal Wilhelm Keitel, Stauffenberg excused himself on the pretext of having forgotten his cap and belt in an ante-room. There, with his three good fingers, he swiftly opened the briefcase, broke the capsule which started the primitive timer, and then calmly rejoined the waiting Nazis. In ten minutes the bomb would explode.

Inside the conference room, Stauffenberg took his place a few feet to the right of Hitler. He placed his briefcase on the floor, against the stout oak leg of the conference table. With four minutes left, he quietly left the room on the pretext of receiving an important call from Berlin. After he left, one of the other officers leaned over to get a closer look at the war map, and found Stauffenberg's case in his way. He moved it to the far side of the massive table support, unwittingly protecting Hitler from the brunt of the blast. At 12.42 p.m. the bomb exploded. Stauffenberg was standing a couple of hundred yards away observing the scene when he saw the building go up in a roar of smoke and flames. Debris flew in the air and some bodies came out of the windows. Stauffenberg had no doubt that everyone in the room was dead or dying.

Although an immediate alarm was sounded, he talked his way past four armed SS checkpoints. At the nearby airfield, he boarded a plane with its engine running and began the three-hour trip to Berlin. 'This was a crucial period,' says Franz Ludwig. 'He was out of communication with any of the conspirators on the ground, and it cost them the most critical time.'

Unknown to Stauffenberg, Hitler had survived the blast. His back was cut by a falling beam, his legs were burned, his hair was singed, his right arm was temporarily paralysed, and his eardrums were punctured, but he was not seriously hurt. Four others died, and many were critically injured. Meanwhile, with Stauffenberg in the air, the conspirators lost their momentum and leadership. The message from the Wolf's Lair was not clear as to whether Hitler was dead or alive, and as a result no one in Berlin issued the Valkyrie orders to start military operations to take over the government. Everyone waited for Stauffenberg's landing, and when he did arrive in Berlin he was stunned to learn the most critical hours had been lost. No one had even seized the radio headquarters or telephone exchanges. He rallied the plotters, and the conspirators did manage, for the rest of the day, to hold some major buildings and detain some loyal Nazi forces, but the open communication lines slowly carried the word that the Führer had survived. Stauffenberg refused to believe it. But once that news spread, some key officers who had been fence-sitting reverted to supporting Hitler. The news also guaranteed that forces loyal to Hitler were energized for a bitter fight.

At 9 p.m. the conspirators were startled to hear a radio announcement that Hitler would shortly address the nation. By eleven that night the dwindling leadership of the conspiracy was sequestered in the war ministry when a group of loyal Nazis burst in. During the ensuing scuffle, Stauffenberg was shot in his remaining arm. Within half an hour, his former superior officer, General Friedrich Fromm, announced that Stauffenberg and three others had been sentenced by a summary court-martial to immediate execution. Stauffenberg, the sleeve of his wounded arm soaked in blood, was led to a courtyard at the back of the ministry. There an army truck's headlights lit a wall where the condemned men were lined up to be shot. 'Long live our sacred Germany!' Stauffenberg shouted as he fell to the floor, dead at the age of thirty-six.

'Of course, we children knew nothing at all before the plot,' says Franz Ludwig. 'Any information of that kind would have been absolutely irresponsible and suicidal. So we had no idea that anything would happen. What happened was that the next day, the twenty-first, my mother came to our room. It was a large, three-level house and our rooms were in a kind of library, converted for that purpose while we were there, and we were playing and my mother came in and said she had something terrible to tell us – "Papi is dead." That is what I distinctly recall. Of course, it took me some time to realize what that really meant. It was not difficult to realize what death meant, but to realize that it was really Papi. My mother was not crying. She told a little more to my eldest brother, who at that time was ten years old – of course, not the whole truth, but she told him there had been a terrible mistake or error.

'Two days later, during the night, my mother and my great-uncle, who had been there at the time, were taken away to prison when we were all asleep. When we came down for breakfast the next morning, we learned about this. We had a nurse, and I think she told us. Then a couple of days later, my aunt went to Berlin to try to see my father's eldest brother, Berthold. But I do not have a very strong memory of this. What is a stronger memory is that a couple of days later we were told that my grandmother and her sister, a retired Red Cross nurse, had also been arrested and taken away. Again, we didn't know about their arrests until we were told. You see, it was a big house, and there were six children altogether, four of us and two cousins, and there was a maid of my grandmother's who was also in charge of the kitchen, there was a girl to take care of the two cousins, so there was a lot of life going on beyond the small number of actual family.'

Unknown to the Stauffenbergs, isolated on their large estate in southern Germany, Hitler and Himmler had embarked on a brutal campaign of vengeance to stamp out all vestiges of the resistance. There was a wild wave of arrests followed by gruesome torture, kangaroo trials, and sadistic death sentences, including the suspension of victims from slaughterhouse meathooks. Relatives and friends of the suspects were rounded up by the thousand and sent to concentration camps. The Stauffenberg arrests had marked the beginning of the sweep across Germany. Within two months the Gestapo arrested more than seven thousand suspects, and 'people's courts' sentenced 4980 to death.

One of those executed was Count Berthold von Stauffenberg, Claus's older brother. 'I remember my uncle,' Franz Ludwig recalls. 'I remember quite well what he looked like. I can always tell from photos whether he is well represented or not. We saw him on certain holidays. He was a lawyer and a navy judge, and for this reason he was in navy uniform and this was quite exciting for us.'

The third Stauffenberg brother was a professor of ancient history at a university and was above suspicion. Still, the Gestapo arrested him because he was a Stauffenberg. With two of the brothers dead and the adults of the family in prison, the Nazis decided to move against the children.

'Just about this time, I don't recall if it was before my grandmother was taken, but I think so, yes, there were two men who arrived at our house and were introduced to us,' Franz

Ludwig says. 'They took over the household. They ate with us, they took us for walks. They were Gestapo. One was a heavy man, quite big and large, and I think he was the boss. The other was smallish and thin. At that age a child realizes a lot and remembers quite a lot, but doesn't deduce logically the meaning of everything around him. A child just takes things as they are, not looking for explanations of what is going on. It simply happens, and if the grown-ups tell you it is all right, then you simply accept it. Of course, it was extraordinary, and I remember I really didn't like these two, but I can't say I disliked them. I just felt they didn't belong to us. But they took over and behaved like the masters of the house. Then, again after a number of days, we were told we would travel away in a car. We were told it was in a car because that would be more exciting – a car was such a rarity.

'Then something happened which I remember quite well. My grandmother's maid was a devout Catholic. She took us to the village priest, and we went the very short walk to the priest whom we knew well, all six of the children. He talked to us, and he gave us a blessing and told us that quite bad and even ghastly experiences might await us, and that we even might land in a pigsty. But that whatever happened we should always remember that our father was a great man and what he did was good. Of course, this was an extremely dangerous and courageous thing for this priest, because if we had told that story to the Gestapo men, he would have been put into a concentration camp. I remember that evening walk and I remember the maid crying. I knew something very emotional had happened but I didn't realize what it was.

'The next day a car came for us, a black limousine, a big, black thing. On the one hand it was exciting, but on the other hand it was sort of uncomfortable, because one didn't know what was going on and where we were going. For me, there was one very important point: I had two older brothers. I just kept close to them, and they seemed quite confident. As long as they accepted what was going on, it was okay for me. I think it would have been quite different if I had been the only child, or the eldest. But since I wasn't, I could draw my feelings from the way they reacted, and they never panicked. So I felt sufficiently reassured.'

The Stauffenberg children were the first to be rounded up by the Gestapo. Under orders from Himmler, they were transferred to central detention centres until the SS could work out what to do with them. Franz Ludwig remembers part of the trip to the centre. 'One of the Gestapo went with us, I believe the smaller one, but I am not quite sure. The first part of the journey is a blurred memory. I remember we went first to a city, and I think it was Stuttgart. Then we arrived at a place we stayed at until after the war. It was a kind of kindergarten in the Harz mountains, near Göttingen. The place is called Bad Sachsa, a small town on the south slopes of the mountains, now directly on the border between West and East Germany. It was a nice place built around the First World War as a kind of country resort for the children of Bremen. It was nicely planned on a big estate and had several houses, built to hold thirty to thirty-five children each, according to age and sex.

'This was either late July or early August. It all happened very quickly. I stayed there for nearly a year, until June 1945. When we arrived, three of us – my second brother and my male cousin and I – were put together in one house, number three. It was for that age group. My eldest brother went to another house while my female cousin and my sister went to yet another. We were the first to arrive. But shortly afterwards the houses were filled with more and more children. It turned out that these were all children of those involved in the plot or connected to the resistance.'

Suddenly, by late 1944, the SS started reducing the number of children detained. 'We later learned they were taken back to a grandmother or a distant aunt, or whatever,' says Franz Ludwig. 'And then there were only ten of us left again, the six in our family and four others. We learned that three of the others were distant cousins of ours. Their father was a first cousin of my father, and was a liaison man for the resistance between Berlin and Paris. He was a real confidant of my father, and of course he was also killed. Then we were all put together in a single house, so I was together again with my brothers and sister and my cousins.'

During the autumn of 1944, six-year-old Franz Ludwig became ill with a chronic middle-ear infection which progressively worsened. The camp's medical ward tried unsuccessfully to treat him; then he was sent to a specialist in the nearby town of

Nordhausen and from there to a hospital in Erfurt. 'I spent about four to five weeks in the hospital in the department for ears, nose, and throat,' Franz Ludwig remembers. 'And one of the best experts in Germany was there to treat me. I went under surgery, and came out absolutely cured. Looking back, the strange thing is that they really didn't know what to do with us. Instead of being quite glad to have one less of us if something had happened to me, they gave us the best possible medical attention available. Maybe this is typically German. As long as nobody made a final decision about us, everyone took their responsibility quite seriously, because no one knew what would eventually be decided and who would be held responsible. So I got the best possible care.

'But I was taken to the hospital under a false name. From that incident I learned we were all in the camp under false names. My brothers and my sister and my cousin, they were given the name Meister. I remember being checked into the hospital under a different name because it didn't work. I was too stupid for it. We went, for example, to the X-ray, and I had to wait in a room with lots of people waiting with us, and then a nurse would come and say, "Müller, please", or "Meyer, please", and then she would come and say, "Meister, please" and I wouldn't react. And the nurse would say, "It is time to go," and I would say, "Why? Did they say Stauffenberg?" It happened several times. I was never punished for this. Later I found that the entire hospital knew exactly who I was. But it did no damage, so there were no consequences.'

'The reason they changed our names was camouflage. By that time everyone knew the name Stauffenberg. It became a key word for evil in Nazi propaganda, a key word for the traitors.'

Franz Ludwig had been sent to the hospital with a kind, elderly nurse, part guard and part servant, and he enjoyed her company. But his time in Erfurt was also his first contact with the real war. Erfurt was an Allied bombing target, and he remembers that after going to the shelters, 'when we came up we saw the damage to the city. It was frightening, but also exciting. I don't remember being horrified.'

Franz Ludwig returned to the Bad Sachsa camp after St Nicholas's Day, the sixth of December. During that Christmas season, the Stauffenberg children, cut off from their family for five months, had their first visit from a relative, a rather extraordinary aunt. Franz Ludwig remembers her and the visit distinctly. 'Alexander, my father's brother who was the university professor was married to a very interesting woman, Melitta. We called her Aunt Lita. She was a flier, a pilot, which was not that common a profession for a woman at that time. She was not merely an adventurer, she was also an engineer and had invented a number of quite important gadgets for night flying. Now, Göring was an extraordinary personality, with the most peculiar traits, and you can hardly understand how Hitler or Himmler even tolerated him. Well, he was a grotesque type of man. Around him, there was a very special core of people all attached to flying, with a kind of team spirit and camaraderie, not necessarily Nazis; quite a number of them found a way to live near him without becoming too infected with Nazi ideology. Some of them had nothing in common with National Socialism, but they were avid flying enthusiasts.

'Now this aunt was known to every flier, to everyone who had anything to do with aviation. She had a number of personal friends in that crowd. When her husband was arrested she tried to do something about it. She was arrested herself. Her friends, with the loyalty of the crew, tried to get her out, and they succeeded. They told the Gestapo that she could have had nothing to do with the Stauffenberg plot and that she was only married to a Stauffenberg and that she was irreplaceable and badly needed in the aviation field; no one else could fill her position. And when released she said fine, but she wouldn't go to work unless they met two conditions. First, she would always know where her husband and the rest of her family was, and she regarded all of us as her family. Second, that she would have the opportunity to visit all of us. She was granted both these requests. She was very courageous; she took a great risk and succeeded. Not only was she promised the information, but she got it. She knew where we were taken, and where my mother was taken, where all the family was, and she visited everyone. So as a surprise, she came to us during Christmas 1944. During the holiday, we were asked to the house of the camp director, a woman, and we went over and there was Aunt Lita. And there was a Christmas tree and she wanted to celebrate with us the way we used to, and since it was difficult to get toys, she had gone to a place where they kept war medals, and she took a handful of them and gave them to us. Of course, we felt like real war heroes.

'As a result of this visit, she also could tell my grandmother where we were and that we were well.

'We loved her. She was very exciting. She told the most wonderful stories of her flying and her planes. Christmas was great with her that year.'

During the time Franz Ludwig and his brothers and sister were in Bad Sachsa, their mother, who was pregnant at the time of her arrest, had another child, a daughter born in January 1945. Although Countess Nina and her new child became quite ill, they were slowly nursed back to health in a hospital in Potsdam. Melitta Stauffenberg visited her there and assured her the rest of her children were safe.

By early 1945, Bad Sachsa had been converted to the headquarters for an army division, a change which Franz Ludwig found 'very exciting'. It was also a transit point for hordes of refugees streaming through from the East.

At the time of his detention, Franz Ludwig did not realize that conditions could have been much worse. Bad Sachsa was the detention centre for children up to the age of thirteen. Children aged fourteen and over were placed in a concentration camp near Danzig. When the Eastern front drew too close, that entire group was moved from one camp to another, always one step ahead of the Russians. For a while they were in Buchenwald. They finally ended up in the Alps under SS guards, and in an unusual twist they were liberated by regular German army soldiers, who later turned them over to American troops in northern Italy. Franz Ludwig had several relatives with the older group, and learned from them later of their experience.

As for the Stauffenberg children, they remained in Bad Sachsa until June 1945, although the camp was liberated by Americans in the last days of April. 'We heard the sound of big guns, a deep thundering noise, and we knew we were losing the war from the German soldiers who were stationed at our location,' Franz Ludwig says. 'We knew the enemy was coming nearer and nearer. Then one day we heard fighting nearby and we had to go to the basement of this medical house to a room used like a tool shop. Someone came in and said tanks had arrived and the

Germans had retreated. Then finally the door was pushed open and a small soldier came in with his gun ready, looking about, and someone said that there were only children here, and then a second soldier came in and they seemed satisfied. That was it. The camp was occupied by American soldiers, the whole camp except our house. And that was the first time I had ever seen chocolate. There was a soldier who made friends with a girl who had brought him some water, and while he was in the camp he gave her sweets which were a luxury for us beyond any description.

'The memory I have of the American soldiers is absolutely positive, and not just because of the chocolate. They were friendly, awfully nice, and they were all very young. They played with us and had fun with us.'

After a short period the troops left, but almost immediately after their departure Franz Ludwig's great-aunt - his grand-mother's sister, the former Red Cross nurse – arrived with a female friend. They had found the children through Melitta's information. They had travelled more than three hundred miles through two Allied zones, even persuading the local French commander to lend them his official car, emblazoned with the symbols of the French army. His great-aunt wasted no time in moving them out of Bad Sachsa. Franz Ludwig remembers the concern and the hasty exit. 'There was real fear at the time about how far the Russians would come, that they would come into Bad Sachsa. And the Russians were the key word for terror. They were a menace. Mentioning the Russians, among all Germans, even at my age, was a cause of absolute fright. We felt safe with the Americans, and fairly safe with the French.

'In Bad Sachsa no one really knew anything. There were many rumours, and no one knew which ones were reliable. So we tried to leave in a hurry, and that was difficult, because now there were some fifteen of us to be transported and my aunt had only one car. So she organized a bus which was run on methanol: it looked like a large stove in the front. This was quite common right after the war because of the shortage of oil products. It was not a very efficient energy combustion system, and it was slow and took a long time. My two brothers and I went in the French officer's car. We went first to my grandmother's home in Lautlingen. The bus didn't arrive for several more days and I remember my grandmother was very worried that the bus was so slow the Russians might have caught it.'

While his grandmother fretted over the arrival of the bus, Franz Ludwig was occupied with a new discovery: he had finally learned what his father did during the war. 'I remember well the first time somebody told me what my father had actually done,' he recalls. 'It was the woman who was in the company of my great-aunt picking us up in Bad Sachsa. She went back with the three of us, my two brothers and me, in the car of the French officer, and on the way back she told us, and I remember it was a great revelation to me. Quite astounding. She told us what had happened. Then later, especially when my mother came back, I learned more about it.'

But when Franz Ludwig first arrived at his grandmother's, no one knew the fate of his mother. In July, the family finally learned she was alive. She had escaped from an elderly guard just before the final Russian onslaught on Berlin. An overcrowded train took her to Saxony, and then she walked, carrying her baby in her arms, until she reached Bavaria and some relatives.

'In the meanwhile, my other aunt, wife of Berthold, and my uncle Alexander were back at my grandmother's house,' recalls Franz Ludwig. 'They arrived in a great Mercedes car, and we were very impressed. It belonged to the cardinal of Munich, who had offered his personal car for the journey. But we received very bad news from my other aunt. Melitta did not survive the war. She was shot down in her small aeroplane during the last days of the war. We now know she was intentionally shot down in Bavaria by German troops. The officer in charge of the anti-aircraft guns was told who she was and they said she was trying to get away with the Stauffenberg family jewels to Switzerland.'

Franz Ludwig's grief over Melitta was tempered when he was reunited with his mother in late August. He had not seen her for more than a year. 'When my mother returned it was a great time for us. I didn't notice any major changes in her, but then it was my mother, I was so glad to see her. She had not been treated that much worse in prison because of who she was. She was fortunate that the guards were regular prison guards and not from the SS.

'My mother settled down in Lautlingen, because the house she had inherited from her parents in Bamberg was badly damaged and then pillaged. So we couldn't move there. And after 20 July the Nazis had taken it over and had converted it into a Gestapo office. For the local people, the fact that it had been a Gestapo headquarters was sufficient justification to get inside and take whatever they needed. And at that time everything was needed. Even the window-panes, the plumbing, everything was taken. It took my mother years to get the house in order. She had no money at all.'

Fortunately, Franz Ludwig's grandmother had sufficient space. After the summer of 1945, all the Stauffenberg children entered a local school. Franz Ludwig, then eight years old, recalls the Nuremberg trial at the end of that year and the beginning of 1946. He listened to it from a much more detached perspective than many of the other children interviewed for this book, whose fathers were in the dock. 'I remember the Nuremberg trial quite well. My great-aunt, the one who fetched us from Bad Sachsa, was always very interested in politics, and she listened on the radio to what happened in Nuremberg. Her specific interest was because she had grown up in Stuttgart with one of the accused, Konstantin von Neurath, formerly minister of foreign affairs. She didn't believe that Neurath was capable of doing something evil, but she also never thought he was fit to be foreign minister. She thought he was a nice boy and basically decent, but not a great genius. She knew him personally, but had no contact with him for a very long time. So I listened to the trial broadcasts quite often, and I still remember the broadcast describing the faces of the defendants when the verdicts were announced.'

Although the Stauffenbergs had been a monied and titled family, the immediate postwar era was difficult for them. 'It was certainly not comfortable for us,' Franz Ludwig says. 'But compared to the fate of many others we were reasonably lucky. That was also true at the end of the war in the Bad Sachsa camp. There were great shortages then, and on Sundays we used to get stewed beets, like those they gave to the cattle, and I hated them. We had shortages, we couldn't get sufficient clothing, but we managed in a decent way.

'At home, there were the normal shortages, but very quickly the life was better in the American zone and worse in the French zone. The best was the American. And there was great smuggling between the zones – cigarettes, sugar, wheat, flour, everything.

The people who managed best at this time were the farmers, but we had no farm. Food was rationed and it was not very good but at least we were not hungry. I remember shortages but we did not suffer real hunger. But it took some time for my mother to get any money. My father was an army officer and she received his pension, but it was not much for her and five children. It was not a life of great luxury by any means.'

At the age of thirteen, each Stauffenberg child was sent to a boarding school near Lake Constance in Switzerland. Franz Ludwig stayed there until his final exams, the equivalent of high school, in 1958. He heard about his father in school, 'but I didn't learn anything new about him. He was always described in positive terms. The name Stauffenberg always rang a bell and people knew who I was. The village where I went to early school was part of a town where the Stauffenberg family had come from. I was not the son of a hero Stauffenberg, because Claus Stauffenberg was also a child of the village. We were just children of the old-time family.'

In 1958, at the age of twenty, Franz Ludwig went to the University of Erlangen. He was not accepted for the military draft due to deafness in his right ear from his wartime middle-ear infection. He was prepared to serve in the army, following a long and distinguished family tradition, and was initially surprised and disappointed that he was not accepted into the reserve-officer programme.

At three universities, he studied both law and history. He passed his first law exam in 1962, and was married in 1965. By 1966 he had passed his final exams. He initially worked at an industrial company, as an assistant to the managing director and a member of the legal department. He stayed there five years. In 1972, at the age of thirty-four, Franz Ludwig Stauffenberg was elected to the Bundestag, and was a member for the next twelve years before changing to the European parliament.

His eldest brother is a brigadier-general in the army; he was formerly the German military attaché in London. His second brother is a successful businessman. His younger sister married and had one daughter, but died of leukaemia in 1966. The youngest sister married a Swiss attorney and lives in Zurich with her four children.

Although his father is a genuine hero, Franz Ludwig has still encountered negative reactions to him. 'Several times I have had bad reactions to my father but always anonymous. No one has ever, face to face, said anything openly negative about him. There were people who were sceptical or negative but they kept their mouths shut, or they worded their comments in cautious forms. So I am still quite intrigued that there have been and still are numbers of people who will not accept my father as a hero, who will not see him, or what he has done, in a positive way. But up until now, they either do not have the courage or do not think it appropriate to tell me so.

'There have been unsigned letters, quite a number of them. Quite nasty in tone. There might be letters that said I was just as evil as my father was. You know, the world is full of fools. And if you take public office, you will automatically be the object of letters of this type. So one should really not exaggerate this point. There hasn't been one of these anonymous letters now for quite a few years. It depends, you read these letters and some of them are medical cases, and others are just nasty because they want to be nasty. I have brought some of them to the attention of the police where I thought there might be some criminal intent.

'It is interesting that you don't have to be a National Socialist to be critical of my father. There have been quite a number of people who were critical because, they said, "Why didn't he just kill Hitler by shooting him down?" questioning the courage of what he did. It is a rather simplistic approach, which I don't think is that surprising. What they really show – these types of approaches, questions, or criticisms – is an insufficient knowledge of the facts. First of all, those people obviously do not know much of my father's role in the plot. His main role was not to set the bomb; it was not to kill Hitler, but to be the key man in the organization. It was one of the great weaknesses of the whole plot, that the same man who was to be the key organizer also had to place the bomb. The second point is that they do not know about the physical impediments, the loss of his hand, and the obstacles he had to overcome even to place the bomb.

'I am sure from my experience that the vast majority in the country react positively to the name Stauffenberg.'

Franz Ludwig acknowledges his father's heritage was not a neutral factor for him as he grew up, but he finds it impossible to say whether being the son of Claus von Stauffenberg was an advantage or a disadvantage. 'It is too complex,' he says. 'I don't think it really can be answered because to answer such a question you must know what would have happened if you were someone else or had a different name. I don't know what it feels like not to be the son of Stauffenberg. But I certainly was not landed with a negative burden attached to my father.'

Franz Ludwig Stauffenberg has worked hard to make a distinguished and independent career for himself, and he has succeeded. 'Eventually you must trust that the people who deal with you in your educational and professional career see enough in you not just to see the son of someone, but instead your own person,' he says. 'But that is the average situation and inevitable experience of all children of well-known people. You are interviewing me now for hours, and not because I am a member of the European parliament, but because I am the son of Stauffenberg. It is really still that way.

'But it is quite acceptable for me because I am proud of my father and I have much love for him. I don't see him as the perfect god on earth. I think he was a very intelligent man with great courage, but I also see him as somebody who had his weaknesses, as any other person. He was a great man, and a very human one. He had some extraordinary and great qualities well worth remembering, not only for his children.

'It is quite understandable that I much prefer being the son of Stauffenberg than the son of a Himmler or the like.

'The memory and knowledge of what my father did will always be very special to me. He is very special to me.'

CHAPTER 9

The True Believer

More than ten million Germans and Austrians joined the Nazi party during its twenty-year existence. The numbers would undoubtedly be higher if Hitler had not closed the membership ranks from 1933 to 1937 because he feared people would join the party for its high-profile success, not because of ideology. Yet even a fair percentage of those who joined prior to the ban were driven as much by ambition as by pure National Socialist fervour.

The true Nazis in spirit were usually those who joined in the earliest days, when the National Socialists were still a fringe political group. These followers risked estrangement from mainstream society, as well as the possibility of imprisonment. Men and women who took such risks had the fanatical commitment to the cause which Hitler sought. Even after the devastating loss of World War II, many of these zealots maintained an adamant belief in National Socialism.

One such man is Ernst Mochar, an Austrian member of the NSDAP in 1927, when there were only several hundred Nazis. He was a front-line soldier during the war, but was not involved in any war crimes. Yet today he remains a committed Nazi, still convinced the party's philosophy was the right one. His adherence to Hitler's cause has created difficulty with his daughter Ingeborg, the youngest of three children. Today, Ingeborg is a psychotherapist in Vienna. But it is not only her life-style which caused confrontations with her father and his political beliefs; the conflict came when she informed her family she intended to marry a Jewish man. For the child of a committed Nazi, the announcement led to recrimination and bitterness. But Ingeborg was determined not to let her marriage split the family. An uneasy truce exists between her and her husband's families, who would have been enemies during the war. Ingeborg is one of two children interviewed for this book whose fathers are still alive.

Ernst Mochar was born in Carinthia, a rural region of Southern Austria, on 30 October 1909. He was the third of four children in a very poor Catholic household. 'They lived in a single room in a house with no running water,' says Ingeborg. 'It was cold and wet and they had almost nothing to eat.'

Mochar's eldest brother was killed during World War I. His father, a blacksmith, was released from a Siberian prisoner-of-war camp, only to be imprisoned by Yugoslavians over an ethnic dispute in Carinthia. There he was beaten to death. On her own with the children, Ernst's mother, a farmer's daughter, barely survived. 'My father grew up with the consciousness of being German and wanting to be German. It was not so clear in his region because there were many Slovaks. He was very discouraged as a boy, because he saw Catholics pray to God one minute and then do or say terrible things to people the next moment. That's why he joined the NSDAP in 1927 and left the church.' His brothers also joined the Nazi party.

Eighteen-year-old Mochar became an electrician, but spent most of his time training young National Socialists in a wide variety of sports. When Austria banned the Nazi party, Mochar was arrested and put in prison from 1929 until 1930. On his release he was deported to Germany, in the midst of the Great Depression. Yet he was welcomed by Germans and party members and quickly took a Berlin course to become a sports instructor. Soon he transferred to Freiburg, where he taught Nazi philosophy to Hitler Youth groups. In 1937 the twenty-eight-year-old met his future wife. She was also a physical instructor for the party, but came from a very different, upper-middle-class background. Her father, killed in World War I, was a doctor, and her stepfather an ex-army general. 'And my mother looked the very image of the pretty German maiden, with blonde hair, blue eyes,' says Ingeborg. 'Very pretty and nice. She still is. They went to Carinthia where my father had a school and my mother got a job as a Bund Deutscher Mädchen [League of German Girls] leader at a nearby girls' camp, and they got married in a great NSDAP wedding.'

When the war broke out in 1939, Mochar immediately enlisted in the army. 'He thought, "I am no good unless I go to war," ' Ingeborg says. 'He went against the advice of almost all his friends.' Mochar was assigned to the Eastern front, where he fought bravely and was slowly promoted to lieutenant. He was seriously wounded when a bullet ploughed through his backpack, and lodged in his back. On his recovery he returned to the front. He was never taken prisoner, and for the better part of five years he served the German war effort, only occasionally returning home on leave.

In the meantime, the Mochars had started a family. In 1941 a daughter was born, in 1943 a son, and Ingeborg arrived on 6 September 1945. When Mochar returned to Carinthia in the spring of 1945, the local police and the British were searching for him. His early affiliation with and enthusiasm for the party were well known, and he was wanted for questioning and de-nazification proceedings. But at the time, his wife was pregnant with Ingeborg, and Mochar did not want to surrender until his daughter was born. His escapades while evading the British troops and Austrian police became popular stories in the local countryside. Mochar sneaked into the house for Ingeborg's birth, and then surrendered to the British. They put him in a small detention camp in southern Carinthia for two and a half years. He was never charged with any offence. Once he tried to escape, but was unsuccessful.

'He was in a very bad mental and physical state,' says Ingeborg. 'My mother could visit him very seldom. I have seen the letters between them during this time and they are all about survival. "I got some potatoes, some sugar", things like that. They had nothing. Everything had been taken away.'

Mochar was home by early 1948. Ingeborg's first recollections of the family date from the following year: 'We were very poor. He couldn't teach any more, they had taken away his credentials. So he started as an electrician again. They had zero. He worked a lot.

'He was so very disappointed from the end of the war. His political life had ended. He was very bitter. All his ideals had been defeated, and he collected experiences which supported his feelings, like stories of crimes committed by the communists. He ridiculed people who had been National Socialists and then had become socialists or gone back to being Catholic. He would say, "I said yes then, and I will say yes today. I keep to it!"

'So as a result he had to reject or ignore any information which showed National Socialism wasn't good. So he would say, "No, that's not true." That is a process which started then and has not yet ended. He was so identified with National Socialism he could not admit to himself that it was an error – he cannot bring himself to say, "If I had known this I would not have done it." He can't do that. He can't waver, can't make any exception. It's his thinking. This is the most difficult part of my relationship with him. It's always the same.'

Immediately after the war, Ingeborg saw her father block out the destruction of the Nazi party by turning to work. 'It was the new drive for him all his life,' she recalls. 'He worked so hard to bring home enough money for us, it was more important to him than playing with his children. But still, I remember him as a very fair father who showed affection to me. I remember him as a strong and handsome man, and I loved him very much. I clearly remember the few times he did play with us, because when he did I enjoyed it so.'

While Ingeborg remembers the family as a 'good one', she also recalls a 'lot of control'. Both parents were strong-willed, and raised their children strictly. Arguing and disobedience were not allowed in the house. 'During those years I accepted my father's ideas about nature, God, about almost everything,' she recalls. 'For instance, I agreed with him on the issue of euthanasia, that if a child is weak or poor and idiotic, then it made no sense to let it live. I thought if you were like that it was not very beautiful to live. There are now many things, like euthanasia, which I have completely changed my mind about.'

One of the subjects about which her father lectured her was the Jews. Since there were no Jews in the region where Ingeborg grew up, she could not judge for herself. 'I grew up with some prejudice about them, but I was also attracted to them because they seemed so opposite. I heard anti-Semitism from both my parents, but my mother's is what I call a "decent, civilized" anti-Semitism. That is not to excuse her but to draw a distinction between the more radical hatred. Her family in Germany knew many Jews, since many of them were also doctors. She appreciated them but would never mix with or marry them. She saw the synagogues burning and said it was terrible, but she blocked it out, forgot about it very soon, and never thought about the ramifications.

'My father believes the total National Socialist theories of race. His only contact with Jews came as a youth when he brought tennis balls to a court and the players were Jewish. They dismissed him and didn't give him any money. This was an unfavourable impression. They were, in his opinion, tight-fisted and aggressive. He believes the Nazi theory that Jews, gypsies and the like are inferior. He thinks Germans are better. He was always afraid that Jews and other groups would undermine the German race.'

Although Ingeborg acknowledges her father's anti-Semitism, she is not convinced that he would have followed wartime orders to murder Jews. 'I am not so sure he would have found killing them the best way of getting them out of German society. I think it's possible he would not have done it.' She pauses for a minute and then continues: 'If my father had been involved in crimes, it would not, I think, be possible to have any real contact with him. My fantasy is that he was in the resistance. But if he was a murderer, it would have been very, very bad. If I was the daughter of Himmler or Mengele, I don't think I could even speak to you.'

But as a child, attending a local school with her brothers, she did not think her father's views were unusual. Many people in Carinthia shared them. Most of Mochar's friends from the war had settled back in the region, and their meetings and discussions reinforced their Nazi leanings. 'It's not nostalgia,' says Ingeborg, 'he is not the romantic type. They are just his beliefs.'

When she was seventeen, in 1962, Ingeborg attended a lecture in her history class which was a revelation to her. 'I learned that National Socialism was not as my father had told me. For the first time, I heard another point of view. Until then I had not even heard about the murder of the Jews. So I came back and confronted him, and he said, "Look at your teacher, he is Slovak, it's not true what he is saying." And I said, "But Hitler started the war," and he said, "That's not true, the other countries started the war." He argued with every point and just ignored reality. That is the first time I realized what a confirmed National Socialist he was.'

A year later, at eighteen, Ingeborg left her parents' home to attend a school sixty miles away. She wanted to become an elementary-school teacher. For one year she stayed with her uncle, her father's brother. While she had just begun to learn that her father was a dedicated Nazi, she was surprised to find her uncle even more inflexible.

'My uncle was a very big Nazi, and is still very active. He has the same philosophy as my father, but he is politically active in fighting against Slovaks. All over the main room of his house he has Nazi material on the walls, whereas my family has put all that away. You don't see it. But my uncle's place is like a Nazi shrine. My father was disappointed after the war and just wanted to be left alone. He was no longer interested since he viewed all political parties as the same, but not my uncle.

'I was considered a complicated daughter by my family. When I was with my uncle, I would quarrel with him, and he was much more radical. He said, "They didn't kill all the Jews, they should have killed more." My father never said that. If he had been my father, I think I would have just said, "Leave me alone." I would be totally estranged from him. But my uncle has children and they don't question him. They love him totally. They say he is just harmless, but for me he is not. It would be horrible if he were my father.'

After a year of constant fighting with her uncle, Ingeborg moved to Vienna to continue her studies. It was the first time she had lived in a major cosmopolitan city, and it reinforced her critical reanalysis of National Socialism and her family's beliefs. It also made for stormy reunions with her father. 'Whenever I came home,' she recalls, 'within five minutes we quarrelled about the Jews. You cannot imagine how bad it was. I was looking forward to seeing him and then I would get home and we would immediately fight. All my thinking was different from my parents', especially my father. My mother tried to be loyal to both of us, and I really don't know what the bottom of her soul looks like. But I knew with my father, and I wanted to change him, so I suppose I started many of the arguments.'

Ingeborg's brothers tried to discourage her from arguing with him. They constantly told her he was a good old man who would not change his opinions, and they implored her to 'leave him in peace'. They accepted him, but Ingeborg could not. Since settling in Vienna she had met several Jewish colleagues, and found them interesting and funny. They were not at all like her father's warnings.

'In arguments, I always tried to make him accept that it was wrong what the Nazis did in the war. He would say it didn't happen. But I would say to him, "You can't tell me it didn't happen when friends of mine tell me their parents, their grandparents, their aunts and uncles, have all been killed. You can't say such awful things." So he would say, "Well, it wasn't six million Jews, maybe it was six thousand." And I would say, "Even if it wasn't six million, isn't it still a tragedy?" And he would say, "They overdo it now, they exaggerate it, and all this is written by the Jewish newspapers and press – it is not true." '

Ingeborg's mother pleaded with her to stop arguing. ' "He won't change, it makes no sense to argue with him, it's over, it's gone, forget it. Leave him alone. You see how he is." ' But Ingeborg was convinced that she could persuade her father to see another point of view, and continued to quarrel with him, in vain.

While she stayed at the university in Vienna, studying psychology, Mochar continued working as an electrician earning a modest salary. By the mid- and late 1960s, a wave of socialism swept Europe, and Mochar could have advanced in his work if he adopted the new leftist philosophy. He refused, still adhering to National Socialism.

By 1973, twenty-eight-year-old Ingeborg had finished her studies and received a doctorate in psychology. Her relations with her sixty-four-year-old father were as confrontational as ever. 'On the one hand we loved each other,' she recalls, 'but when we started to talk, especially on politics, I just continued to fight his stubbornness and stupidity.' Ingeborg now believes she was trying to establish a different life for herself in all respects, and politics was merely the catalyst. Her father always tried to tell his children that if they lived like him, everything would be all right. 'That philosophy almost killed my brother,' says Ingeborg. 'He never finished school, never had a profession, and my father always pushed him to make something of himself. He never accepted my brother because he was not like him. I was the most like my father in nature, but not in thoughts. Maybe that is why we quarrelled so much.'

During her final Vienna studies, Ingeborg had lived with a man in Vienna. Although he was not Jewish, he was very philo-Semitic, loving Jewish literature, music and art. He supported her in the confrontations with her father. Although their relationship ended in 1973, with the conclusion of her studies, he had given her the factual basis and encouragement to continue challenging her father's anti-Semitism. But in the same year, Ingeborg's relationship with her parents underwent a significant change. 'I had started my own practice in Linz at the time, and things suddenly became very good between us. I visited them, I loved them, we did not quarrel and we had become quite close.'

Three years later, at a symposium on group dynamics, Ingeborg met her future husband, Ronnie Scheer. He was a paediatrician – and Jewish. Although his parents were both non-practising Jews, earlier generations were very religious – some were rabbis – and he had lost relatives in the Nazi death camps. His parents were shopkeepers who had escaped to Palestine. In an interview with a British journalist who reported on their unusual relationship, Ronnie commented on his initial feelings regarding her family: 'I knew from the very beginning that Ingeborg's parents had a Nazi past. It was a hard time then. We had known each other only a short time and we liked each other very much. I think it brought us even more together that both families objected.'

Within six months Ingeborg and Ronnie lived together. (They didn't marry for another six years, although they had two children during that time.) Before moving in with Ronnie, she told her parents. 'My mother was on the phone. I said, "I have a nice guy, he's Jewish, and I want to show him to you." And she said, "Well, is this really necessary?" In a second call she said, "Please don't have children with him, because they are such a poor breed." This is one of her prejudices, that these children are very neurotic, weak and so forth. My father said, "You must know my feelings, but I do not think it is any good." Later I learned that one of the first things Ronnie's mother said to him was, "Don't have a child with her." Eventually, when I got pregnant, she said, "Oh, my God, what now!"

'So then I brought him home. At the first meeting, my mother was polite. My father was very reserved, but he is always like that. They didn't say he couldn't come into the house, they invited him and were kind to him. And my husband said, "You know, during the war, we would have been on opposite sides, so we just can't sit here as though everything is perfect." And my mother said, "Oh no, I am not interested in this," but my father interjected, "Yes, you are right." '

Ronnie and her father never discussed politics but neither gave room for the other to compromise. On the few occasions when Ingeborg and Ronnie visited, the Mochars' friends stayed away from the house. None of the neighbours ever came to introduce themselves to her new lover. Ronnie recalled the dinners 'as calm affairs on the surface. It is impossible to fight with my father-in-law because he will not get into any fights with me. We had a quarrel only once. They had a neo-Nazi newspaper there, and I said, "What bloody stuff are you reading?" and he said, "That is not bloody stuff." But that was all.'

Whenever he stayed overnight at the Mochars' house, Ronnie had nightmares of Nazis coming to take him away. 'They were really terrible dreams,' Ingeborg recalls. 'It was hard for him at my parents' house, and not just because of the dreams. My mother liked him and tried to make him comfortable. My husband tried to make a personal connection with my father but it was not possible. They are opposites in almost every way. Ronnie is an intellectual, my father the opposite; he is not sporty, my father is very athletic; he is very sophisticated, my father not. In their thinking, their living, their food, they were totally different. This was all important to me. He represented such a complete break with my past and the way of life with my father. I liked this in him.'

When Ronnie and Ingeborg had their first daughter, the relationship with her parents patially improved and partially worsened. 'I was quarrelling more again,' Ingeborg recalls, 'but I went often. Before Ronnie, things were nice, but I didn't go so often.'

In Ingeborg's opinion, part of the problem with her father was that her Nazi uncle incited him to quarrel over her relationship with a Jewish man. 'My uncle simply would have told his daughter. "No Jew in my family". He prodded my father all the time about this. So I wanted my uncle and aunt to meet Ronnie and I pushed for it. We went to their house and it was extremely unpleasant. The Nazi memorabilia was all still displayed. Looking back, it was a mistake to take him there. But I really wanted them to accept him. They almost refused to give him their hands, and my mother forced them. My aunt and the young people were nice, but my uncle was terrible. We stayed too long. I was too stubborn to see what was going on, and I should have left immediately. It embittered Ronnie for quite a while.'

In contrast to her family, Ingeborg loved the relaxed and carefree atmosphere she discovered in Ronnie's family. To Ingeborg, his mother seemed 'more like a girlfriend than a parent'. She admired the warmth and laughter they shared. His father was also outgoing and enjoyed playing with the grand-children. 'It was so different from the controlled atmosphere in my household.'

Soon after they began living together, Ronnie started attending services at the only major synagogue left in Vienna. Of two hundred thousand Jews in Austria before the war, only eighteen hundred were left in 1945. The remaining community is close-knit. Ingeborg accompanied him to services, standing in the women's balcony, watching her husband participate in the ritual below. 'When I look up at her during synagogue services, I have mixed feelings, but mostly proud she is there,' Ronnie said. 'In this mixed marriage, with one generation representing the victims, and one the murderers, maybe we can help our children get over the guilt.'

Ronnie said that in a 1987 interview; since then the marriage has changed: he met another woman. Ingeborg is very honest in talking about what has happened to their relationship. 'It is so difficult now because not only does he have another woman in Graz, where he works, but she had a child by him about six months ago. She gave him a boy; he wanted one, and I only gave him daughters. I knew everything of this relationship but I couldn't stop it. I used to say to him, "Please leave it," but he'd say, "It's not me doing it, it's her." She is Jewish, and very possessive. The opposite to me. So now I live in Vienna and he lives there, more or less with her. She is a doctor and they work together. He comes to Vienna on weekends to see his children and stay with me, but it's not good for me. They have had a relationship for three years, and I never fought her, so I can't blame him that she won.'

Ronnie's relationship with another woman has angered Ingeborg's parents. 'They are very angry about it. My father said, "I don't understand him; I wouldn't do this to a woman, and that's not correct. He shouldn't do it to you." He has never said a word about this being a Jewish trait, but it has probably increased his prejudice against Jews. He knows there are many troubled relationships today without a Jewish partner; maybe inside he feels it is part of our problem, but he doesn't talk about it. I don't think I would let him. I mean, I haven't talked to my uncle now for four years, ever since the time they were so terrible to Ronnie.'

One of the things her father cannot understand is that Ingeborg still has feelings for her husband. 'He doesn't understand me this way. Ronnie says he doesn't know what is correct and he can't solve it. I am angry, but I see he can't choose. So I must choose. We will always have some contact because of our children. We don't have to fight and hate each other. But I don't have to see him every weekend as my husband – I don't think it's right.'

The split in her marriage has caused her to rely on her parents for some emotional support, and as a result their relationship has improved again. 'It is much better,' she says. 'They are really trying to help me. I wrote a letter to my father about six months ago. I thought he is old and maybe he will die soon and I will suffer because I quarrelled with him so much. While this conflict still exists between us, I wanted to tell him that I loved him. Even if our opinions, our lives and ways, are so different, I accept his life. I don't accept his opinions, but I accept that I love him. He was very happy with that letter. He wrote a long letter back that it is the same for him.'

Recently, Mochar visited his daughter in Vienna after an absence of several years. It was a good visit. 'One year ago, he finally said to me, "Maybe it was a mistake what the Nazis did to the Jews. Maybe." It took me almost twenty years and I could only get him to "maybe". But for him it's a change. He loves me so much, and we had quarrelled so much about this subject, that it had cost him part of his relationship with me. So I believe he made this step to improve the relationship. It was the first time he had not totally rejected something I said.

'I understand there is a connection between his person and his politics. To him, if he rejects that period he must reject himself. And that's the point I can't accept.'

During our meeting in Vienna, I telephoned the Berlin Document Centre, the largest repository of Nazi documents in the world. All Nazi party and SS membership files, captured intact at the end of the war, are maintained under US control. After some hesitation, Ingeborg allowed me to check her father's file. He had always told her he was a simple soldier on the Eastern front, never involved with the SS or any other criminal organization. If he lied to her, the Berlin Document Centre would have the original evidence. I had requested the information several weeks earlier; when I telephoned, the centre had extracted Mochar's file. As I received the information, Ingeborg sat next to me, obviously tense at the thought that she might discover her father lied about his wartime service. Mochar had told his daughter the truth. Although he was a very early party member, he was a mere soldier, unconnected with the SS. When I told her the news she was near tears, relieved that she did not have to confront a final betrayal from her eighty-one-year-old father.

Despite her rejection of his beliefs, Ingeborg does not think she would have turned her father in to the authorities if he had been a fugitive charged with war crimes. 'It's hard to say, but if he had been charged with crimes . . . I don't know. It's very difficult. I don't think I would have turned him in '

Her relationship with her father is still evolving. 'It is better, but it's not perfect. All I want from my father is for him to be reformed. All I want is for him to say, "In that time I thought it was all all right, but now I do not think it is all right." That is the sentence I want to hear from him. But he won't say it.'

CHAPTER 10

Little Princess

When Hermann Göring checked into Mondorf prison during the last week of May 1945, he lived up to his reputation as the leading Nazi officer of opulent and extravagant over-indulgence. The five-foot six-inch Göring weighed 270 pounds and needed two men to lift him from his car. His face was flushed, his hands trembled, and his breathing seemed erratic. He was accompanied by a five-member kitchen crew: a valet; his wife, Emma; his daughter, Edda; and their maid and nurse. He had sixteen monogrammed leather suitcases and a red hat-box. One of the suitcases was crammed with cash, while two others were packed with gold, silver and precious stones, including a museum-quality Cartier diamond watch. Another suitcase was bursting with over twenty thousand codeine pills, which he took at the rate of forty a day. He had left behind an unfinished railway tunnel near Berchtesgaden, stuffed with priceless art stolen from every corner of Europe and enough champagne and caviar to last a lifetime. Upon his arrival he insisted he would speak to no one but General Eisenhower.

Edda Göring, seven years old at the time of her father's arrest, was his only child. She lived a pampered and privileged life as the daughter of the Reichsmarschall, with her own private section of a grand château as a playhouse. After changing her mind several times before meeting me, she finally gave a three-hour interview, regretting her cooperation only later. She maintains a complete set of her father's unpublished correspondence with his wife and other family members. She had ignored or rejected all earlier requests for interviews, except for a Swedish television docu-mentary about her father, whose producers not only paid her for her participation but gave her final control over what was aired.

Her insistence on similar control in this project eliminated further discussions. Yet her limited comments still provide an interesting insight into her feelings towards her father.

Hermann Wilhelm Göring was born in Bavaria on 2 January 1893, into a middle-class Catholic and Protestant household. His family life was harmonious and he excelled at school, where he showed early signs of an erratic brilliance. In 1914, at the age of twenty-one, he joined the infantry and entered World War I. Soon he was a pilot, and became one of Germany's most decorated heroes, credited with twenty-two confirmed dogfight kills. He finished the war with a Pour le Mérite, the country's highest medal. 'He was a genuine war hero,' says Edda. 'He was a real patriot, and that is one of the reasons the German people loved him so much.'

After the war, Göring earned a living by performing in aerial shows in both Scandinavia and Germany. During that time, he met his first wife, a married Swedish countess, Carin von Kantzow. She was slender, five years older than he, and suffered from heart disease and tuberculosis. Yet she left her husband and eight-year-old son for the handsome and adventurous German pilot; they married in 1923. Göring discovered Hitler shortly after their marriage. During the Beer Hall Putsch that November, Göring led the party's battle squad and was seriously wounded in the Munich mêlée.[22]

While Hitler and Hess went to prison for their role in the putsch, Carin took Göring first to Austria, then to Italy, and finally to Sweden. In recovering from his wounds, he was given morphine to ease the pain, and by 1925 he was a confirmed addict. After he had attacked a nurse in an opiate-induced daze, he was put in a Swedish mental hospital on 1 September 1925. After two long stays in the hospital, he returned to Germany in 1927, and became the Berlin representative for BMW. He had been gone four years.

In Germany, Göring's reputation as a World War I hero was still intact, and as a facile conversationalist he used his new position to climb into Berlin society. Hitler, seeking to capitalize on Göring's popularity, had him run for the Reichstag in 1928. He was one of twelve Nazis elected. Soon the word spread that Göring was anxious to be bought. Lufthansa appointed him its Reichstag lobbyist while Fritz Thyssen gave him 150,000 marks to buy an elegant new apartment. I. G. Farben and Krupp formed special relationships with him. The 1930 elections, in which the Nazis jumped to 18 per cent of the total vote, suddenly made him a powerful politician.

Göring was a greedy man who desired great personal wealth and endless power. He often fought for control of other Nazi fiefdoms. His adeptness at scheming and intrigue propelled him: he helped remove Hjalmar Schacht from the Reichsbank presidency so he could be responsible for economic questions. After Fritz Todt, chief of armaments, died in a 1942 plane crash, Göring was bitterly disappointed when Hitler gave the ministry to Speer instead of to him. He fought with Himmler for control of the police and security apparatus. Not only did he head the Luftwaffe, and the very lucrative Hermann Göring Works industrial conglomerate, but he constantly prodded Hitler for more titles and positions. Eventually Göring was rewarded in the Machiavellian hierarchy. Not only was he named Hitler's official successor, but he was commander of the storm troopers and the German air force; prime minister of Prussia; speaker of the German parliament; Reich master of forestry and game; special commissioner of the Four-Year Plan; president of the state council; chairman of the Reich Defence Council; chairman of the Scientific Research Council; and Reichsmarschall of the Greater German Reich. In addition to these titles, he was the architect of the Gestapo and planner of the concentration camps.

Yet his obsession with personal aggrandizement led to detached and poor management of the Luftwaffe. By 1941, the Germans had lost control of the skies, a factor which was crucial in the deteriorating war effort. Like other ranking Nazis, as the war worsened he turned to clairvoyants and psychics. He paid millions of marks to a rainmaker for help with his battle plans. At other times he used clairvoyants for predictions on strategy and planning. His chief intelligence officer saw him swing a diviner's pendulum across a table map, trying to guess where the British and French might attack Germany. Yet, despite his excesses and eccentricities, his sharpness of wit and personality kept him one of Hitler's personal favourites until the last days of the Reich.

Göring, who proudly referred to himself as a 'warlord', was

unrivalled in his corruption and megalomania. By 1940, Nazi art experts had scoured Western Europe to stuff his castle home, Carinhall, as well as his hunting retreats and summer lodges with some of the best works of art from the defeated nations. Some were stolen outright, and others were 'bought' at ridiculously low prices from Jewish families forced to emigrate or face a concentration camp. Eventually, truckloads of Rembrandts, Rubens, da Vincis, and the best nineteenth-century Impressionists, worth hundreds of millions of dollars, found their way to Göring. The walls of his massive homes were covered with old masters, three and four to a tier. In Carinhall, his fifteen-hundred-square-foot study was renowned for a collection of furniture and decorative sculpture rivalling that of any museum.

He often strutted about his Teutonic château carrying a spear, dressed in floor-length coats and silk blouses. On his fingers he wore six to eight rings, often flawless multi-carat emeralds and diamonds. Hjalmar Schacht said, 'His greed was boundless, his lust for jewellery, gold and silver unimaginable.' A woman invited to tea found him wearing a toga and jewel-studded sandals; his hands were covered in rings and his lips were lightly rouged. He held gluttonous parties that rivalled the worst Roman excesses. He created a series of new uniforms and medals for public appearances, and his military baton was gold and silver, encrusted with precious stones. Government buildings, the commissioning of which was under his jurisdiction, were to be marble palaces, complete with dens for his favourite African animals, lions. At Göring's direction, Speer designed him a Berlin palace. A mixture of Versailles and the palace of Caesar, it was intended to have twelve hundred rooms and to be built of thousands of tons of imported marble. To Göring's disappointment, the war prevented it from being built, although several small-scale mock-ups existed. On his birthdays, Göring withheld part of the salaries of thousands of men under his command so he could buy himself another piece of art at their expense. German industry was coerced into supplying him with ever-increasingly valuable gifts. In 1943, when Goebbels called for commitment to 'total war', he demanded that all luxury restaurants be closed in beleaguered Berlin, but Göring sent troops to keep his favourite one open as a private club, and continued to have lavish meals although food was scarce throughout Germany.

Edda Göring does not attempt to defend her father's personal excesses. Instead, trying to change the discussion's focus, she bitterly complains about the German government. 'The German people were good to my mother and me after the war, but the government was terrible. They took everything, and not just what he had acquired in World War II, but also all the property my parents had before the war, except for a beach house on the island of Sylt. They even took the jewels my father had given my mother before the war. They didn't even let me keep his wartime medals. The Americans stole his special baton, and it is on display at West Point. Is that right? A Japanese man said he would be willing to spend a million dollars for it. The Americans stole a lot, and they also gave a lot to the German authorities. In 1972 in Munich, the German government sold six hundred and fifty thousand [Deutschmarks] worth of my father's belongings at auction. It was all profit for the government, and of course. I did not receive anything. I thought of suing them, but it was too expensive and no one wanted it on a contingency. All over Munich, even today, there are pictures of my father and me that are sold for several dollars. Everyone makes money from him, but not me.'

Göring's family life had changed with his accumulation of power and money under the Nazi régime. The sickly Carin died in 1931, at the age of forty-three. In 1935, Göring married Emmy Sonnemann, a provincial actress his own age, in a wedding to rival any royal nuptial. Thirty thousand troops lined the route while thousands of Berliners cheered the popular Göring and his wife in a car awash with tulips and narcissi. Göring had wanted a wedding reserved for an emperor, and he received it. As Hitler stood quietly in the background, two hundred planes flew in salute overhead. 'They had a wonderful marriage,' says Edda. Although Carinhall was filled with pictures and paintings of his first wife, Edda says, 'My mother was never jealous. She allowed the pictures of Carin to be all around. She felt that if he could love one woman that much, then he could love her the same. It was a terrible loss for my mother when she lost him.'

Three years later, in the spring of 1938, Edda was born. Göring was ecstatic. Some historians claim she was named after Mussolini's daughter of the same name. 'That is ridiculous,' says

Edda. 'My father did not even like Mussolini. I was named after an old German heroic tale that my father and mother were very proud of.' More bothersome to Göring at the time of Edda's birth was the accusation by the party's leading Jew-baiter, Julius Streicher, that Edda was conceived through artificial insemination. Göring was infuriated, and although Streicher retracted the allegation, the Reichsmarschall never forgave him. He appointed a commission to investigate Streicher's personal life and business dealings, and as a result Streicher was dismissed from all party posts.

With the Streicher controversy settled, Emma and Hermann Göring had Edda christened on 4 November 1938. Reich Bishop Ludwig Müller presided and Hitler acted as godfather. The presence of leading industrialists and ranking party officers ensured that the infant received a stunning array of gifts. The fact that the ceremony was religious annoyed some in the Nazi hierarchy; six days later Rudolf Hess opted for the party's pagan naming ceremony in 'christening' Wolf. Hitler again acted as godfather. But Göring ignored the criticism and set about pampering Edda as if she were an infant princess. Half a million Luftwaffe men even donated money to build the child an exact miniature replica of the Sans Souci palace, complete with grand halls, kitchens, and dolls. Edda's birthdays were great celebrations, with even Hitler taking time from the losing war effort, on 2 June 1944, to help her celebrate her sixth birthday. Göring, often away from the family, still tried to telephone his wife and daughter daily. At home, Edda remembers her father often holding and kissing her, playing with her for hours at a time, and accompanying her to ballet class, which started when she was five.

Göring's grand life-style and facile charm remained popular with the German masses. He later said, 'The people want to love and the Führer was often too far removed from the masses. Then they clung to me.' But his decadent behaviour worked to his disadvantage in the Nazi inner circle, where he was eventually condemned as a corrupt man whose drug problem rendered him ineffectual. By the close of the war, Göring had come to symbolize the worst of Nazi excesses. Edda believes that the tilt against her father in the rest of the party hierarchy was precipitated by Martin Bormann, Hitler's secretary, whom she calls the 'grey eminence'. 'He was my father's real enemy,' she says. 'He poisoned Hitler and others against my father.' When I mentioned that Bormann's eldest daughter felt very positive about her own father, Edda shrugged and said, 'I don't care. She would be no friend of mine.'

Edda also has her own version of Göring's activities on 'the Jewish question'. She acknowledges her father's desire to please Hitler, but disputes the overwhelming evidence that he condoned the persecution of Jews and did his best to force them out of German economic life. 'I can understand that Jewish writers would write bad things about my father,' Edda says. 'Terrible things did happen to them and it must be impossible to forget. But my father was never fanatical. You could even see his eyes were always calm. In contrast, Hitler was fanatical, especially about the Jews. My mother used to tell me that when someone mentioned the Jews to Hitler he just went into a fit. He had become so violently anti-Semitic during his years in Vienna. My father's problem was his loyalty to Hitler. He had sworn personal fealty to him and would never abandon it, even when Hitler had gone too far. The things that happened to the Jews were horrible, but quite separate from my father.'

In the final days of the war, Göring relaxed in his lavishly appointed mountain villa at Obersalzberg, together with his wife and Edda. Hitler was trapped in Berlin, but Göring made no effort to help his beleaguered Führer. On 23 April when he received a report suggesting Hitler might be dead, he sent a telegram to the Führerbunker offering to take the reins of government unless he heard to the contrary by 10 p.m. Hitler and Bormann were incensed and ordered the SS to arrest Göring. One day later, an SS contingent surrounded the Göring retreat and forced him and his family into the limestone tunnels which snaked under the villa. Emma and Edda, in their nightgowns, stayed in the tunnels without food or water for two days. Finally, some food was brought on the third day, although the opiate-starved Göring had fallen into a deep depression. However, by 28 April the charismatic field-marshal had revived enough to convince his SS guards to let him and his family leave the heavily bombed Obersalzberg. In his armour-plated Maybach limousine he went with his wife and Edda to his castle in Mautendorf, while an SS platoon followed in trucks. There he resumed his pashalike life-style, until he drove to a rendezvous with an American general on 7 May. He took his wife and daughter with him, hoping to have a personal meeting with Eisenhower. It was his last day of freedom: the Americans arrested him and took away a crying Emma and Edda.

Göring underwent a major metamorphosis in Allied custody. Forced to kick his drug addiction, he lost more than eighty pounds, and seemed a different man. In his cell, a source of strength in abandoning his addiction was a single picture of Edda. Scrawled on the back was her note: 'Dear Daddy, come back to me soon. I have such longing for you. Many thousand kisses from your Edda!!!!' Albert Speer noticed the difference in Göring within several weeks: 'Ever since his withdrawal cure he had been in better form than I had ever seen him. He displayed remarkable energy and became the most formidable personality among the defendants. I thought it a great pity that he had not been up to this level in the months before the outbreak of the war and during critical situations during the war.'

During October 1945, as Göring languished in Nuremberg prison, Emma was arrested by American troops and placed in Straubing prison. Edda was put into an orphanage. On 24 November, seven-year-old Edda was allowed to join her mother in prison. By February 1946, the Allies feared that imprisonment of the defendants' families might be used in their trial defences to win public sympathy. As a result, on the last day of February Emma and Edda were released from jail and were permitted to live in a cottage deep in Sackdilling forest. The hut had neither water nor electricity. Edda hated her new home. It was quite a change from the villas of her pampered childhood. 'I was an only child,' she recalls. 'That made it harder for me. I had no one else my own age to rely on.'

Meanwhile at Nuremberg, a revived Göring became an unofficial cheerleader for the other defendants, coordinating their defences and bolstering their flagging spirits. During the trial he grumbled, loudly interjected comments from the witness box and shouted congratulations to witnesses with favourable testimony. He took great interest in presenting his defence, one in which he portrayed himself as being equal in importance to Hitler in the rejuvenation of Germany but totally ignorant of the atrocities. His testimony was forceful and made an impression on many at the trial. He hoped that Emma and Edda were listening on the radio, but without electricity in their cottage they could not. Speer saw through the blustering charade: 'His whole policy was one of deception. Once in the prison yard something was said about Jewish survivors in Hungary. Göring remarked coldly: "So, there are still some there? I thought we had knocked them all off. Somebody slipped up again."'

Göring told the prison psychoanalyst, 'I'd rather die as a martyr than a traitor. Don't forget that the great conquerors of history are not seen as murderers – Genghis Kahn, Peter the Great, and Frederick the Great.' He predicted that in five years Hitler would be an idol of Germany again, that in fifteen years the Nuremberg proceedings would be a disgrace, and that 'in fifty or sixty years there will be statues of Hermann Göring all over Germany. Little statues, maybe, but one in every German home.'

Besides trying to convince his captors that he was a great historical figure, Göring spent much of his solitary time doting on his wife and child. In June 1946 he sent a letter to Edda for her eighth birthday. It has survived intact and its words are a source of pride to his only daughter.

> My darling, sweet child! My golden treasure!
> Now's the second time that your birthday has come around and I can't be there. And yet, my darling, today I'm especially close to you, and send you my warmest and most heartfelt greetings.
> I pray to Almighty God from the bottom of my heart to look after you and help you. I can't send you any gift, but my boundless love and longing is all around you and always shall be!
> You know, my little sparrow, how fond I am of you! You are always so sweet and tender. You'll always be our happiness and joy.
> Mama has told me what a brave little helper you are everywhere and how good you are being. I'm proud of you.
> I hope the weather's fine so you can spend your birthday outside in the wonderful forest. My little sweetheart, once more all my warmest wishes for today and always; fondest hugs and kisses from your Papa.

This letter symbolizes Edda's rememrance of her father. 'I loved him very much,' she says, 'and it was obvious how much he loved me. My only memories of him are such loving ones, I cannot see him any other way.'

Edda wrote back to her father, filled with excitement that she might visit him with her mother: 'I'm sooooo fond of you and it's so awfully long since I saw you. Oh, Papa, if only I could come too!' Edda did see her father, for the first time in sixteen months, on 17 September 1946. 'I was only eight years old,' she recalls, 'but I remember the day very clearly. Maybe I just didn't understand it at the time. It was very unusual because I had such a wonderful relationship with my father, it was strange to see him at Nuremberg through a glass window with an American soldier with a white helmet standing next to him. I remember seeing two of the Frank children.' (She shakes her head at the mention of the Frank name. 'That Niklas Frank, I cannot understand him. I do not have a problem with him drawing a distance from what his father did, but I can't accept the mean way he said it.')

Returning to the single time she saw her father in prison, she remembers standing on a chair to see him better, and then reciting parts of ballads and poems she had learned for the occasion. Hermann Göring cried freely on the other side of the glass, unconcerned about the presence of the other defendants.

Fifteen days after their meeting, the tribunal handed down its judgement. Göring's use of slave labour, and his cavalier attitude about concentration camps and the Final Solution, worked to his disadvantage. His defences were rejected, including that Germany's taking of occupied territories was no different from the Americans 'grabbing Texas'. Despite his bravado, he was found guilty on all four counts and sentenced to be hanged. Emma and Edda had obtained a working radio by this time, and heard the judgement live. Göring showed no emotion when given his verdict, but when Schacht was acquitted he slammed down his earphones in disgust.

On 4 October, Göring's lawyer petitioned that he be executed by a firing squad instead of the hangman. The petition was denied. But he cheated the hangman by one day. On 15 October 1945, the American guard watching his cell screamed, 'Chaplain, Göring's having a fit!' Within seconds Göring was in convulsions and his breath rattled deep in his throat. He had crushed a glass suicide capsule in his mouth, and within a minute he was dead. The source of that capsule has baffled investigators since the war. The official American investigation concluded that Göring had the capsule with him and that either it was hidden in his wooden pipe or he repeatedly swallowed it and passed it in his stool, saving it until the crucial moment. However, prison letters from Göring, published in 1989, indicate that the final poison capsule (two had already been removed from his luggage) was provided by someone on the prison staff. The most likely suspect is an American officer, Lieutenant Jack G. Wheelis, a hard-drinking six-foot Texan who formed a close bond with Göring. The two were impassioned huntsmen, and Wheelis not only accepted mementoes from Göring but helped him smuggle letters to Emma and Edda. Wheelis died in 1954, taking the possible solution of the Göring death to his grave. But in our discussion, Edda Göring let slip an important fact when talking about her father's death. She laughed at first when she spoke of the suicide, and then said: 'The Americans were so careful. But it was so much better this way. If it had been a firing squad instead of hanging, my father would probably have accepted it. That would have been like a soldier. But hanging was like a criminal. It took much strength to kill himself.' Near tears, she continued: 'I will always be grateful to the man who did this for us.'

She could tell that I was surprised at the admission, which meant that someone had smuggled the poison to her father. It meant the official Allied report on his death was wrong. She quickly collected herself and adeptly dodged further attempts to elicit more information. She knew she had already said too much, and seemed almost angry at having allowed her emotions to take control, even if only for a moment.

At this point, Edda started drawing our conversation to a polite close. It was as though a temporary spell had broken. As we finished the last cup of coffee, she commented on some of my questions, but in a more deliberate manner. She did not understand the need to express positive feelings about her father in a book, since 'I actually expect that almost everybody has a favourable opinion of my father, except maybe in America'.

Although she is quite bitter over her father's fate, she thinks that Hess's forty-six-year imprisonment was worse. 'To languish all those years,' she said. 'That would have been much worse for me.' She agrees with Wolf Hess that the Allies finally killed the ninety-three-year-old prisoner.

Edda stressed that her case was very different from those of some of the other children I intended to interview for the book. 'As for Mengele, there is no comparison at all. This is very clear. It is easier for me to speak than if I were the daughter of Himmler. It's very difficult for her. She has some real problems when it comes to her father's role.'

By this time, Edda had closed the family album filled with pictures and unsolicited letters praising her father. The fifty-one-year-old daughter of the former field-marshal began to lecture me. For a moment she sounded surprisingly life Wolf Hess. 'The Americans wanted that trial and result. They took away my mother's right to earn a living as an actress until she was too old to have a career. We were treated miserably after the war by the Americans. And for a long time they have been telling the world how to run things, under the guise of human rights. The US spends so much on its military, so little on social progress. Now that the US is saturated with drugs, these will come to Europe next. Another problem the US has given us: I see your country increasingly as one of rich and poor, not like Germany where there is an active middle class. Only Frankfurt is really bad, with crime, drugs and all; it's like Chicago – really terrible.' She still resents the country which she blames for her father's conviction as a war criminal and for his death. She has never visited the United States, 'never had any desire, never had any interest in that type of society'.

As we finished our afternoon meeting, she emphasized the difference between her current life and the opulence she lived in for seven years as a child. 'I work now for a cataract surgeon. I must earn my living. I have no time to write a book about my father because I can't afford to take the time off.'

I glanced around once more at the small fifth-floor flat, decorated in 1960s Scandinavian modern. The living-room is dominated by a beautiful 1937 oil painting of her mother. It is in a simple frame because, Edda tells me, 'the German government took away the precious frame after the war'. Other portraits fill the apartment: crayon drawings of her and her mother; a portrait of both her parents; a large framed photo of the three of them, Göring in a spectacular white uniform; a watercolour of her father with his World War I medal proudly displayed around his neck; a wartime painting of Edda; and a large Göring family crest. At the doorway, I looked one last time at Edda Göring, who bears a remarkable resemblance to her father. 'I will let you know if we will meet again,' she said. 'But you know how I feel. I love him very much, and I cannot be expected to judge him any other way. He was a good father to me, and I have always missed him. That is all you need to know.'

CHAPTER 11

Betrayal

Some of the children discussed in the preceding chapters have had great difficulty coping with their fathers' wartime crimes. Although the families were seldom forthright about a father's involvement in the Third Reich, most had parents so famous that they quickly learned about them at school or in books. With the exception of Rolf Mengele's family, who deceived him for sixteen years about his father's identity, it was difficult for the families to hide a father's Nazi past. And in the Mengele case, Rolf had so little emotional connection with his biological father that the truth was somewhat easier to bear.

This chapter is quite different. It is the only one concerning a child who had a loving and close relationship with her father, only to discover at a much later date the truth about his wartime involvement. Adding to the difficulty, she made that discovery herself. The betrayal was devastating. Dagmar Drexel is the youngest child interviewed for this book, the only one born almost a decade after the end of the war. Her father is still alive, and they are totally estranged. She spoke to me after great hesitation, only under the condition that her story should not be printed in Germany as long as her father lives.

Max Drexel was born on 2 May 1914, in Boeblingen, the eldest of three brothers in a middle-class Lutheran family. His father was a police officer who ran an authoritarian and politically conservative household. 'But the real strict influence in my father's life was his mother,' says Dagmar, the younger of two Drexel children. 'His mother was extremely strict, and she even ruled my mother in the beginning of my parents' marriage.'

The right-wing family atmosphere encouraged Drexel to join the Nazi party at the age of nineteen in 1933. He was an ambitious and ideologically committed member. Although he volunteered for service in the Wehrmacht, he was rejected because of a knee injury. Instead, he served as a Jungvolkführer, a Hitler Youth leader. At the end of 1936, after the ritual trawl through four generations to ensure untarnished Aryan heritage, Drexel joined the most elite group within the party, the SS. The twenty-two-year-old was selected for the Totenkopfverbände, the Death's Head battalions, and was tranferred to Stuttgart, where he worked in Heydrich's Sicherheitshauptamt (central security department).

It was also during this period that Drexel was able to show his superiors the degree of his commitment to the Nazi cause. Under SS policies, a member's wife had to be cleared for racial purity before the marriage was approved. While Drexel's proposed wife satisfied the racial check, the Nazi investigators discovered that his future father-in-law was an alcoholic. The initial recommendation was against marriage. Drexel produced a flurry of letters attesting to his fiancée's domestic nature, love of children, and other good Aryan values. Moreover, he ordered his future father-in-law to enter a detoxification programme. Finally, he stated that if the man's drinking problem did not improve, or if the SS saw any likelihood of a genetic predisposition towards drunkenness, he would abandon the marriage plans. Any soldier willing to prefer National Socialist theory over true love was the type of zealot Himmler's SS desired.

This commitment to the cause was rewarded with a transfer to Berlin, where Drexel began legal studies. But his judicial training was interrupted by a 1941 posting to the Eastern front and the 'Einsatzgruppe D', a special mobile commando unit under the jurisdiction of the Sicherheitsdienst (SD). The Einsatzgruppen were charged with massive liquidations of the civilian population, with an emphasis on Jews, communist officials and partisans. Using brutal methods of mass arrest, these killing units used single rifle shots and a handful of gas vans to kill an estimated two million civilians in an eighteen-month period. Letters from Einsatzgruppen commanders to Berlin head-quarters often complained about the waste of live ammunition involved in the executions, as well as the toll such personal involvement in mass murder took on the troops. Such complaints eventually led to more impersonal means of murder: the large gas chambers of extermination camps in Poland.

By the time of his transfer to the East, Drexel was an Obersturmführer, or first lieutenant. He volunteered for control of his own commando unit, and was stationed near Simferopol, in the Ukraine, from the spring to the autumn of 1941. One of the war's worst recorded bloodbaths took place there, with thousands of Jews and Slavs summarily executed. Most of the victims were lined up along the edges of mass graves and killed with a single rifle shot into the back of the head. Drexel, who constantly exhorted his troops to speed up their shootings, watched the slaughter from a nearby hill. Entire families were eliminated. To conserve his squad's ammunition, he ordered that mothers hold their infants in such a way that a single shot could kill both of them. Beyond the mass shootings, he also hanged many of his victims. This was his personal decision, contrary to the practices of most other Einsatzgruppen.

The SS considered Drexel's service exemplary, and he was promoted to Hauptsturmführer (captain). After finishing his duties with the mobile killing units, he returned to Berlin, where he completed his legal studies. While he also spent a short time in France, his Eastern service was finally rewarded with an honoured SS assignment: he was sent to Bayreuth and became part of the personal bodyguard of Winifred Wagner, daughter-in-law of the Nazi-worshipped composer Richard Wagner. Having served the Third Reich in the murderous Einsatz-gruppen, Drexel was allowed to finish the war in the genteel surroundings of the annual Bayreuth festivals with the cultural elite of National Socialist Germany.

'My father used to come home during the war,' says Dagmar, 'and the family says he was so proud and cocky in his uniform. All his family had either joined the party or were very sympathetic to it, but my father was the most proud. No one could believe that this meek teacher had suddenly reached such a high rank and was now a ravager of the Eastern populations. I think almost everybody dismissed his bragging as a lie. No one really knew what he was doing, but also no one believed he was capable of anything too terrible. They just thought he was trying to make himself more important by his stories.'

At the end of the war, Drexel knew that his Einsatzgruppen service would subject him to Allied prosecution for crimes. He avoided arrest and de-nazification proceedings by giving the name of an ordinary soldier on his detention. In the midst of hundreds of thousands of detainees and ongoing searches for prominent, missing Nazi officials, the Allies overlooked Drexel's simple ruse, and he was released. His real identity and role were not uncovered. Yet, still afraid that he was on a wanted list for war crimes, he fled to the Swabian Alps, a sparsely populated, rural region in southern Germany. There, under a false name, he worked as a farmer for five years. The farm's administrator was his brother-in-law. During his time under cover he left his wife and his only son, who was born in 1944, in Leonberg, near Stuttgart. Occasional visits were his only family contact.

Finally, by 1950, Drexel felt comfortable enough to return to a normal life in Germany. The majority of the war crimes trials were over, and the Allied High Commissioner, John J. McCloy, had only recently commuted the sentences of all the convicted industrialists and most of the medical personnel. The war crimes fever had subsided, much to Drexel's relief. Moving back to Leonberg, he again started teaching in elementary school. No one asked where he had been for five years, and certainly no one discussed the war. It was a subject better forgotten. Soon, he moved to Henbach, a small town of five thousand, and again earned a living from teaching.

Dagmar was born on 5 February 1953. Her parents had decided they wanted another child in addition to their son, then ten. She was raised in a middle-class German family which, to outside observers, seemed very normal.

'My earliest memories of the family, especially my father, are rather positive. I remember he took me to the sports arena and bicycle riding, and I was allowed to sleep with him and even bathe with him. In comparison to my brother, my father was always very nice to me. My mother also took very good care of me, but it was obvious to me that during that time she was very depressed, and spoke a lot about death. My father did not take any notice. He didn't work against it, but it bothered him that she wasn't healthy. She did not fulfil his ideal of a wife, and he had no qualms about letting her know this. He made it quite clear to her.'

It was obvious to Dagmar that her parents did not have a good relationship, although neither took out their frustration on the children. One day in 1959, her mother took her to a friend's house. Dagmar remembers that her mother 'said good-bye to the friend in a very odd way'. Then she asked to borrow some rope. After she had not returned for several hours, the friend telephoned Drexel, who together with some colleagues, began searching for his wife. They found her in the forest, hanged.

'I think there was a suicide note, but I have never seen it,' says Dagmar. 'The poor relationship of my parents was one of the reasons she killed herself. It was a bad time for us, but I was only five and a half years old and did not realize the full significance of everything that happened. But those first couple of months after my mother died, my father took good care of me. I really loved him then.

'Today, thinking back on my mother's suicide, it seems eerie that she hanged herself, when my father used to hang so many of his victims.'

Almost a year after Mrs Drexel's death, the family housemaid moved into their home and began living as a lover with Drexel. 'The family just assumed they had an affair before my mother's death,' says Dagmar. 'We lived in such a small town, and people talked so much that they had to marry very quickly.' Dagmar's brother, sixteen years old, was sent to a boarding school.

Drexel and his lover married in 1961. The new wife's relationship with eight-year-old Dagmar was 'very bad. I had been longing for another mother, but my stepmother came from a bad background and she had no way of dealing with children. She worshipped my father slavishly and served him with no questions asked. That was enough for him.'

While Dagmar struggled to understand her mother's suicide and to cope with her stepmother, an event took place the following year that would make everything else seem insignificant. In 1962, her father went to Stuttgart to bury his forty-two-year-old brother,[23] who had died of cancer. Without any warning, forty-eight-year-old Drexel was arrested by German police and taken to a jail in nearby Schwäbisch-Gmünd. 'Later that same day, my stepmother was visited by two police officers and they searched the house. It was very uncomfortable for me. It bothered me a great deal as a child to see these two men search the entire house. And my stepmother and members of the family who lived nearby were beside themselves.'

The arrest and surrounding events confused Dagmar. 'About

the meaning of his arrest I wasn't told anything. When I visited him in jail he said he was not guilty of anything, had not done anything, and anyhow I wouldn't understand why he was charged. He just said he would be coming home with us soon and it would be the same as it used to be. That was all he said.'

Being left alone with her stepmother was far from ideal for nine-year-old Dagmar. Her mother's two sisters decided to take her into their household while Drexel was in prison. Dagmar recalls the day they approached him with the suggestion. 'When we first visited him in Landsberg prison, I went with my stepmother and my mother's two sisters. He was very depressed, and cried, and was beside himself. Then one of my aunts said he shouldn't worry so much, and told him that they would take care of my brother and me. "Don't worry, the children will be all right," they told him. Then my father said, "I am not concerned about my children, that's not the question – I am worried about my wife, we have only been married a year!" Whereupon my two aunts stormed from the visitors' room with me in tow and were really incensed. I couldn't really understand the dimensions of what had happened.' Before Dagmar could move to her aunts', her father was released on bail. He had been in prison for almost five months. When he returned to his small town, he found little had changed as a result of his arrest.

'All our friends and neighbours knew about his arrest,' says Dagmar. 'But no one spoke to me about it. The charges were totally unknown to me. Except for the family, no one in the town really knew what he had done. They knew it had something to do with the war, which they didn't find that terrible. Nobody understood or wanted to know the range of his deeds. Some of the upper class didn't want anything more to do with my father, but that was because of his second marriage. His second wife was not up to their standards. It had nothing at all to do with his Nazi past.'

The arrest meant Drexel could no longer teach. A friend gave him a job at a local factory. He continued to be active in his social clubs, and within a month of his release everything appeared to return to normal. But for Dagmar, ignorant of the reason for her father's arrest, and unable to discuss it at home, the pressures took their toll in a different way: she began failing at school. Instead of trying to help his daughter overcome her learning difficulties, her father decided to cover them up. It was one of the reasons why he finally sent her to live with her two aunts in 1965. 'In this way,' says Dagmar, 'he could tell the neighbours I was doing fine at school. Since I was out of the town, no one would know any better.'

For the next seven years Dagmar stayed with her aunts, and had contact with her father only through family visits. He remained a loving but distant figure. Unknown to her, the first charges brought against him were quietly dropped when the prosecution failed to put together a case they considered watertight. Meanwhile, Dagmar had begun to hear about the war and the atrocities, for the first time, in school. 'It was shortly after I arrived at my aunts',' she recalls. 'I was about thirteen years old, and I learned the real horror stories of what had happened during the Nazi period. I just never connected them with my father. And I could never bring it up with my father or my aunts. They had both been National Socialists during the war, and they were the same as the rest of the family. It was taboo to talk about the war or about sex. I asked one of my aunts once and she gave a very one-sided account. She made the war sound heroic, and said everything we were taught about it was a lie. She had been there and said young people couldn't judge or criticize. In my family, they had always groaned, "Oh, not the bloody Jews again. They couldn't have killed that many, they are still everywhere – in the press, in industry, all over America."

'So I just kept these things to myself. My aunts talked ill of my father. They blamed him for killing their sister. But none of their criticism was ever because of his Nazi past or what he had done in the war.'

By 1968, amid dramatic left-wing political movements and student revolts sweeping Europe, fifteen-year-old Dagmar became politically active. She joined the Young Socialists, became a spokeswoman for her school, and participated in numerous student demonstrations: 'I was engaged in everything that dealt with issues of oppression.' But at home with her family she avoided any discussion or confrontation, still refusing to challenge her father about his wartime activity. Still accepting his authority, Dagmar did not bring her newfound political activism home. 'I was brought up to be silent and to listen absolutely to authority,' she says.

The only political discussions with her father were 'highly abstract'. But Dagmar soon discovered that her father liked to provoke her. Since he knew of her left-wing bias, he often teased her, saying, 'Oh, you are all cowards, you don't make a revolution, we made a revolution.' Sometimes when she returned home to visit him, he chided her about socialist government crises or problems, provoking her to argument. 'He was always like that.'

In July 1970, Drexel was arrested a second time. This time the prosecutors had prepared a much more damning case. The indictment, which also charged Drexel's personal translator assigned to the Einsatzgruppen, ran to more than two hundred pages. It charged Drexel with being the commander in dozens of organized executions, each of which claimed from twenty to seven hundred victims. He was indicted for personal responsibility in murdering more than 2600 people, including entire families. The indictment left no doubt about the nature of his wartime service, stating that he had acted with extreme cruelty regarding the executions of Jews: 'In no way, shape, or form did he behave humanely. On the contrary, he distinguished himself through his precision, his performance.' Again Drexel was released on bail after a short stay in prison. Once again, Dagmar was not informed about the details of his arrest or the charges against him. Although she was seventeen years old, and politically rebellious at school, she could not bring herself to confront her father. The rest of the family remained silent.

Dagmar dropped out of school around this time, never finishing her college entrance exams. In 1972, at nineteen, she married, but the marriage lasted less than three years.

While she tried to establish her own life independent of her family, her father prepared for his eventual trial. A group of ex-Nazi officers dubbed Stille Hilfe (Silent Help) offered Drexel money for his defence, and he hired a right-wing lawyer. One of his first manoeuvres was to have the trial postponed on the basis of poor health. This tactic worked for nearly five years. In 1974, Dagmar accompanied her father on one of his trips to a Munich doctor. It was a day that permanently altered her view of him.

'I had to wait for him for a long time. His files were in his open briefcase and I just started to look at them. And for the first time I found out exactly what he had done, what the trial was all about, what crimes he had committed. I saw the indictment, and I intended just to have a brief look at it. But then there were some notes in the margin in my father's handwriting that caught my attention. I could see immediately that these notes were meant for his lawyer. Some of the notes accused his translator, very specifically, regarding the number of guards and that fewer Jews were brought to the executions. For example, when it said that four people were led to the pit, he had crossed it out and written that it was only two or eight, or whatever the correct number was. In this way he had altered the entire indictment. I was shocked. I realized not only what he was charged with, but that his memory was very exact, in great detail. He used to say he couldn't remember, that nobody could after all this time. I was paralysed. I was not able to talk about it even later because the shock was so great. I didn't tell him what I had seen. For a long time I did not talk about it to anyone.

'I still cared for him, and was present at the verdict in Munich. But I was so agitated I don't remember the details. Also, at that point I had the belief that two wrongs don't make a right – I couldn't punish him just because he had done a wrong. He was still my father and to me personally he had not done anything wrong. I had private problems with a divorce from my husband, and that helped me avoid thinking about the many things connected with my father. Only much later did I understand the dimensions of the whole thing – actually, I would have to say only within the last few years.'

Dagmar believes she was the first member of the family to see the indictment and understand the full scope of the charges against Drexel. Alone, she tried to reconcile the newly discovered image of a criminal with that of her loving father.

The trial started in 1975. He asked her not to attend, and except for one occasion when she sneaked into the courtroom, she followed his order. She did not hear any of the witnesses tesitify against him. 'But I do know,' says Dagmar, 'that many of his friends came to testify what a good man he was. He was very proud of that.' Drexel also impressed the judge by admitting certain crimes and expressing remorse at his SS service. 'I now know he admitted only those things which had already been proven one hundred per cent,' says Dagmar. 'As for the expressions of remorse, he was always a good actor. I know he has no remorse, no regrets for what he did. He believes he did his duty, it was the right thing, and he is proud of it, not ashamed. He has never felt any pity for any of his victims. But he knew he could not say this to the court.'

Dagmar was in the courtroom on the day of the verdict. Drexel was found guilty of directing or assisting in twenty executions totalling 746 murders. The sentence was twenty years. But the judge, who was impressed by his apparent remorse, almost immediately reduced the sentence to five years in a minimum-security prison. Drexel did not start serving his sentence until June 1977, when his appeals were exhausted.

'When the verdict was announced I was not surprised by the dimension of the punishment,' says Dagmar. 'I don't want to be a judge of what is fair and what is not fair. You can't measure crimes like his by the length of a prison sentence. If he had been indicted right after the war he probably would have got a life sentence. But even if he was put behind bars for the rest of his life, the suffering of the people he killed and their relatives cannot be compensated. Not even with a life sentence.

'I visited him frequently in prison. But I definitely want to point out that I never, never accepted what my father did. On the contrary, he carries a heavy burden for what he did and his actions can never be excused.'

Drexel was eventually given credit for time he served during his previous arrests, and spent only two and a half years in prison. The convicted murderer was free by the 1979 Christmas holidays.

'And on the return to his home, none of his friends avoided him,' says Dagmar. 'They totally accepted him, and are of the opinion that a great injustice was done when he was sentenced and had to serve time. He also feels that way, that the government did him a great disservice and treated him unfairly. It is interesting, but not a single person in the town ever criticized him. He actually moved up in social circles!'

Shortly after her father's release, two important events took place for Dagmar. She married a second time, and soon had her first child, a son. She had her first discussions about her father with her husband. From the beginning, he helped her place her father's crimes into their proper perspective, and bolstered her independence. After the birth of her son in 1980, Drexel began visiting more often, anxious to see his first grandchild. During this time Dagmar was still unable to talk to her father about his past. He still did not know she had seen the indictment or knew the truth about his Einsatzgruppen service. Their relationship was strained, but he never knew why. She tried to limit his contact with her children (a daughter was born in 1982), afraid of the influence he might have on them.

In 1985, Dagmar met another daughter of a Nazi father, Dörte von Westernhagen, who was researching a book on children of non-prominent Nazi officers. The book, *Die Kinder der Täter* (Children of the Perpetration), appeared in Germany in 1987, and Westernhagen included a chapter on Dagmar and her father. This was shortly after the publication of *Born Guilty*, a collection of anonymous interviews with the children of Nazis.

'One day my father was at my house and he saw a copy I had of *Born Guilty* and he jokingly said, "What do you have there? Are you in here too?" And I then asked him, "What would you do if I was in there?" He dismissed the suggestion totally: "Nonsense! Nonsense!" '

Two years after Dagmar's interview was published in Westernhagen's book, a cousin told Drexel about it. He was furious. 'He probably would never have found out otherwise,' says Dagmar. 'He doesn't read anything like this, nothing about the period. He was outraged, as were most of the family. They considered it a fouling of the nest in public. Most of them broke with me over it.

'My father just could not deal with it. He didn't speak to me about it but his aggression got stronger and stronger, and affected my children.

'Some time later I received a long letter from him in which he tried to deny everything I said. He attacked me. One example is when he said, "To make a point that could serve as an excuse for you, I would say you are a psychopath, as you have admitted yourself, who in this notorious interview has acted wildly." He also said he would like to justify his behaviour to his grandchildren. After that letter I decided not to have any further contact with him. A second letter followed but I refused it, in order to protect myself.'

Although they live only forty miles apart, Dagmar has not spoken to or seen her father for two years. 'I know how much it hurts him to be cut off from his grandchildren. He suffers from that! But he has created this situation for himself.'

She does not feel any hatred towards him: 'I lived, and I still live, in a conflict. I have never been able to understand the image of a good and loving father and that of a criminal. It has been better in the last few yers since I have no contact with him. In this way the image of the loving father has receded. I see him more now as a human being who has burdened his soul with the murders of many people. If I feel anything for him, it is compassion. Pity.'

Because of her father's crimes, Dagmar has made a special effort to raise her children in an open and liberal atmosphere. They attend the Steiner school, studying a liberal-arts curriculum; her father's Nazi department had closed the school during the war. 'I hope very often that none of my father's traits are in me or in my children,' she says. 'I think so much of it is controlled by the environment in which you grow up, and my husband and I are really trying to raise our children differently. We teach them to be humane and tolerant of everyone, that everyone is created equal. We explain that you must honour everyone's rights. I never want my son to be in the military and I try to instil pacifism in him.

'I have not told my children yet about their grandfather's role in the war. They are too young [eight and ten]. But when I think they are old enough to understand, I shall give them the trial transcripts, and books and everything about him, so they may know the truth.'

Dagmar has also been active in social causes. 'I help foreign families here in Germany. It starts with the language and ends with social integration. In my modest way, I try to help these less fortunate families with their social problems. I think with this type of work I am trying to make up for his actions.'

She recently visited Israel, 'a wonderful experience', and plans to return. Dagmar also encourages her children to play with Greek and Turkish children whom the rest of the village often shuns. These actions are her effort to establish an identity quite separate from her father. 'He won't change at all. He still thinks there are some races not as worthy of life as the Aryan race. Other people think like that too. If I were as brutal as he is, nothing would ever change – not in our family, not in anyone. I have to act differently from him.

'He could have done something for society; he could have made some attempt at reparation. There are some things in your life you can never make right again, but you can do your best, and he has never even tried.'

As I sat with Dagmar in her home, she showed me a photo album her father had put together and given her in 1983. It is a nostalgic look at his family and his Nazi service. Included were photos of young men in Nazi uniforms, of National Socialist sporting events, of her father resplendent in his SS uniform – even his original wedding announcement, complete with the SS insignia on the front. On one page he had written the heading 'My Chiefs' and included photos of Heydrich and Göring. In other parts of the book he had meticulously drawn the SS lightning bolts insignia.

'These were his mementoes,' said Dagmar. 'At the time he gave it to me, it had somehow become a burden for him, all the photos of my mother and all. It's typical of him, when things are difficult to deal with, he pushes them away, as he did with this book. But it shows how he still feels.' She shook her head slowly as she looked at the pictures. 'We are all so tired of hearing "I was just doing my duty",' she said softly, talking more to herself than to me.

Her cousin, Ute, was present during our meetings. She tried to help me understand the conflict Dagmar still faced. 'Dagmar is waiting for someone, like magic, to come and lift this great burden from her. She hoped when she spoke about it for the first time, it would be cathartic, off her mind once and for all. But it has become worse each time she speaks about it. It's her father's intransigence, his unwillingness to change that is so maddening for her. It's his refusal to acknowledge, even for a moment, the barbarity of his actions during the war.'

Dagmar interjected, 'He's so convinced he's right. Never any remorse or any guilt. I can't understand that he's my father and is like this.'

When I approached her to be included in this book, she was torn about what to do. Part of her initial hesitation was that the book would include a number of children of prominent Nazis. She was not sure if her father belonged in a book with Nazis of such high rank or notoriety. 'I finally decided that rank doesn't really matter,' she says. 'What counts is the destruction of every single person. Every death of a human being was a murder. It is enough what my father did.

'For a long time I debated whether I should again go public with my personal story. And I am doing it only because I spoke to you for a long time. In the meantime, I am not afraid any more, I don't fear my family's repressions or threats. But I do think of my children, and they should not suffer from this. I have arrived at this after a long process of thinking that one cannot make up for what happened. But by listening to my story people may realize they have to react sensibly to political change and that every individual is responsible to ensure that something like this never happens again. People have to engage themselves to fight for freedom and peace, and most of all for humanity.'

CHAPTER 12

The Nazi Legacy

The Palace of Justice in Nuremberg is intact. The great complex spreads over several acres, the main building still grand with its endless stone corridors and more than six hundred and fifty rooms. Past mysterious nooks and crannies which lead off the staircases is the enormous second-storey courtroom that was the site of the main war crimes trial in 1945. Its magnificent clock and ornate chandeliers have been replaced with fluorescent lights, and the press gallery for two hundred and fifty reporters has been dismantled. But the room is remarkably like that shown in photos of the accused Nazis sitting two deep in the defendants' box. In this room the fathers of Wolf Hess, Edda Göring, Ursula Dönitz, Cordula Schacht and Niklas and Norman Frank had their fates decided. It was from this room that most of the world learned the details of the Final Solution and the massacres of millions of civilians.

The empty Nuremberg courthouse was also the site of a bitter 1987 pilgrimage for Niklas Frank. In contrast to the almost circus-like frenzy which gripped the room in 1945, the tall ceilings and hard surfaces accentuated the silence of Niklas Frank's solitary vigil. In the austere surroundings, he concentrated on the climax of the British prosecutor's summation: 'It may be that the guilt of Germany will not be erased, for the people of Germany share in it to large measure. But it was these men who, with a handful of others, brought that guilt upon Germany and subverted the German people. That these defendants participated in, and are morally guilty of crimes so frightful that the imagination staggers and reels back at their very consideration, is not in doubt. Let the words of the defendant Frank be always well remembered: "Thousands of years will pass and this guilt of Germany will not be erased." '

Niklas stared at the wall where the large defendants' box had been, at the very place where his father sat one generation before. 'A fantasy of mine,' says Niklas, 'is to sit here every year, and wait for my father to appear. And he will say "I am guilty, I am really guilty!" And then he will say why he is guilty, and in which year he became a criminal. I am waiting for this. It's my dream, but it's never happened.'

The sins of the father: they affected a second generation of Germans in ways little understood or appreciated. The children of those who served the Third Reich have had to deal with their dark legacy to a much greater extent than the rest of the German nation.

Those who broke with their fathers' politics and crimes are often troubled by shame and guilt. Some, like the Frank brothers, are haunted by images of mounds of twisted corpses or Jewish families being packed into a ghetto. Yet, even without these chilling memories, many are confused by their heritage, almost sharing the guilt for their fathers' crimes. 'I am afraid,' says Dagmar Drexel, 'that if the people I meet know what my father did, they won't want anything to do with me.' 'I would like to go to Israel,' remarks Niklas Frank, 'but how can I go? I am ashamed to meet those people.' 'I *do* apologise to all the victims for what my father did,' says Rolf Mengele. The most extreme example is that of Norman Frank, who decided not to have children because 'after what my father did, I don't think the Frank name should go on'.

The conflict between the image of a good, loving father and the criminal described in documents and by witnesses is seldom resolved. The men described in this book did not exhibit to their families any of the overt signs of psychopathic behaviour for which analysts often search. Those who survived the war never again reverted to their criminal Nazi behaviour. Murderers like Mengele and Drexel returned to quiet, mundane lives, unburdened by guilt. It is that lack of remorse that some of the children find most disturbing. The second generation often has greater moral outrage over the atrocities than any of their parents, the actual perpetrators.

For those who condemn their parents, the quest for understanding their motivation is both arduous and perplexing. Ambition and weakness, often cited as motivating factors, explain only part of their fathers' actions. Not every ambitious person is capable of murder, and weakness alone does not suffice to illuminate hateful and barbarous statements. Mengele blames his father's ambition, but still thinks of his parent as 'an alien'. Norman Frank is still troubled that he cannot uncover any rational basis for his father's extreme conduct. Dagmar Drexel has abandoned the effort: 'I will never understand my father.'

At the opposite end of the spectrum are those children proud to defend their fathers. They are often consumed by the desire to deny any wrongdoing, and they seem as anachronistic as the hateful theories of National Socialism. Wolf Hess is as burdened by the defence of his father as any child who fights against his or her parent. Ursula Dönitz and Edda Göring, with mementoes of their fathers and of World War II sprinkled around their houses, show that part of their souls is still connected to their fathers' wartime glory. Their justification of their parents' actions has not freed them from the emotional turbulence left over from the Nazi era. By denying their fathers' complicity in monstrous crimes, they attempt to justify the pureness of their love. Since they refuse to acknowledge any criminal taint, they do not feel compelled to explain or excuse their feelings. None of them is haunted by Niklas Frank's conflicting images of an indulgent, cultured parent who was steeped in German music and poetry and of a monster who sent over two million Polish Jews to their death. These defenders draw the line at the 'excesses in the East', and if they admit to the Holocaust, the blame is put on others.

Whether the children defend or condemn their parents, the more famous the family name, the greater the public pressure. These 'prominent' children are often thought of in the light of their parent, and judged as much by his career as by their own. Stauffenberg and Schacht energetically strove to create lives independent of their fathers' strong reputations, while Rolf Mengele complains that he still has to be careful every time he offers a political opinion 'since people will say that is the son of Mengele, and oh, listen to what he says about this or that'. All these children have been subjected to meticulous public scrutiny.

Yet such offspring also have an advantage. They never had to rely on their fathers for information about their Nazi past.

Because of their high positions or notoriety, the historical record is replete with information. Mengele and Schacht both used the available sources to learn objectively about their parents' deeds. Yet, others, especially Hess and Göring, have ignored the written record and dismissed most of it as 'lies and propaganda'. In those cases, they have missed a rare opportunity to confront the truth and break symbolically with the past. Denial is a powerful emotional tool. In the case of Nazi parents who themselves deny any wrongdoing, it is not surprising that some children should forgo an aggressive search for the truth at the expense of a more benign, less threatening judgement.

The children of less well-known Nazis may have avoided the public scrutiny, but they were not spared the torment associated with their heritage. Certainly the stormy relationships of both Dagmar Drexel and Ingeborg Mochar with their still-living parents eliminate any speculation that these children had an easier time. In one way, their task is more difficult: since there is no public information on their fathers, they must rely on their families to divulge the truth. It is not a subject that many German parents discuss freely. Drexel only discovered her father's past because she accidentally stumbled across his indictment. Mochar's father told her what he did in the war, but she was never able to check the facts until I obtained his Berlin Document Centre file. She worried that her father had lied and she was about to uncover a criminal past.

The generation responsible for the crimes closed all discussion. They refused to be honest and forthright. This silence did not eliminate the family friction, but only submerged it, often into the child's psyche. Years after the parent's death, some of the children seek to have the public discussion about their feelings that their fathers denied them.

Since the perpetrators remained silent, the burden of seeking the truth and acknowledging the responsibility was passed to another generation. Only Mengele and Mochar accepted the challenge inherent in this burden and confronted their fathers. Mengele made no headway in quarrelling with his father, eventually abandoning the effort to get him to admit some remorse or guilt. Mochar argued with her father for twenty years and has only recently been able to get him to admit that 'maybe' the extermination of the Jews was a mistake.

Some never had the opportunity for confrontation, since they were only infants when their parents were executed. Niklas Frank would probably have challenged his father, but now he is left with a void. In other cases, even in those where the fathers are alive or lived for decades after the war, the children could not bring themselves to confront their wartime records. While many wanted their parent to admit that his Nazi allegiance was a mistake, or that he was sorry, they refused to be the catalyst to force that admission.

'My generation,' Niklas Frank reflected sadly, 'has lost its fight against our parents. We never asked them what happened, especially, you my dear father, or you my dear mother. Why were you weak at this time? Why were you a coward? What did you really know about the Jews in your village, your town, your city, your neighbourhood? What happened to them? When all the old Nazis are dead, then our children will be able to make a genuinely fresh start.'

'It is enough now,' says Rolf Mengele. 'I know there is nothing I can do about this. I guess it's my fate to be his son. But I know if you talk to other Germans my age, very few of them think of the war, the Nazis, the crimes, as much as I must. My father did these things, and now I must answer for him. But it cannot go on to my children. This heritage must end with me.'

'And I think it's important for the victims and their families,' says Dagmar Drexel. 'They should know that we, the children of these men who are guilty of crimes, that we don't just forget about the Holocaust. Instead, we try to deal with it. The murders of millions of people, especially Jews, can't be redressed. We try to do our little part to prevent it from happening ever again. It is our special obligation.'

Notes

1. *Born Guilty*, by Peter Sichrovsky (New York: Basic Books, 1988), and *Legacy of Silence*, by Dab Bar-On (Cambridge, Mass.: Harvard University Press, 1989).
2. A son, Klaus junior, died in 1981 in a hang-gliding accident in Bolivia.
3. In December 1946, US authorities brought twenty-three leading SS physicians and scientists to trial at Nuremberg. On 20 August 1947, fifteen of the defendants in the so-called 'doctors' trial were convicted.
4. Technically, Auschwitz was outside Frank's bailiwick, but it was only thirty miles from his Cracow headquarters.
5. In this instance, Norman's recollection is faulty. The Nazis did expand the ghetto and construct large walls around it.
6. Lasch was executed on 1 June 1942, after an SS trial for corruption. Hans Frank did nothing to save his old friend.
7. Dr Alfred Seidl, the same Nuremberg attorney who defended Rudolf Hess, also represented Frank. He used these four speeches – in vain – as a cornerstone of the defence.
8. During my research I discovered that da Vinci's 'Lady with an Ermine' is on display at the Czartoryski House in Cracow. Polish authorities had quietly recovered it after the war. Niklas was relieved to learn that his father was not responsible for the permanent loss of a great work of art.
9. Although referred to as a diary, the books were primarily a record maintained by his staff, and only partially Frank's personal account.
10. Ilse Koch was dubbed the 'Bitch of Buchenwald'. Her husband was a camp commandant whose behaviour was so notorious that the SS executed him in 1945. She was a sadistic taskmaster whose hobby was collecting lampshades, book covers and gloves made from the skin of dead inmates. She committed suicide in her prison cell in 1967.

11. *Eichmann in Jerusalem*, by Hannah Arendt (New York: Viking, 1963).
12. Haushofer was arrested as a member of the resistance after the 20 July 1944 assassination attempt on Hitler. He was executed by the SS on 23 April 1945 only days before the end of the war.
13. Some of the other children agree with this sentiment. Norman Frank, the elder son of the executed governor-general of Poland, Hans Frank, said, 'It would have been much worse if my father had been imprisoned like Hess's father for all those years. That would have killed me, knowing he was in prison while all of us were free enjoying our lives' (see Chapter 1).
14. Nicholas Ridley, the British Minister for Trade and Industry, resigned his Cabinet-level post in July 1990, following uproar after his published comments warning against Germany's resurgence and comparing Britain's entry into the European Community with capitulation 'to Hitler'.
15. While the director-general, Dr Bartscherer, may have been anti-Nazi, Fritz Thyssen, the company chairman and family heir, was one of Hitler's earliest and most influential backers.
16. Wernher von Braun was a German rocket scientist. He was hired by the United States after the war and, together with other former Third Reich scientists, formed the nucleus for research and development at NASA.
17. Saur was not the only top Speer aide to escape prosecution. Dorsch was not only freed but started an engineering firm which is extremely successful, with branch offices in New York, Tokyo, Delhi, South Korea and Latin America.
18. Cordula told her father, 'Ich mag dich gut leiden.' It is a typical North German expression, difficult to translate because it means more than merely 'I like you' but somewhat less than 'I love you'.
19. A picture of Rolf and Josef Mengele in Rosenheim is in the photo section.
20. *Bunte* eventually gave more than $100,000 to a New York-based survivors' group. When Rolf allowed me to use his father's papers in a biography, *Mengele: The Complete Story* (New York: McGraw Hill, 1986), he requested that I donate 20 per cent of my profits to survivors. I did so, giving the money to a group of surviving twins, all victims of his father's experiments.
21. His formal title is Graf (Count) Stauffenberg. The informal use of his name is Franz Ludwig, as used in this chapter.
22. The 1923 Beer Hall (or 'Munich') Putsch, so called because it was plotted in a beer hall, was an attempt by Hitler to overthrow the Bavarian government. During the five-year prison term (reduced to less than a year) which followed, Hitler wrote *Mein Kampf*.
23. His deceased brother had also been an SS member.

Bibliography

Books and articles

Benton, Wilbourn, and George Grimm, eds, *German Views of the War Trials*. Dallas: Southern Methodist University Press, 1955.

Bewley, Charles. *Hermann Goering and the Third Reich*. New York: Devin-Adair Co., 1962.

Conot, Robert E. *Justice at Nuremberg*. New York: Carroll & Graf, 1983.

Davidson, Eugene. *The Trial of the Germans: An Account of the Twenty-Two Defendants Before the International Military Tribunal*. New York: Macmillan, 1966.

Dawidowicz, Lucy. *The War Against the Jews*. New York: Holt, Rinehart & Winston, 1970.

Dönitz, Karl. *10 Jahre un 20 Tage*. Frankfurt: Athenäum, 1958.

—. *Mein wechselvolles Leben*. Göttingen: Musterschmidt, 1968.

—. *Deutsche Strategie zur See im zweiten Weltkrieg*. Munich: Bernard & Graefe, 1969.

Dulles, Allen. *Germany's Underground*. New York: Macmillan, 1947.

Ferencz, Benjamin B. *Less Than Slaves*. Cambridge, Mass.: Harvard University Press, 1979.

Fishman, Jack. *The Seven Men of Spandau*. New York: Rinehart and Co., 1954.

Frank, Hans. *Im Angesicht des Galgens*. Munich: Beck Verlag, 1953.

—. *Das Diensttagebuch des Deutschen Generalgouverneurs in Polen, 1939–1945*, Stuttgart: Deutsche Verlagsanstalt, 1975.

Frank, Niklas. *Der Väter: Eine Abrechnung*. Munich: Bertelsmann, 1987.

Frischauer, Willi. *The Rise and Fall of Hermann Goering*. New York: Ballantine, 1951.

Gilbert, Dr Gustave M. *Nuremberg Diary*. New York: Farrar, Straus and Co., 1947.

—. 'Hermann Göring, Amiable Psychopath', *Journal of Abnormal and Social Psychology*, Vol. 43, No. 2 (April 1948).

Gilbert, Martin. *The Holocaust: A History of the Jews of Europe During the Second World War*. New York: Holt, Rinehart and Winston, 1985.

Göring, Emmy. *My Life with Göring*. London: David Bruce and Watson, 1972.

Hess, Wolf Rüdiger. *My Father, Rudolf Hess*. London: W. H. Allen, 1986.

Hilberg, Raul. *The Destruction of the European Jews*. Chicago: Quadrangle Books, 1961.

Höhne, Heinz. *The Order of the Death's Head*. Translated by Richard Barry. New York: Ballantine, 1971.

Irving, David. *Göring: A Biography*. New York: William Morrow and Co., 1989.

Kelley, Douglas. *22 Cells in Nuremberg*. London: W. H. Allen, 1947.

Kempner, Robert M. W. 'Blueprint of the Nazi Underground', *Research Studies of the State College of Washington*. (June 1945).

Kersten, Felix. *The Kersten Memoirs, 1940–1945*. New York: Macmillan, 1957.

Knieriem, August von. *The Nuremberg Trial*. Translated by Elizabeth D. Schmidt. Chicago: H. Regnery Co., 1959.

Kranzbühler, Otto. 'Nuremberg, Eighteen Years Afterwards', *De Paul Law Review*, Vol. 14 (1964).

Manchester, William. *The Arms of Krupp, 1587–1968*. New York: Little, Brown and Co., 1968.

Manvell, Roger, and Heinrich Fraenkel. *Göring*. New York: Simon and Schuster, 1962.

—. *Hess*. London: McGibbon & Kee, 1971.

Padfield, Peter. *Dönitz: The Last Führer*. New York: Harper & Row, 1984.

Parker, John J. 'The Nuremberg Trial', *Journal of the American Judicature Society 30* (December 1946).

Rees, John R., ed., *The Mind of Rudolf Hess*. New York: W. W. Norton, 1948.

Reitlinger, Gerald. *The SS, Alibi of a Nation*. London: Heinemann, 1956.

Rowe, Harvey T. 'Im Schatten der Väter', *Quick,* 6 November 1986.

Schacht, Hjalmar. *Account Settled*. London: Weidenfeld & Nicolson, 1948.

—. *Confessions of the Old Wizard*. Boston: Houghton Mifflin Co., 1956.

Schlabrendorff, Fabian von. *The Secret War Against Hitler*. New York: G. P. Putnam's Sons, 1965.

Shirer, William L. *The Rise and Fall of the Third Reich*. New York: Simon and Schuster, 1960.

Speer, Albert. *Erinnerungen*. Berlin: Propyläen, 1969.

—. *Spandau: The Secret Diaries:* London: Collins, 1975.

Swearingen, Ben E. *The Mystery of Hermann Goering's Suicide*. New York: Harcourt Brace Jovanovich, 1985.

Published government reports and studies

Nazi Conspiracy and Aggression. 10 vols. Washington, DC: US Government Printing Office, 1947.

Trials of War Criminals Before the Nuremberg Military Tribunals. 15 vols. Washington, DC: US Government Printing Office, 1951–1952.

Unpublished government reports

National Archives, 'Report of Board of Proceedings in Case of Hermann Göring (Suicide)', Captured German Records Section, Washington, DC, October 1946.

Archive sources

Berlin Document Centre, West Berlin; British Library, London; Bundesarchiv, Koblenz; Department of the Army, Military Intelligence Files, Fort Meade, Maryland; Hoover Institution of War, Revolution and Peace, Stanford, California; National Archives and Records Services, Modern Military Branch, Washington DC; Wiener Library, London; Zentralstelle de Landesjustizverwaltungen, Ludwigsburg, West Germany.

Index